Saints and Stirrers

Edited by Geoffrey Troughton

Saints and Stirrers

Christianity, Conflict and Peacemaking in New Zealand, 1814–1945

Edited by Geoffrey Troughton

VICTORIA UNIVERSITY PRESS

TE WHARE WĀNANGA O TE ŪPOKO O TE IKA A MĀUI
VICTORIA
UNIVERSITY OF WELLINGTON

VICTORIA UNIVERSITY PRESS
Victoria University of Wellington
PO Box 600 Wellington
vup.victoria.ac.nz

First published 2017

A catalogue record for this book is available from the National Library of New Zealand.

Printed by Your Books, Wellington

Contents

Contributors

Peter H. Ballis was most recently Head of Campus, Gippsland for Federation University Australia, and Head of Federation Business School, having served previously at Monash University as Pro Vice Chancellor at the Gippsland Campus. His primary expertise is in the sociology of work and organisations. Major publications include *In and Out of the World: Seventh-day Adventists in New Zealand* (1985) and, with Gary Bouma, *Religion in an Age of Change* (1999).

Allan K. Davidson taught at St John's College and the University of Auckland for many years. He has published extensively on the history of Christianity in New Zealand and the Pacific, most recently, *New Zealand Methodist Chaplains and Ministers at War* (2016). In 2010 he was awarded an ONZM for services to history.

David Grant has published on many aspects of New Zealand's social, cultural and political history. A leading historian of dissent, his books include: *Out in the Cold: Pacifists and Conscientious Objectors in New Zealand during World War II* (1986), *A Question of Faith: A History of the New Zealand Christian Pacifist Society* (2004), and *Field Punishment No. 1: Archibald Baxter, Mark Briggs and New Zealand's Anti-militarist Tradition* (2008).

Harold Hill is a retired Salvation Army officer and adjunct teacher for Salvation Army Colleges in Wellington and Sydney. He has published *Leadership in the Salvation Army: A Case Study in Clericalisation* (2007) and *Saved to Save and Saved to Serve: Perspectives on Salvation Army History* (2017).

Stuart Lange is a Senior Research Fellow at Laidlaw College. His publications include *A Rising Tide: Evangelical Christianity in New Zealand, 1930–65* (2013) and, with Geoffrey Troughton, *Sacred Histories in Secular New Zealand* (2016). He is also the writer and presenter of *Te Rongopai: 200 Years of the Gospel in New Zealand, 1814–2014* (DVD, 2014).

Peter Lineham is Professor of History and Director of the College of Humanities and Social Sciences at Massey University, Albany. He has written extensively on New Zealand religious history, the history of British Protestant sects, and trends in contemporary religion. Among his recent publications is *Destiny: The Life and Times of a Self-made Apostle* (2013).

John Stenhouse teaches in the Department of History at the University of Otago. He is currently editing (with Diane Paul and Hamish Spencer) *Eugenics in British Colonial Contexts: New Zealand, Australia, Canada and South Africa* (forthcoming, 2017). Other projects include an historical geography of religion in New Zealand and a book on missionaries, science and medicine in the modern world.

David Tombs is the Howard Paterson Chair of Theology and Public Issues at the University of Otago. He has a particular interest in religion and violence, and in public and contextual theologies. He is author of *Latin American Liberation Theology* (2002).

Geoffrey Troughton is a Senior Lecturer in Religious Studies at Victoria University of Wellington. His research focuses on religion in New Zealand, the history of Christianity, and contemporary religious change. Major publications include *New Zealand Jesus* (2011), *The Spirit of the Past* (2011), with Hugh Morrison, and *Sacred Histories in Secular New Zealand* (2016), with Stuart Lange.

Preface

Yearning for peace is a fundamental human aspiration. To be secure, safe from threats, and free to flourish and thrive: these are common desires, shared by people the world over. As simple and unremarkable as they may seem, sadly, for too many people in too much of the world, such desires remain largely unfulfilled or realised all too fleetingly. New Zealand has never been immune from conflict and turmoil. Yet, as has often been noted, the nation has also been blessed with relative peacefulness. Surprisingly, however, this experience has not led to extensive critical exploration of the peace dimension in New Zealand history, or of the roots of the nation's peace traditions. Nor have religious contributions received significant attention. This lacuna is predictable but also regrettable. For as the following accounts attest, New Zealand Christianity is replete with remarkable and often complex stories of peacemaking and opposition to war.

This volume aims to provoke fresh thinking about these issues, and about the history of peaceable ideas and practices within New Zealand. It focuses on various expressions of Christian opposition to violence and warfare, and provides the most substantial and broad-ranging examination of this theme to date. The book should be read as part of a larger project on Christianity and peace in New Zealand: another forthcoming volume, *Pursuing Peace in Godzone: Christianity and the Peace Tradition in New Zealand*, will address Christianity's relationship to peacemaking in more recent times. Both books are collaborative efforts; the impetus for them has arisen out of my recent focus on the peace dimension in early New Zealand missionary Christianity and its legacies.

Many thanks and acknowledgements are owed. I am grateful for the gracious, cheerful and energetic efforts of the authors who have contributed to this volume. I also express my appreciation to the reviewers, and others, who scrutinised sections of the book and offered valuable advice. My colleague Philip Fountain has been especially generous in his support and encouragement of this book, as well as offering insightful critique; he has also been a superb collaborator in the larger peacemaking project. As ever, I am grateful for the support of a remarkable group of colleagues in the Religious Studies programme at Victoria, and also for the outstanding work of the team at Victoria University Press. I thank Rowan Heap who has produced another superb, evocative cover design. I also appreciate the generous and timely support of various archives and libraries, including: the Alexander Turnbull Library, Wellington; the Hocken Library, Dunedin; the Presbyterian Archives Research Centre, Dunedin; and the Library and Image Services at Victoria University of Wellington.

This volume would not have been possible without generous support from a Royal Society of New Zealand Marsden Fund Grant (ID: VUW1412), and also from the Faculty of Humanities and Social Sciences at Victoria University. Most of the chapters that follow were initially delivered as papers for a conference that I organised with Professor Chris Marshall in November 2015: '"Peace, not war, shall be our boast": Historical, theological and contemporary perspectives on peace and Christianity in New Zealand'. I acknowledge his support and the contributions of others on the organising committee, along with the Religious History Association of Aotearoa New Zealand, the College of St John the Evangelist, the National Centre for Peace and Conflict Studies at the University of Otago, and St John's in the City, Wellington. Finally, I acknowledge the support of family and friends for their encouragement of this project, including and especially Adrienne, for her continuing love and forbearance.

Geoffrey Troughton

1

Christianity, Peace and Opposition to War

Geoffrey Troughton

The question of peace has long haunted Christianity in New Zealand. Throughout the nation's history there have been frequent efforts to oppose war and promote peace based upon Christian convictions, often drawing upon longstanding traditions within the faith. Despite such impulses, refusal to participate in war has never been the dominant stance in New Zealand. Activist commitment to peace has been a remarkably consistent but largely marginal concern within the church as a whole. This book brings new attention to the relationship between Christianity and peace in New Zealand. It focuses on Christian peacemaking and opposition to war in the period from the nineteenth century until the end of the Second World War. In so doing, it provides critical insights into New Zealand Christianity, as well as peace activism, politics and New Zealand society more generally.

This book has been written during a period of extended commemoration of the First World War, when questions of war and peace have taken on especial significance. In New Zealand, as elsewhere, the centenary of the Great War has stimulated a remarkable range of public exhibitions, activities and projects designed to mark key events and promote reflection on their ongoing importance.[1] Anzac Day and other occasions for remembrance have received substantial support from government, media and the wider community. Many historians have been kept busy. Their labour has yielded evaluations of diverse issues—from the wartime home front, to aspects of the memory, material culture and social and cultural history of the war.[2] Yet more militant emphases have also been apparent.

Campaign histories and studies of hardware, technology and strategy have proliferated and still tend to predominate within the war history market.

Arguably, one effect of all this memorialisation has been a sharpened emphasis on war as a maker of national unity and identity, and a related strengthening of New Zealand's Anzac civil religion—a form that has been shaped in part by Christian symbols and imagination.[3] In this tradition, war is ultimately regarded as a unifier and peace-bringer, however much the costly destruction and sacrifices involved may be lamented. Counter-traditions of opposition to war fit uneasily with such outlooks. They raise questions about the shape of nationalist mythologies, and implicitly challenge deep-seated ideologies of redemptive violence. Yet such questioning is important in liberal democratic societies.

War resisters and opponents of militarism have received some recognition during the centennial commemorations.[4] The harsh treatment of Archibald Baxter, Mark Briggs and others of 'the 14' objectors who were sent to England and the Front has attracted renewed attention.[5] Such stories have become a little better known, and helped to illuminate the societal hostility that has often been directed towards those who failed to participate in the nation's wars. Yet the space for questioning of war is still narrow. The propriety of honouring war service is relatively uncontested, but the lines between remembering and celebrating war remain fraught. There is an awkward relationship in New Zealand between pride in the nation's reputation as a peaceful country and contributor to global peacemaking on the one hand and a chariness about anti-war campaigns on the other. Civil religions have their saints, and they are not usually the doubters, critics or war resisters.

Questions about the peaceable character of Christianity have taken on renewed urgency in recent times, though it seems strange in some ways to even pose them. After all, peace was established as a central ethical norm in early Christianity, and remains a significant theme for Christians. Jesus taught his followers to love their neighbours (including their enemies); he blessed the peacemakers, and promoted non-violence. Christians worship Jesus as saviour and hail him as the prince of peace. And for many years the earliest Christians held to pacifist ideals.[6] Yet such ideals were clearly not sustained as central emphases throughout subsequent Christian history. Since the eighteenth century, a key dimension of the Enlightenment critique of religion has been its purported complicity in conflict and violence. Far from being regarded as peace-bringing, Christianity has been imagined as a breeder of violence and division. This polemical characterisation has been widely criticised, but it continues to hold sway in much contemporary thinking. It has been taken up, for example, as a central factor in 'new atheist' claims and calls for a 'new Enlightenment'.[7] Such sentiment is now sustained in large part through concerns about global terrorism and religious nationalism.

In New Zealand, concerns about a nexus of religion and conflict have had some purchase, despite the nation's relatively peaceable reputation and longstanding secular political arrangements. Religious commitments—and differences—have frequently been viewed with anxiety as potential sources of division, threatening social order and the body politic. Thus, while sectarian tensions between Protestants and Catholics were never as sharp in New Zealand as in many other parts of the world,[8] they have featured as a staple of discussion on religion in national histories.[9] Religion, often of a detraditionalised kind, has also been deployed in the cause of national unity, with God put to work in service of the national interests during war and at other times. In the political theology of patriotism, the 'lord of battles' has always been more important than the 'prince of peace'—as a seldom-sung third verse of the national anthem, Thomas Bracken's 'God Defend New Zealand', makes clear:

> Peace, not war, shall be our boast,
> But, should foes assail our coast,
> Make us then a mighty host,
> God defend our free land.
> Lord of battles, in Thy might,
> Put our enemies to flight,
> Let our cause be just and right,
> God defend New Zealand.[10]

Such language suggests that religion has been deeply entwined with nationalist feeling and the projection of State power. Yet generalised assumptions about the interplay of religion, conflict and violence need to be tested and carefully examined. To date, there have been few attempts to do this in New Zealand.

Christianity and New Zealand peace traditions

The essays that follow focus on Christian peacemaking and opposition to war. For reasons that will be addressed below, the book focuses on the years from 1814 to 1945, a timespan that incorporates the beginnings of organised Christianity in New Zealand through to the end of the Second World War. Christian peacemaking and opposition to war is addressed in this period through a series of case studies drawing from an array of Christian traditions. There are stories of various Māori and Pākehā saints from mainline denominations through to those from an assortment of smaller and lesser-known groups, and also from independent types who eschewed institutional affiliation but were nevertheless believers.

Through these various accounts, this book seeks to provide fresh perspectives on the histories of peace activism and Christianity in New Zealand. There is much to be explored in both of those domains. For while New Zealand enjoys a contemporary reputation as a peaceable, peace-loving country, analysis of the nation's peace traditions has been surprisingly limited, and partial in certain respects. There have been relatively few studies of anti-war and anti-militarist traditions,[11] and those that do exist have tended to focus particularly on pacifism and conscientious objectors. There have been even fewer examinations of religion-based anti-militarism, or the application of Christian commitments to peace conceived in broader terms. Studies of Christian opposition to war have generally focused on individuals, and organisations such as the New Zealand Christian Pacifist Society and the Anglican Pacifist Fellowship.[12] No broad, single-volume examination of Christian peace traditions in New Zealand has previously been undertaken.

The focus on opposition to war in New Zealand is restricted in this book to the period up to 1945. The post-Second World

War era was a crucial time in the crafting of New Zealand's contemporary image as a tolerant, liberal, independent and peaceable nation. It was also the period in which a distinctive post-war peace movement emerged. That movement focused initially on issues related to nuclear weapons, disarmament and related Cold War era concerns. As the movement broadened in scope, the framing of peace also changed. Considerations of peace and justice became more explicitly aligned so that issues such as racism, women's liberation and human rights all came to be viewed as part of a wider peace agenda. There is a story to be told about the place of Christianity in post-1945 peacemaking, peace activism, and peacebuilding more generally—not least because this has been largely neglected in existing accounts.[13] That later era warrants its own analysis, however, and another forthcoming volume will attend to this time period.[14]

The limited attention afforded to Christianity in the period following the Second World War is consistent with analyses of earlier opposition to war. In important works on opposition to the South African War and on early twentieth-century women objectors, for example, Malcolm McKinnon and Megan Hutching respectively recognise the Christian commitments of some of their key subjects, but provide little exploration of relevant religious and theological factors.[15] McKinnon's analysis discusses five categories of opposition to the South African War; interestingly, religious opposition does not feature as a distinct or particularly significant form. By contrast, the Labour leader Harry Holland's well-known tract, *Armageddon or Calvary*, famously noted four somewhat overlapping types of conscientious objector during the First World War: religious, socialist, Irish and Māori.[16] Holland listed religious objectors first, and deployed powerful Christian symbolism and rhetoric in framing his entire work. As his primary purpose was political—the volume was consciously written as a polemical pre-1919 election statement—emphasis was placed upon socialist and labour-based opposition, even where Christian and socialist commitments cohered. This orientation, and Holland's focus on conscientious objectors, characterised much subsequent thinking about opposition to war, though it represents only a very particular strand of criticism and a narrow strain of peace commitment.

The question of peace in New Zealand has been shaped by participation in conflict and war. In the period to 1945, these conflicts included some wars that were fought on New Zealand soil and others that were waged elsewhere. In the nineteenth century, intertribal warfare among Māori (including the 'musket wars' of the 1820s and 30s), and wars fought between settlers, the Crown and Māori, were key instances of conflict. From the end of the nineteenth century, imperial connections led New Zealanders to participate in wars in other parts of the globe, beginning with the South African War of 1899–1902, and then more extensively in the world wars of 1914–1918 and 1939–1945. New Zealand's contributions to these wars were relatively small in the context of the conflicts as a whole, yet the impacts upon New Zealand society were extraordinary. The advent of modern industrial war, mass conscription and deployment of total war in the twentieth century enmeshed all of society, reconfiguring New Zealand life. Understandably, these moments of conflict also shape the contents of this book, forming key focal points for many of the case studies that follow.

The nineteenth century

This collection of essays addresses a broad range of Christian engagements with peace and opposition to war, cohering particularly around three key nodes. These relate to the nineteenth century, opposition from within sectarian Christianity and case studies of individuals associated with the mainline denominations. With respect to the nineteenth century, one key focus concerns the development of peace ideals within missionary and Māori Christianity. Nineteenth-century Māori had well-established peacemaking protocols and procedures.[17] Nevertheless, evangelical Christian missionaries regarded their message as a gospel of peace that spoke generally to the needs of all humanity, and directly to Māori circumstances. An emphasis on peace teaching and peacemaking developed; this came to feature prominently in characterisations, particularly of the Church Missionary Society (CMS) and a number of its leading figures.[18] A peace emphasis thus became strongly associated with the earliest forms of Christianity in New Zealand.

The first chapter in this volume examines the character of peace ideals in the earliest years of the CMS mission, which was established under Samuel Marsden's direction in the Bay of Islands from December 1814. Beginning with Marsden himself, the chapter confirms that peace teaching and anti-war advocacy were evident from the outset, before the beginnings of the musket wars. The mission's peace gospel sat within an evangelical theological framework of salvation and redemption. In this, peace was set forth as a gift of the gospel—spiritually, but also in temporal terms, as a requirement and outworking of true faith. The CMS did not advance an absolutist pacifist message, but its peace gospel did entail renunciation of retaliation, principled commitment to peacemaking and pursuit of non-violent conflict resolution. These elements were closely tied to notions of Christian law and civilisation, and were characteristic of a broader pattern that became more obviously influential by the 1830s.

Missionaries in the mission boat *Herald* accompany a taua with the aim of acting as peacemakers. Source: William Yate, *An Account of New Zealand* (1835), 184.

Two subsequent chapters explore the development of this peace tradition in connection with the CMS. In the first of these, Peter Lineham examines the place of peace in the CMS mission of the 1830s as it spread southward from Northland and into the Waikato and surrounding regions. This area was embroiled in a complex set of conflicts, and was also the setting of one of New Zealand Christianity's most famous stories—the story of the young girl Tārore, and the extraordinary instances of forgiveness and reconciliation that followed in the wake of her murder.[19] Lineham's account is not principally concerned with Tārore, but teases out essential elements of the context in which those events occurred. He demonstrates the centrality of peace to the CMS mission, and clarifies the logic and shape of the teaching, indicating ways in which the demand for peace became established within various expressions of Māori Christianity in the region.

Stuart Lange's careful account of the deaths of two Christian Māori, Te Mānihera Poutama and Kereopa Hemi Patene, in 1847, illuminates precisely this dynamic in another setting, further to the south. Te Mānihera and Kereopa were Ngāti Ruanui Christian converts from southern Taranaki who were killed in the process of seeking to evangelise their tribal enemies, Ngāti Tūwharetoa, in the central North Island. In the period following their deaths a commitment to non-retaliation prevailed as Ngāti Ruanui worked together with the Pūtiki-based CMS missionary Richard Taylor to pursue reconciliation with the evangelists' killers. Lange sees in this story an almost paradigmatic case of the embrace of Christian reconciliation—from the initial risky evangelistic mission to the subsequent peacemaking expeditions. Evangelistic considerations remained a core dimension of the evangelical peace message; the implications were never seen to be merely 'spiritual', however, but were also social and political. The story illustrates the interweaving of those elements, and the way that new Christian understandings came to be expressed within Māori norms and expectations. It also demonstrates the pivotal role that Māori Christians played in extending this peace ethic, and some of the costs and risks associated with doing so.

Similar stories abound, as Māori and missionary Christianity emphasised peace in different settings around the country, from Northland to the deep south.[20] Commitments to peace and reconciliation were complex, however, and the legacies of this earlier intense emphasis on peacemaking need to be carefully probed. The embrace of a kind of Christian peace ethic was part of a broader engagement with Christian modernity—including dimensions such as law, education and economy.[21] Like missionaries, and Pākehā Christians, Christian Māori responded in different ways to the conflicts of the nineteenth century.[22]

Nevertheless, remarkable instances of peacemaking and non-violence emerged out of this milieu. Some later examples, like the Parihaka story, are relatively well known, though many are not. Oddly, many accounts emphasise the non-violent resistance of Parihaka, but downplay the 'religious' dimensions of the story and the intense spirituality of Te Whiti O Rongomai and Tohu Kākahi.[23] Evaluation of the significance of Christian influences also tends to be limited. Danny Keenan's recent account notes Te Whiti's early interactions with the Lutheran missionary Johann Riemenschneider, but his overall interpretation emphasises the repudiation of missionary authority in the development of the Parihaka settlement.[24] Yet it seems more than incidental that Riemenschneider, and Wesleyan teachers including John Whiteley, were active promoters of a Christian peace ethic on the North Island's West Coast,[25] and that leaders like Te Whiti, Tohu and Te Ua Haumēne all interacted closely with them. The movements they initiated seemed to work creatively with multiple traditions—including a Christian peace tradition.

Elsewhere, at Ōtaki, the CMS missionary Octavius Hadfield emerged as one of the main voices of humanitarian opposition to the Taranaki War. His criticisms of the war were not overtly founded on a pacifist ethic so much as on a basis of justice, rights and objection to settler acquisitiveness.[26] A Christian peace ethic was, however, promoted and Christian Māori connected to the Ōtaki mission became influential advocates in different parts of the country. In 1843, Tāmihana (Katu) Te Rauparaha and Hēnare Mātene Te Whiwhi went to the South Island with the aim of evangelising and brokering peace between Ngāti Toa and Ngāi Tahu. Both were influential in the development of the Kīngitanga (Māori King movement), and in seeking to establish the Wellington area as a peace zone during the 1860s—though they did not prohibit participation in fighting in the wars being waged further north. In the Manawatū, another Christian teacher, Hoani Meihana Te Rangiotū, actively mediated between iwi and between Māori and settlers. He built a church in the style of a marae, calling it Te Rangimārie (peace), to commemorate an accord established between Rangitāne and Ngāti Raukawa. With Te Peeti Te Aweawe, he agreed with Te Whiwhi's suggestion that the new town square in Palmerston North be named Te Marae-o-Hine (the Courtyard of the Daughter of Peace), in honour of one of Te Whiwhi's ancestors and as an expression of desire for peace between Māori and Pākehā in the district.[27]

The complex relationship between Māori, Christianity, conflict and the State persisted into the twentieth century. In 1919, in the wake of the First World War, the report of the Religious Objectors Advisory Board to the Minister of Defence commented on the fate of imprisoned Māori objectors. None of them had objected on 'bona fide religious grounds', but the Board argued that their cases warranted 'most earnest attention'. The report highlighted one particular reply from a Māori objector who had been interviewed in Auckland, and whose arguments the Board took 'fairly to represent the Maori Objectors point of view'. That reply highlighted not only the emphasis on peace within the Christianity of the missionary era that Māori had received, but also the discrepancy between this Christianity and the later demands of the State: 'At the Treaty of Waitangi we signed to make peace and they put a Bible in our hands. They have now taken the Bible away and put a sword into our hands and wish to make us fight.'[28]

Smaller and sectarian denominations

Prior to the twenty-first century, the vast majority of New Zealanders identified, at least in census terms, with Christianity. Historically, affiliation was concentrated in four main denominational groupings. The 1901 national census, for example, reported that 89% of New Zealanders affiliated religiously as either Anglican (41%), Presbyterian (23%), Catholic (14%) or Methodist (11%). By 1945, affiliation with these churches remained high at 81% of the population.[29] Yet an array of smaller and sectarian Protestant groups also flourished, and it was within these communities that the strongest cultures of pacifist and anti-war sentiment tended to exist. Surprisingly, there have been relatively few studies of these smaller churches and denominations.

The Religious Society of Friends (Quakers) is perhaps the best known of the smaller groups, due in part to its prominence in regulations about 'exemption' from war service—notably with respect to section 18 of the Military Service Act 1916, which allowed for the possibility of exemption from combatant service on religious grounds. Quakers were one of the few religious groups recognised under the narrow provisions of the Act, and so became widely identified as a key example of religious opposition to war.[30] Indeed, religious opposition to war has sometimes been taken to indicate allegiance to the Friends. There certainly is a long tradition of Quaker opposition, dating back to the founder of the movement in the seventeenth century, George Fox. Fox considered war to be incompatible with the Holy Spirit and the 'Inner Light', and the Society's 'peace testimony' became associated for many Friends with repudiation of the 'carnal weapons' of warfare.[31] Quakers were instrumental in the development of the first British Peace Society in 1816, known as the Society for the Promotion of Permanent and Universal Peace. They also became prominent in later anti-war campaigning.

New Zealand Quakers were a tiny minority group, however, and their attitudes to war can be easily misrepresented. Between 1881 and 1916, the number of Quakers nearly doubled according to census figures, though the numbers remained small—rising from just 232 to 431. Affiliation actually declined as a proportion of the population during that time, from 0.05% to 0.04%. Furthermore, Quaker attitudes to war were ruled by a doctrine of conscience rather than commitment to absolute pacifism. In England, some Quakers were conscientious objectors during the First World War. Yet the brothers Laurence and Egbert Cadbury, sons of the Birmingham cocoa and chocolate maker George Cadbury, famously exercised their consciences in different forms of war service—Laurence serving in an ambulance unit, Egbert fighting as a pilot. Similar diversity could be found among New Zealand's Quakers. We should not assume, therefore, that the Quaker peace testimony was always expressed in outright objection.[32] Nevertheless, the Society of Friends did make significant contributions to anti-militarist activism in New Zealand from the nineteenth century.[33] It produced leaders such as Egerton Gill who founded the New Zealand Freedom League, an organisation that received support from Friends in Auckland and Wellington as it campaigned for repeal of the Defence Act 1909.[34] Another important early New Zealand peace organisation, the National Peace Council, was founded in 1911 and apparently financed in part by English Quakers.[35]

One of the founders and leading figures of the National Peace Council was actually a Baptist, Charles Mackie, the leader of the Canterbury Baptist Lay Preachers' Association. A number of Baptist colleagues supported him in this endeavour, as well as in his pacifism and opposition to militarism within the churches.[36] The Baptist Church was the largest of the smaller Protestant denominations in New Zealand, accounting for about 2% of census respondents in the early twentieth century. Baptists, like Quakers, emphasised freedom of conscience; they also brought to New Zealand a long history of critique of the State and dissent from State interference in religion. Such priorities often aligned with anti-militarist conviction, and for a number of radical Baptists they did. J. J. Doke and A. H. Collins were among a relatively small group of Christian ministers to articulate strong opposition to the South African War of 1899–1902, and to criticise atrocities. Other Baptists expressed similar views before and during the First World War, while pacifism and social gospel Christianity also proved attractive to some in the interwar period.[37] Baptist opinion varied, however, and the Church never developed a strong radical tradition in peace activism or the social gospel. The radical Baptist tradition was always remarkably thin in New Zealand.[38] Mackie and Thomas Nuttall discovered this in their pacifist campaigning during the First World War. Their attempts to enrol the support of the newly formed Linwood Baptist Church in Christchurch backfired as the majority of Church members remained committed to militaristic patriotism and an imperialist outlook.

This volume contains ground-breaking studies exploring the tensions and challenges that faced a number of smaller and sectarian Protestant groups, in relation to the First and Second World Wars. Less well known than the Quakers or the Baptists, these groups were nevertheless often either as active or unified in their opposition to war (if not more so). They consequently experienced greater hostility and were typically more prone to being misunderstood. A number of the issues highlighted above were critical for smaller Christian groups as a whole. Even within relatively unified sectarian forms, diverse opinions and theologies created internal tensions and contestation. There were also tensions generated by commitment to doctrinal and ethical purity, set against the desire for influence and respect within the community. The requirements of religious distinctiveness sometimes clashed with hopes for social peace and security, as did competing claims for loyalty to God and to the State. The ways that groups responded to such challenges often had profound implications.

Harold Hill's analysis of the Salvation Army during the First World War provides a rare insight into attitudes to war and peace within that movement in New Zealand. Curiously, given the organisation's martial name and styling, its founder William Booth and many of his family had pacifist sympathies. Though the movement never formally adopted a pacifist stance, this instinct was quite widespread within the Salvation Army internationally, and Hill perceives traces of it within the local organisation. His chapter identifies many instances of warm, liberal commentary about Germany and German Salvationists in the Salvation Army publication *War Cry* during the war years—commentary that was strikingly at odds with the prevailing tone of anti-Germanism in New Zealand society at that time. Hill's explanation highlights local, international, institutional, social, theological and ministry-oriented factors that helped shape the Salvation Army's outlook. He argues that the Army's internationalism, evangelical imperatives and 'theological universalism' were particularly important elements. These served to promote humanitarian values and a cautious witness to peace rather than outright opposition to war.

A number of other small Christian groups were more unambiguously pacifist in orientation, though their small size, sectarian character and unfamiliarity to non-members has meant that their stories have largely gone untold. Their intense biblicist religiosity has also often been portrayed as fundamentalist or fanatical, and led them to be dismissed. In addition, not all sectarian groups maintained a strict opposition to war over the longer term. Pentecostals, for example, became more closely aligned with patriotic political theologies later in the twentieth century, and so their more radical earlier outlook is easily overlooked. Peter Lineham, the nation's foremost expert on radical and sectarian Christianity, addresses this lacuna in a chapter on sects and war. Lineham surveys a diverse array of sectarian groups ranging from Christadelphians, Pentecostals and Seventh-day Adventists, through to the Plymouth Brethren and obscure groups such as the so-called Cooneyites, or Testimony of Jesus. These groups suffered remarkably high levels of imprisonment on account of their conscientious objection, and Lineham's account helps to explain who they were, why this occurred and some of the effects of their wartime opposition.

As Lineham's chapter demonstrates, sectarian Christian groups shared an eagerness to remain separate from the wider religious and secular world, but they often disagreed sharply with one another. Their theologies and experiences were by no means uniform. In another important account, Harry (Peter H.) Ballis explores the differing experiences of the Seventh-day Adventists and Jehovah's Witnesses during the Second World War. Both churches had a history of pacifist objection, which had been expressed during the First World War. Circumstances had changed by the Second World War, and the churches faced new questions and decisions. Ballis's study explores the pressures created by the churches' stance and their marginality within New

Zealand society. It highlights tensions inherent in maintaining principled commitments—tensions that were complicated in these cases by theologically grounded belief in the importance of loyalty to the State. The Seventh-day Adventists and Jehovah's Witnesses chose different paths during the Second World War, and both churches transformed accordingly.

Saints and stirrers in the mainline denominations

None of the four largest settler denominations established a particularly pacific reputation during the years prior to 1945. Consequently, with some notable exceptions, there have been few studies of peacemaking initiatives within these churches.[39] Various works have examined religious responses to specific wars, including the work of chaplains to the armed forces, and considered the effects of war upon the churches.[40] Unsurprisingly, the mainline churches have featured prominently in such works. A key emphasis to date has been on the wartime patriotism and 'loyalty' of the larger churches, particularly during the First World War.[41] The emergence of support for internationalism during the interwar period has also been noted. Within the churches, a few prominent leaders, such as the leading Presbyterian minister and 'patriot into pacifist' James Gibb,[42] were key supporters. So, too, were a younger generation of emerging leaders. Many of these were connected with the Methodist and Presbyterian Bible Class movements and the university-based Student Christian Movement.

Interestingly, Presbyterianism features prominently in four of the chapters that follow, though in different ways and illustrating diverse issues. Each case focuses on an individual. In two instances, the subjects were prominent Presbyterians, though at different points in their careers. John Stenhouse's chapter focuses on the Reverend Rutherford Waddell, a figure most commonly remembered for his outspoken campaigning against sweated labour, which contributed to the introduction of important social legislation during the 1890s. It is less well known that Waddell was also a vocal critic of war. Stenhouse details Waddell's war criticism and draws a connection between this and his social campaigning, arguing that these were related expressions of Waddell's 'puritan' vision for the creation of a cohesive, peaceable society. Waddell's ardent criticisms were not based on an absolutist pacifist principle, however, as became clear in his stance during the First World War. Yet neither was he a Holy War crusader. His opposition was more in keeping with a rigorous just war ethic. As Stenhouse argues, that part of the ethical spectrum has been inadequately represented in the New Zealand historiography of religion and war, though it was nonetheless highly significant.

Allan Davidson's chapter on Alun Richards focuses on the interwar period, and the debate over compulsory military training (CMT) during that time. Richards was a young Presbyterian university student who in 1927 refused to undertake military training—on the basis of his own Christian objection to war, and bolstered by a recent Presbyterian Church statement that such military training was 'wrong in principle'. The Court's refusal to grant Richards exemption on religious grounds created broad discontent not only from pacifists, but also from pacificists within the Presbyterian and other churches, and a wider base of those concerned about issues of militarism and religious freedom. Richards' case, and stance, captured public attention, garnering both support and criticism. He soon became a central figure in a widening national debate. Davidson's analysis of these events highlights the influential role that individual Christians and churches played in the debate over CMT. It also illustrates the strength of debate within and beyond the churches as New Zealanders grappled with issues of peace, war and alternatives to war. For younger Christians like Richards, these events were formative and shaped an ongoing witness for peace in church and society.

Richards was not a lone activist. There were numerous small, peace-oriented organisations operating in New Zealand during the interwar years. Despite this, John Cookson has noted that no '"peace movement" based on a coalition of pacifist and pacificist bodies' emerged at that time.[43] A number of Christian-based groups existed, and new organisations formed. The most prominent and influential of these by the start of the Second World War was the Christian Pacifist Society (CPS), founded in 1936. Ormond Burton was the leading figure within that organisation, and arguably the nation's most high-profile pacifist of the period. Burton grew up in the Presbyterian Church, but entered the Methodist ministry in the 1930s. David Grant tells his story, focusing particularly on his role in the CPS's anti-war demonstrations during the Second World War. Christian pacifism dominated Second World War pacifism in New Zealand,[44] and Grant's narrative outlines the CPS's activities, Burton's particular contribution and the opposition that he encountered—from the State, society and within his own Church. His account confirms the illiberalism of the New Zealand State at that time, and something of the intolerance arising from 'the insecurities of a small, relatively homogenous society'.[45] Burton was also an uncompromising character, and his story highlights the significance of personality as well as the character of the debate about war within the churches.

The fourth study of an individual with Presbyterian connections is something of an outlier—in part because the extent of the Presbyterian connection is less certain, but more importantly because so too is the nature of his Christian faith. Archibald Baxter is New Zealand's best known conscientious objector, though he did not characterise himself in those terms. It is widely accepted that Baxter's objection to war was based in some measure upon religious principles, but the notorious vagueness of Baxter's comments about his faith have led to a wide range of interpretations. David Tombs' chapter provides the first detailed assessment of the evidence concerning Baxter's religious convictions, and concludes that he was indeed a Christian—more deeply and committedly so than has often been assumed. Part of the significance of Tombs' interpretation lies in the well-known fact of Baxter's lack of church affiliation at the time of the First World War. Baxter's convinced but unaffiliated faith is a reminder that Christian ideas, convictions and frames of reference were widely diffused in New Zealand before the Second World War. Christianity's role in shaping moral imaginations and convictions about war and peace could reach beyond the churches, and thus be more extensive than is expected or readily traceable. This raises questions about the boundary lines of 'Christian' thinking about war, and traditions of opposition. It also provides a corrective to any tendency to bind Christianity too tightly to church institutions, even in earlier periods of higher affiliation and church attendance.

Cumulatively, the chapters in this volume reveal a rich range of Christian peace stories in New Zealand that deserve to be better known. The traditions of opposition to war that they represent warrant more extensive investigation, alongside others that are not addressed in this book. They also need to be more carefully integrated into broader accounts of the New Zealand peace movement and of anti-militarism.

The accounts that follow do not demonstrate that New Zealand Christians were uniformly or impeccably peaceable, or even that particular expressions of objection always indicated consistent or strict anti-war outlooks. In the most capacious New Testament sense, saints are simply those 'in Christ'—Christian believers, followers of Jesus. In a narrower sense, there are saints who are especially recognised as such on account of their exemplary character and devotion. All of the subjects in this volume are identifiable as saints, though there may be debate as to the category that best describes them. These saints were invariably stirrers. Even in reputedly peaceable nations like New Zealand, to question war apparently required an element of provocation. While some saints evidently delighted in the role, there was also much variation. This is not altogether surprising. For although peace is widely commended within Christianity, there have always been debates over the ethics of war—and different modes of stirring.

2

Samuel Marsden and the Origins of a New Zealand Christian Peace Tradition

Geoffrey Troughton

Samuel Marsden may seem an unlikely figure to propose as the father of a peace tradition, in New Zealand or anywhere. It is well known that his reputation in Australia is mixed. Notwithstanding his remarkably wide-ranging contributions to life in the New South Wales penal colony, Australian writers have often cast him as a harsh and belligerent figure. This reputation largely derives from his actions as a colonial magistrate, particularly his alleged treatment of convicts and run-ins with various colonial notables such as Governor Lachlan Macquarie.[1] His reputation in New Zealand has generally been more favourable, though not unequivocally so; his more saintly and heroic status as the Apostle to New Zealand has also come under more critical scrutiny in recent years.[2]

There is no doubt that Marsden could be difficult. Even a key supporter, Josiah Pratt, the Secretary of the Church Missionary Society (CMS) in London, referred euphemistically to Marsden's 'decisive character', which led to tensions with colleagues who considered him to be overly harsh.[3] His leading twentieth-century biographer, A. T. Yarwood, claimed that hypersensitivity to 'slights and criticism' rendered Marsden unable to live in 'peace and harmony' in New South Wales.[4] Similar troubles dogged his relationships with a number of New Zealand missionaries. Nevertheless, Marsden provides an important starting point for examining the relationship between Christianity and peace in New Zealand history. A strong case can be made for placing him at the origin of a New Zealand Christian peace tradition—partly because he was the crucial figure in the establishment of a settled Christian presence in New Zealand, but also because of the place that peace occupied in his Christian understanding and in his agenda for the CMS mission among Māori.

Building on claims that have been made elsewhere, this chapter argues that, for reasons of evangelical conviction as well as strategic expediency, peacemaking was a foundational emphasis for Marsden and the early CMS mission in New Zealand. Early Christian missionaries to New Zealand cast themselves as bearers of a 'gospel of peace' and emphasised their role as peacemakers: 'peace' was an important aspect of their message, and a peacemaking role shaped their self-image and was also a key feature of their subsequent reputation.[5] The CMS's peacemaking emphasis and campaigning against war is sometimes treated as a later development—dating to the period after the death of Hongi Hika in 1828,[6] or perhaps earlier, from the arrival of Henry Williams in 1823.[7] Both moments were significant turning points for the mission, and later missionary commentators recognised them as such, including William Yate as early as the mid-1830s.[8] Yet, as this chapter demonstrates, a peace emphasis was evident from the outset of the mission. There were important continuities between this early opposition to war and later CMS peacemaking. Marsden's approach did not make him a peace activist in the contemporary sense, but he was concerned to promote peace in distinctive ways, and his framework and ideals were characteristic of an influential strain within New Zealand Christianity.

Marsden and the background to the mission

The CMS mission to New Zealand was one of the earliest the Society established, following its initial West African mission of 1804. It was established at Marsden's instigation—a product of his mission-oriented evangelical outlook and years of prior interaction with Māori.[9] Marsden's initial associations with New Zealand were established via the New South Wales penal colony where he arrived in 1794 as assistant to the first chaplain, another evangelical clergyman, Richard Johnson. At the request of Governor John Hunter, Marsden soon became a magistrate, and by 1800, after Johnson's return to England, he had become the senior chaplain in the colony. Well connected in British evangelical circles, Marsden's extensive network of influential friends and mentors included the likes of Charles Simeon and William Wilberforce. Indeed, these connections were instrumental in Marsden's rise from relatively humble origins, and in the shaping of his outlook.[10] Marsden was an early supporter of the evangelical missionary movement, and apparently conceived of his chaplaincy in these terms. He became more directly engaged in the mission to the 'heathen' through his contact with fugitive missionaries from the first (London) Missionary Society (LMS) station at Tahiti. By 1800 he was an adviser to the Society's Committee, and from 1812 he was one its few Foreign Directors.[11]

By the early 1800s Marsden was also befriending Māori, including Te Pahi and Ruatara, who arrived in Port Jackson on trade ships and were invited to stay at his Parramatta farm. His positive assessment of these travellers fuelled a desire to establish a New Zealand mission. The CMS granted its support for this project while Marsden was in England between 1807 and 1809. An initial pair of 'mechanic missionaries' was recruited during this time, including a carpenter, William Hall, and his wife Dinah, and cobbler and rope-maker John King—school teacher Thomas Kendall and his wife Jane subsequently joined them in New South Wales, and they too were part of the first cohort of missionary settlers. Delays meant that the mission only finally commenced at the end of 1814, inaugurated during the first of Marsden's seven visits to New Zealand between 1814 and 1837. Though he was not himself a missionary, and never resided permanently in New Zealand, Marsden was clearly the dominant figure in the formation and early oversight of the mission.

Early symbols and peacemaking

Peace symbols played an important role in the framing of the early mission, and there is evidence that concern about violence and conflict was also a significant factor in Marsden's thinking and strategy. In October 1814, prior to the departure of the initial settlers, he wrote of his 'intention to visit New Zealand and see what can be done to promote the eternal welfare of the inhabitants of that island'. In addition to lofty spiritual aspirations, Marsden expressed another immediate desire: 'in some measure, to put a stop to those dreadful murders which have been committed upon the island for some years past, both by the Europeans and the natives'.[12]

Two stories from the earliest period convey something of the symbolic and strategic significance of peace. The first anecdote concerns Marsden's interactions with Ruatara, the Ngāpuhi rangatira (chief) who became the CMS's first sponsor and protector. Marsden tended to Ruatara when he discovered him sick and distressed on board the *Ann* as they both returned from England in 1809, and subsequently hosted him, initially for eight months, in New South Wales.[13] This hospitality paved the way for the mission. During his stay with Marsden, Ruatara apparently became convinced about the benefits of European agriculture and technology. He also came, in Marsden's view, to revere the Christian religion and pay 'the greatest Respect to the Sabbath Day'.[14] On leaving Parramatta, Ruatara declared his intent to institute a Sabbath in New Zealand upon his return. To promote this, he requested 'a Colour' that could be hoisted to advertise the Sabbath and ensure that his people desisted from their labour. Marsden's response was to offer some white muslin, for as he explained to Ruatara, the 'white flag was the Signal for Peace'.

Sabbath observance was an important feature of the evangelical piety of this period, and instructions to early CMS missionaries emphasised the importance of diligence in Sabbath-keeping. Indeed, directives on Sabbath-Day observance were accorded first priority in the CMS's instructions on 'religious conduct' that were delivered to Hall and King as they departed for New Zealand.[15] The importance of Sabbath observance also featured prominently in the missionaries' own teaching to Māori. This practice proved to be one Christian innovation that Māori accepted relatively readily—perhaps partly out of respect for a day that missionaries had cast as Rātapu, and thus spiritually potent and restricted.[16] A willingness to abstain from fighting on the Sabbath was just one expression of such accommodation.[17]

Marsden shared this contemporary commitment to strict Sabbath observance. Malcolm Falloon has astutely noted that Marsden's Sabbath ideas were concomitant with his emphasis on habits of 'industry' and his antipathy to idleness.[18] It represented a providential day of rest and worship to counterbalance strenuous exertion. Marsden's commitments were also grounded in his understanding of the Sabbath's appointed place in bringing about salvation:

> God hath . . . instituted the Sabbath day for promoting man's spiritual welfare and on this day he more especially converts sinners to himself. He commands his word to be preached upon this day. Sinners hear the joyful sound. The Spirit applies the word with power and men are converted to God by it.[19]

In this context, the image of Ruatara's flag was both striking and significant. As a key emblem of Christianity, the flag was intended to symbolise the peace of the gospel, not only in cessation of labour but also in the ending of strife as part of the total scheme of salvation. White flags continued to act as signals for Sunday observance through the following decades.[20]

Rongopai flag, a symbol of the good news of the gospel of peace, flying at the CMS's mission station at Waimate. Source: William Yate, *An Account of New Zealand* (1835), 197.

A second early anecdote dates to December 1814, upon the arrival of the first party of missionary settlers in New Zealand with Ruatara and a cluster of other northern rangatira. En route to their destination, Hohi in the Bay of Islands, one of this party's first acts on New Zealand soil involved an attempt to broker 'reconciliation' between Ngāpuhi and Whangaroa Māori. Marsden and Ruatara were the key initiators of this interaction, though they were supported by the leading Ngāpuhi rangatira Hongi Hika and Korokoro, who were also accompanying the voyage.[21]

The reconciliation in question took place around Matauri Bay in Northland on 19–20 December 1814. It followed in the wake of the *Boyd* incident of 1809, in which some local Māori carried out a reprisal attack on the visiting ship as it lay at anchor in Whangaroa Harbour. The ship was destroyed and most of its crew were killed. Important consequences followed from these events, including a halt on shipping to New Zealand, postponement of the CMS mission, and a cycle of conflict—particularly between Ngāpuhi and Ngāti Uru. The episode was also significant for more generally cementing New Zealand's reputation among European observers as a dangerous corner of the Pacific.

Marsden's interest in pursuing reconciliation partly arose out of a desire to ascertain the truth of what had transpired in 1809. Marsden believed that injustices had been perpetrated against Te Pahi. This particularly concerned him because Te Pahi had earlier been prepared to act as the protector of the mission. But he was blamed for the attack on the *Boyd* and died in 1810 following a retributive assault on his pā (fortified settlement) by European whaling ships.[22] Marsden's letter of October 1814 no doubt had these events in mind. Crucially, his interest in brokering reconciliation reflected a concern to ensure the safety of the missionary settlers—a condition that he had emphasised as a requisite for the mission in his negotiations with Ruatara.[23] Stability would also foster the shipping and trade that would make the missionary venture viable. These benefits of peace had been threatened by frequent skirmishes at Te Puna, in the area where the mission was to be established, following the *Boyd* incident.

Landing of the Reverend Samuel Marsden in New Zealand, 19 December 1814. Published in *Annals of the Diocese of New Zealand*, edited by Sir Charles Jasper (London: Society for the Promotion of Christian Knowledge, 1847). Source: PUBL-0191-frontis, Alexander Turnbull Library, Wellington.

Given the problems that LMS missionaries had experienced previously in Tahiti, and the warlike reputation of contemporary Māori, the parties' desire for peace evidently evoked surprise as well as delight. Marsden reported his wonder 'at the mysteries of Providence. . . . Never did I behold the blessed advantages of civilization in a more grateful light than now.'[24] From Matauri Bay, the party headed south to Hohi, where Marsden soon after preached his famous Christmas Day sermon from Luke 2, heralding the start of the mission there. That sermon is well known. Earlier commentators were also impressed with the significance and symbolism of the earlier reconciliation, though it is less well remembered now.[25] As one nineteenth-century biographer of Marsden remarked:

> Seldom since the words of the prophet were first uttered have they had . . . a more significant, or a more correct appropriation than they now received. 'How beautiful upon the mountains are the feet of him that bringeth good tidings,

> that publisheth peace; that bringeth good tidings of good, that publisheth salvation.'[26]

The central themes of the Christmas sermon had been well rehearsed in those preceding events.

Marsden as peacemaker

These vignettes from the establishment of the mission are suggestive. Yet there is also further more substantial evidence that Marsden spoke widely against warfare, and that Kendall and others supported this orientation from the beginning of the settlement.[27] Despite only occasional appearances in New Zealand, Marsden repeatedly sought to act as an intermediary in disputes and broker reconciliation. Prior to 1828, he was arguably more successful than the settlers in doing so.

Marsden's journals recount a number of occasions in which he attempted to act as peacemaker, including efforts to conciliate in disputes between Māori and European whalers in 1815.[28] Similar entreaties were made in 1819, 1820, and 1823 between various Māori leaders in the Bay of Islands, Tauranga, the Hokianga, and the Thames–Waikato region.[29] In 1830, he was present when the so-called Girls' War broke out at Kororāreka, and along with resident missionaries Henry Williams, Richard Davis and Gilbert Puckey played a significant part in negotiating a ceasefire. Invariably, these exchanges occurred in places where Marsden already had significant relationships with Māori—often established though New South Wales connections, and previous travel—or where he was seeking to extend them. Marsden's own hospitality to Māori in New South Wales, his status as the father of the mission and his largesse in dispensing sought-after goods all built mana (prestige, authority, influence), and paved the way for his involvement in mediation. For the role of peacemaker, or intermediary, was a traditional one that fell to men of standing who had connections to both the contending parties.[30]

Not all interventions were successful or long-lasting. Indeed, even the initial Matauri Bay reconciliation proved far from durable. By 1817, quarrels reignited during a 'naval mission . . . to obtain peace' with Hongi Hika's 'enemies at the North

Cape'.[31] When Marsden returned to New Zealand in 1819, he found that Hongi was once again set to wage war against Whangaroa Māori. According to Marsden's account:

> I told him we had heard of his intention to go to war with the people of Wangarooa [Whangaroa], and remonstrated with him upon the folly of carrying on a continual warfare one with another. Several of the subordinate chiefs urged me to speak to Shunghee [Hongi] to give over fighting as they wished to live at peace, and some of them requested me to take Shunghee with me to Parramatta, and that this would tend to promote the general quiet.[32]

Despite deploying 'every argument . . . to dissuade him from fighting', Hongi simply laughed—though he did also agree to desist from waging war, at least while Marsden was around. Impermanent peace was not unusual. Such deference to Marsden's wishes was, however, striking. It indicated a level of respect and a sense of responsibility, and that Hongi understood the value of placating and thereby protecting his missionary assets. It also demonstrated that the opposition of Marsden—and more generally of the CMS—to such warfare was well understood even at this early stage.

Another expression of peacemaking may be seen in the CMS's emphasis on education. In this context, opposition to war entailed efforts to undermine patterns of conflict and violence. Between 1815 and 1827, Marsden hosted a 'seminary' for young Māori—primarily the children of rangatira—at Parramatta. Recent analyses have highlighted this institution as a place of mutual education.[33] The seminary was created with several purposes in mind. As well as direct instruction and interchange, Marsden explicitly claimed to be working to promote peace by fostering relationships among the offspring of influential adversaries:

> It is very pleasing to see the Sons of the rival Chiefs living with me, and forming such mutual Attachments. . . . By the Sons of Chiefs living together in civil Life, and all paid equal attention to, they will form Attachments that will destroy that Jealousy, which has kept their Tribes in continual war.[34]

This longer-term strategic approach was apparently more generally embraced, for later descriptions also characterised the function of schools for Māori as means of 'counteracting native ferocity'.[35]

The peace ethic and the evangelical missions

Marsden's opposition to war within Māori society was not a pacifist campaign. Peter Brock, Martin Ceadel and others have identified the growth of a rigorous peace movement in Britain in the 1790s that extended beyond Quakerism.[36] It is not evident that Marsden was specifically influenced by this turn. Nor is it clear that this movement had a substantial impact among evangelical Anglicans generally, despite the pacific tendencies of William Wilberforce and others who expressed distaste for the carnage of war.[37] There were some, including Henry Williams, who became more principled in their opposition after the Napoleonic Wars, partly because of their war experience.[38] Reflecting in 1819 on his move from the navy to Christian ministry, Williams wrote: 'I rejoice that He called me out of darkness into His marvellous light, and from the pursuit of war . . . to convey the Gospel of peace to a far distant nation.'[39] Yet campaigning anti-war organisations such as the first British Peace Society (the Society for the Promotion of Permanent and Universal Peace), founded in 1816, were more strongly influenced by Quaker and Nonconformist support than Church of England evangelicalism.[40]

The peace gospel and peace programme established under Marsden was therefore not representative of the nascent British anti-war movement, but reflected a peace ethic shaped by more widely shared evangelical emphases. His ideas about peace were ultimately grounded in the gospel of peace with God through the atoning death of Christ.[41] An analysis of Marsden's sermons delivered in New South Wales reveals that his usual way of preaching about peace emphasised its relationship to the gospel gifts of life and salvation—gospel peace was a gift of spiritual tranquillity and rest.[42] Violent conflict, hostility, turmoil: these were external manifestations of spiritual hostility against the Creator. In the missionary context, warfare, unrestrained by rightful authority, demonstrated that Māori were held under Satan's thrall and therefore in need of salvation. Spiritual and temporal peace were thus seen to be bound together. To Marsden, missionaries were servants of the gospel of peace, with a 'roving commission' to 'sound the silver trumpet of jubilee'; their call was linked to texts such as Isaiah 11, with its millennial expectation of a new age of global justice and goodwill.[43] This binding of temporal peace with the 'eternal peace held out by Jesus Christ' was explicitly articulated by CMS missionaries during peacemaking deliberations.[44]

Thus formulated, the notion of a peace gospel permeated much missionary discourse of this period. So, Thomas Haweis, in a famous sermon launching the Missionary Society in 1795, proclaimed: 'We meet under the conduct of the Prince of Peace; and unfurling the banner of his cross, desire to carry the glad tidings of his salvation to the distant lands sunk in heathen darkness, and covered with the shadow of death.'[45] Significantly, Haweis's message explicitly eschewed violent conquest as a means of advancing Christianity, thus distinguishing the voluntary missionary society from coercive State power, and persuasion from the application of force. His message also emphasised the importance of amity between Christians for the sake of Christian witness.

In the New Zealand mission, those ideals were taken up as part of the call for missionary peacemaking from the outset. The CMS Committee's instructions to King and Hall emphasised that their duty was 'to instruct the natives how to build houses and boats, &c., &c., and not to fight.—but to teach them to live in harmony as you do.'[46] Josiah Pratt's prayer for King and Hall in 1811 was that they would have 'peace and harmony together'. Pratt later charged Kendall to be 'a steady and determined peace-maker', invoking the words of Scripture: 'If it be possible, as much as lieth within you, live peaceably with all men.'[47] As it turned out, the early mission was beset with internal strife. By May 1816, William Hall was reporting that '[t]hese several weeks Hall the Smith has been living in enmity with Mr Kendall'. Soon after, Kendall attacked Hall with a chisel; a firearm was discharged in response, with the smith accidentally shooting his own wife through the arm.[48] Amity was in short supply for much of the first decade.

The Committee's instructions to Hall and King were made in the context of forbidding them to participate in any local wars, recognising that 'wars are not uncommon in New Zealand'.[49] Marsden's comments at the time of the Hohi land purchase in 1815 made explicit that this prohibition extended to the supply of weapons. Bay of Islands rangatira were advised that 'the smith should make them axes, or hoes, or any other tools they might stand in need of, but that he was on no account to repair pistols or muskets or make any warlike instruments, not even for the greatest chief upon the island'.[50] A few years later Marsden emphasised his personal opposition to the diffusion of muskets among Māori, explaining something of his rationale:

> Muskets and gunpowder I disapprove of, as they tend to inflame the warlike spirit of the Natives. Saws, spades, hoes, and axes will civilize them, and induce domestic and commercial habits; will give them something to eat and to sell, and will prepare them for receiving the Gospel.[51]

This opposition, and his admonitions to avoid violence or force against Māori, represented a rare change of opinion.[52] In 1801, in the wake of faltering in the Tahiti mission, Marsden had advised the Missionary Society directors in London of his view that any subsequent mission there should be large and well-armed enough to defend itself 'from the violence of the Natives', and be protected from local rivalries.[53]

Yet the question of arms remained highly contentious. Marsden opposed the trade in muskets among Māori for a variety of essentially strategic reasons.[54] The role of muskets in escalating the scale and devastation of intertribal conflict was clearly a factor, but opposition to the trade preceded this becoming a substantial consideration. Early trading had occurred largely out of necessity, although desire for leverage among Māori was also a salient factor. Significantly, when Marsden contended with Kendall about Kendall's continued arms dealing, he conceded that muskets were civilised weapons.[55] He evidently appreciated their utility in approved contexts, and furnished some arms to settlers on that basis. Marsden never questioned the role and legitimacy of the armed forces either, though he accepted that they were not always virtuous. Indeed, Marsden expressed respect for sailors who 'fight our battles, defend our country, expose themselves to every hardship, and support our church and state against all foreign enemies', even as he fretted about the 'want of the sacred ordinances' among them and their consequent neglect of God.[56]

Sarah Dingle has argued that, overall, the New Zealand CMS did not repudiate warfare per se, but accepted its legitimacy when prosecuted by civilised nations where just causes could be attributed.[57] Marsden and his colleagues thus fitted within a just war tradition that sanctioned the use of rightly authorised and applied force. They were more pacificist than pacifist—principled in opposition to war, yet more prudential than absolutist, and shaped by specific considerations. They were highly critical of the Māori tradition of utu (reciprocity, payback), which was seen to perpetuate and escalate violence, and work against gospel values of forgiveness and reconciliation. Yet Marsden also accepted the legitimacy of capital punishment in the Māori context. And in discussing Māori justice-making, he admitted that force was sometimes warranted in redressing wrongdoing—even if loss of life was regrettable.[58] The Ten Commandments prohibited killing, or murder, but there were nevertheless conditions where the lawful shedding of blood was accepted.

Peace, civilisation and the political theology of empire

As the preceding discussion has suggested, the relationship between peace and 'civilisation' was a crucial factor in Marsden's understanding, and in the peace ethic established within the mission. It is well known that Marsden promoted civilisation as the route to Christianisation. Industry, agriculture and trade were all identified as key indicators of civilisation, and means for its advancement among Māori. Crucially, these pursuits were all specifically contrasted with the evils of idleness and warfare, and presented as means for peace and prosperity. The logic of this contrast formed the basis of Marsden's message at the Matauri Bay reconciliation in 1814, where he sought to persuade local chiefs 'how much more it would be for their interest and happiness to turn their attention to agriculture and the improvement of their country than continue to fight and murder one another'. European presence would help, he argued, and 'if they would only attend to the cultivation of their lands and lay aside all wars and murder, they would soon become a great and happy people'.[59]

Similar comments were made on many further occasions as Marsden commended the virtues of the 'peaceful arts'. In 1820, for example, he reported spending one evening with a group of Māori 'conversing on the various consequences of war, the advantages of peace, civil government, agriculture, and commerce'.[60] In 1823, he lamented that warfare flourished because Māori presently lacked alternatives to 'exercise their active minds', adding: 'Should the arts of peace in time open to them the field of commerce to find them employment, they will then have less inclination for war.'[61] And again in 1823, he reflected:

> If they would turn their attention to agriculture and commerce, these would furnish a field sufficient to occupy their minds. They would increase their wants and their means of supplying them. Until something of this kind is adopted, I cannot conceive how their wars are to be prevented.[62]

If peace was the fundamental measure of civilisation, then agriculture and trade provided the essential pathway.

Civilisation also required government. In Marsden's estimation the want of this, and associated law, was another factor in the perpetuation of conflict. As he told one rangatira, Te Toko, in 1820: 'I lamented much that they should live in such a continual state of warfare and be exposed to such public calamities; but I hoped, in time, an end would be put to these wars, and that they would have a regular government which would afford them protection.'[63] As early as 1815, Marsden had argued that the proliferation of so many chiefs, without centralised governance and power, was a leading cause of endemic violence and warfare. In England, war could only be rightfully declared by the king. Therefore, he claimed, 'there were no fighting and murdering one another in England as there were among them'.[64] A social contract was needed to secure more peace-producing political structures, as exemplified in the British model. In this, the king had authority and rights in war but was constrained by the rule of law—limiting their use even of lethal force, for example in the application of the death penalty.

The Reverend Samuel Marsden, engraved by James Fittler in 1808, as the idea for a mission to New Zealand took shape. Source: Acc 23,602, Hocken Collections, Uare Taoka o Hākena, University of Otago.

Marsden continued to promote the idea of centralised kingship, and spoke to various rangatira on the matter. As Hongi Hika's war campaigns stretched ever further, Marsden independently suggested to Waikato and Rewa that the best prospect for a general peace would be to make Hongi king—so long as he would promise to protect them.[65] Few imagined, however, that Hongi would be willing to renounce war, or that he was ambitious for national rule. Much later, Māori did adopt kingship in the face of concerns about land loss under the new colonial government. That move was initiated and strongly promoted in large part by Christian Māori; it needs to be understood in the context of Christian Māori experimentation with new forms of social and political organisation, and as part of a long tradition of Christian promotion of kingship as a means for fostering justice and peace.

In this earlier period, Marsden had no plans to see British models, law or rule imposed upon Māori. Rather, as others have noted, he seems to have imagined the ideal polity as a kind of Christian Māori theocracy, supported by missionaries, but grounded in Māori leadership and the Bible. In this, he may have hoped for the formation of something like the kingships that emerged under Pōmare in Tahiti and Kamehameha in Hawai'i.[66] Judith Binney observes that the notion of ture (law) was introduced in New Zealand as a new category by Marsden and the missionaries, drawing upon a term derived from the legal codes Pōmare introduced in Tahiti. The term may refer to 'codes of behaviour that the missionaries and their congregations adopted'.[67] Ture was therefore an intermediate category, distinct from English law and traditional Māori ritenga and tikanga (customs and protocols), in which legal interpretation finally rested with Māori as they engaged with missionary understandings of Christian law. It supposed the possibility of a new kind of Christian polity.

Where Marsden did promote application of British law, he typically did so with the intent of protecting Māori from the depredations of European whalers and traders—as occurred from the outset of the mission.[68] In 1830, in the wake of the conflict at Kororāreka, Marsden cautioned against the establishment of a military settlement in New Zealand. Nevertheless, he recommended to Governor Darling that 'a small armed King's vessel' be dispatched during the whaling season to prevent 'mischief' from whalers, and to apprehend runaway convicts.[69] British intervention eventually increased in the 1830s. Missionary opposition gave way to reluctant support, invariably framed around ideas of 'peace and good order' and 'protection'.[70] Notably, those terms featured in the 1835 Declaration of Independence and the Treaty of Waitangi in 1840. The shift towards support for a more interventionist empire in the late 1830s was dramatic and fateful. It represented a change of policy and strategy, but not of missionary goals or political theology.

Conclusion

In 1814, when Samuel Marsden reflected upon the launch of the New Zealand CMS mission to New Zealand he expressed his awe at the working of providence, in which God was using a penal colony 'to make a way for His missionary servants . . . [to] publish peace to the heathen world'.[71] This reflection was striking, not only for its providential interpretation of the British empire, but also for the centrality of peace in Marsden's articulation of the mission's purpose. Such language was rhetorical, but not merely so. Neither did it invoke a gospel of peace conceived purely in spiritual terms as peace with God through Christ.

Marsden's peace gospel was not pacifist in an absolute sense. Yet it was rigorous. It sought literally to implement the biblical visions of Isaiah and Micah, of a day when swords would be beaten into ploughshares, spears into pruning hooks, and when warfare between 'nations' would end.[72] The peace gospel promoted ideals of reconciliation and non-violent resolution of conflict, as well as reorganisation of the social and political order to address patterns of conflict and warfare. Marsden's criticisms of Māori society and ideas about peace were deeply grounded in his convictions concerning civilisation. The cultural biases of his outlook are obviously susceptible of criticism. Yet it is important to recognise that Marsden was primarily committed to the advancement of Christian civilisation rather than the reach of the British empire, and that the two were not coterminous. The latter was useful, and providential, so far as it facilitated the creation of the former among Māori. Empire aided God's plan for the salvation of Māori, primarily by promoting civilisation—expressed through the peaceful arts of agriculture and trade, and through models of godly government, law and good order.

It is well known that there were important debates within the CMS over strategy, and the merits of the so-called 'civilisation first' policy that Marsden advocated. Significantly, adherence to the peace gospel transcended such differences. Ideas about peace were broadly influential within the mission, and over time became increasingly important in terms of Māori engagement with Christianity. Missionary settlers witnessed the conditions and consequences of warfare at close hand, but had little initial capacity to exert tangible influence. They became more engaged, and effective, in mediation as the mission became more independent, and as Māori began to pursue peace more vigorously from the late 1820s. Missionary peacemaking flourished from that time as Māori invited them to act in this traditional mediating role. In many ways, this flourishing was the outworking of a peace ethic that had been established much earlier. Missionaries had been preaching peace from the outset. They continued to do so as the CMS opened new stations, spreading south from the Bay of Islands.

3

Te Waharoa's War and Missionary Visions of Peace

Peter Lineham

The Church Missionary Society (CMS) took a major step in 1833 when with the permission of the parent committee in London, and the support of the local committee of missionaries, it commenced the establishment of a new branch of the mission out of the Bay of Islands in the Thames, Waikato and Bay of Plenty regions. In the new context the work of brokering peace was as crucial as it had been in the north, and as interconnected with evangelism. An intertribal war partially destroyed the mission, and missionaries were despondent at the outcome, so deeply connected were peace and evangelism. In the minds of the converts, too, peace and the Christian gospel were interconnected, and the significance of the young girl Tārore's death and the shaping of Wiremu Tāmihana Tarapīpipi Te Waharoa's vision for Kīngitanga (Māori King movement) were consequences of that CMS mission and its failure. The Christian vision for peace succeeded at its point of seeming defeat. In retrospect the mission succeeded in unexpected ways.

The missionaries in the new CMS outreach insisted on the maintenance of peace between Waikato and Bay of Plenty Māori as a condition for placing missionaries in the area. The position of the senior missionary, Henry Williams, in negotiations during his southern visit in February 1833 was clear. He pointed to 'the unhappy consequences of war, involving them in perpetual confusion, and restraining them from hearing and receiving the truths of the Gospel of Jesus Christ'.[1] He believed that the desire for missionaries was so great that he could demand a commitment to peace between the Waikato and Bay of Plenty tribes. Interpreting the effects of intertribal warfare in spiritual terms, he described war as Satanic and made it clear that the mission would leave immediately if peace was not declared.[2] Alfred Nesbit Brown, the senior missionary sent south, shouldered the responsibility of keeping the peace, negotiating peace between tribes on the grounds that 'Jesus Christ . . . commanded all men to love one another'.[3] When the peace collapsed he made the decision to close the key mission station at Matamata. So peace proved to be not just a goal but also a condition of the mission.

The vision for the CMS southern mission

In 1831 a deputation visited the Bay of Islands from Rotorua, pleading for missionaries to be sent there.[4] Late in 1831 and in March 1832 exploratory visits were made, 'to see in what temper of mind [the natives there] may be in at present'.[5] Then in February 1833 Henry Williams and a team of missionaries made an extensive visit to the Waikato and Bay of Plenty, travelling by canoe up the Waihou River to Te Aroha and then hiking to Matamata and back.[6] Their goal was 'the promotion of peace among the native tribes' and an appraisal of the disposition of the tribes towards their coming. They were caught up in peace negotiations as they travelled:

> we determined to change our route and go direct to Maketu, see the contending parties and endeavour if possible to moderate their feelings, at least to see them and shew them how contrary are their proceedings to the peaceful spirit of the Gospel of Jesus Christ.[7]

They were besieged with requests for missionaries to reside in the area with the hope that their presence would 'check the evil which abounds'.[8] As the missionaries prepared to leave the territory of Ngāti Hauā, the principal inland Waikato tribe, they received a delegation which 'urged the necessity of not leaving them to themselves, but that we must return, and that some Missionaries should be here to move continually amongst them to preserve peace'.[9] Te Arawa, the great Bay of Plenty tribe, took the same outlook when the missionaries visited them, and Henry Williams 'expressed our desire to see peace established in order that Missionaries might come amongst them'.[10]

Missionaries passing through a swamp, with support from Māori guides, en route to Matamata. The missionaries are, from left to right: Henry Williams, Alfred Nesbit Brown, William Fairburn, and John Morgan, who is being assisted, having slipped into a hole. Source: Missionary Register, September 1836, 438.

Once the parent committee in London had approved the funding of the new station, the missionaries returned searching for suitable sites. The decision to settle at Pūriri just up the Waihou River was because the friendly tribes of Ngāti Whanaunga, Ngāti Tamaterā and Ngāti Maru were all close at hand. The Pūriri Mission Station was opened by James Preece and John Morgan at Christmas time in 1833 although the swampy setting soon proved its unsuitability.[11]

An invitation from the paramount chief of Ngāti Hauā, Te Waharoa, decided the location of the second base.[12] At his suasion Williams and colleagues visited the great inland pā (fortified settlement) at Matamata.[13] Matamata offered ready access to other Waikato tribes.[14] On 9 April 1835 a station was opened just outside of Te Waharoa's pā at Matamata by Brown and Morgan. A second Waikato station was opened in a remote location at Mangapōuri, near Pirongia, by James Stack and James Hamlin. In August 1835 a station was opened at Tauranga by Morgan, William Wade, Philip King and John Flatt. At the same time a station was opened at Te Koutū near Rotorua, by Thomas Chapman and Henry Pilley. Missionaries were rotated between these stations over the next two years. Thus in just 18 months a whole new mission district developed, founded on the assumption of peace.

Tensions in the region and Te Waharoa's role

Māori society seemed more violent to outsiders than to those within. The rules of utu (reciprocity, payback) called for an act of equivalent violence to respond to violent or offensive acts. Māori were insistent that reparations must be made by the wronged person, should an offence be committed. The right to revenge for wrongs and defence of status merged in acts of muru (reprisal raids). Given the lack of settled tribal boundaries, increasing population pressures and the arrival of European arms, these traditional procedures were increasingly bloody. Missionaries who attended tribal gatherings struggled to understand the rapid swings in attitude and found the sudden resort to violence very troubling.

The new missionary bases were in territory dominated by the Tainui tribes and their competitors the Te Arawa people. It had been a war-torn area over the previous 15 years. The Ngāpuhi aggression at Thames in 1821 had forced Ngāti Maru inland, thus inflaming its relationships with Ngāti Hauā, which was itself caught in an ongoing conflict between the eastern and western hapū (sub-tribes) of Tainui.[15] There were traditional Ngāti Hauā landholdings in Matamata and in Tauranga, and the tribe was thus in an exposed position.[16] Te Waharoa showed great skill in maintaining Ngāti Hauā's position.[17] Evelyn Stokes argues that his overall aim was a highly rational one, to secure future kaimoana (shellfish, seafood) for his hapū, along with coastal access and contacts with European traders.[18]

In August 1834 at a meeting with William Williams, Brown and Morgan, Te Waharoa played his cards well in seeking a missionary who might help him to believe.[19]

> Old Waharoa said, that his residence was at a cross-path; and that, while sitting there, he should see a white man coming toward him, whom he should find to be a Missionary from Tauranga, passing through his place on a visit to the Missionaries at Waipa: that afterwards he should see another white man coming along, who would prove to be a Missionary from Waipa, going to Tauranga, or else to the Thames Station. . . .[20]

The missionaries for their part depended on Te Waharoa's support since the inland location of Matamata made it more vulnerable than any of their coastal stations.

The Pūriri and Matamata mission stations were 87 kilometres apart, while Matamata and Thames were 67 kilometres apart, and Tauranga was situated 50 kilometres over the Kaimai hills and 63 kilometres from Rotorua. Thus the stations were far further apart than those in the Bay of Islands, and more separated by tribal boundaries between Te Arawa and Ngāti Maru and the other Tainui tribes, and between Ngāti Maru and Ngāti Hauā. There were further tensions between Ngāti Hauā and Te Arawa at Rotorua, and they were exacerbated by Ngāti Hauā's interests at Tauranga on the coast. These were the realities of the situation that confronted the missionaries in their new stations.

Te Waharoa saw the value of the missionary call for peace in this tense environment. The missionary offer to broker peace was convenient. William Yate, ever prone to exaggeration, reported a chief's speech made at the arrival of the missionaries at the Thames station:

> 'The Missionaries', he said, 'are come to blunt the points of our spears—to snap our clubs asunder—to draw the bullets out of our muskets—to bury our bayonets in the ground—to bring this tribe and that tribe together—and to make all, all to live in peace.' A loud shout then burst from the whole assembly—'We will have them! We will have them!'[21]

The work of peacemaking was a high priority for the missionaries in the southern district. Warfare was a serious threat to their work—and to the investment in the new stations.

The collapse of the peace

There were skirmishes between Ngāti Hauā and Ngāti Maru in September 1834 which caused significant problems for the mission. Fortunately peace was restored.[22] When Brown and John Wilson sought to go up river to Matamata on 29 January 1835, one pā demanded a toll but they were assured that, 'although we were going to reside with Waharoa's tribes, we were Missionaries to them as well as to the Nati haua, and would visit them as we passed up and down the river'.[23] On 9 September 1835 Brown wrote to the chiefs of Ngāti Whanaunga, Ngāti Maru, Ngāti Pāoa and Ngāti Tamaterā at Thames, pleading for peace.[24] Ngāti Maru agreed to open negotiations, and sent a letter to Te Waharoa.[25] Te Waharoa promised peace so long as the Thames hapū stayed away from Matamata.[26] This truce lasted for the next few months but Te Waharoa built up a stock of arms in order to protect his interests.[27]

Ngāti Hauā's relationship with Te Arawa faced a deeper crisis a few months later, when on 25 December 1835 Te Hunga of Ngāti Hauā was killed while visiting Rotorua by Haerehuka, of Ngāti Whakaue from Ōhinemutu, a local Rotorua marae.[28] The missionaries at Rotorua buried his severed head with respect and warned of the consequences.[29] Te Waharoa was under immediate obligation to respond to the insult to Ngāti Hauā under the laws of utu. At Matamata, Brown approached Te Waharoa seeking to negotiate peace and avoid an act of muru but Te Waharoa was emphatic on the need for revenge and soon departed to his Ōtūmoetai pā at Tauranga to prepare for the attack. Nevertheless Brown was permitted to go to Maketū to make contact with Te Arawa, and he negotiated the safe departure of Te Arawa people unconnected with the killing.[30] Tainui allies of Te Waharoa, including Ngāti Korokī and Ngāti Maniapoto, assembled at Matamata. On 23 March 1836 the Tainui warriors left for the Bay of Plenty.[31] The first engagement was at Maketū on 29 March.[32] Te Tumu, also on the Bay of Plenty coast, was the site of the next battle.

Sacking of the mission stations at Rotorua and Matamata

Over the next few months the noose tightened on Rotorua itself.[33] War parties marauded across the forest paths between Matamata, Tauranga and Rotorua. In August Te Waharoa took his warriors to the Ōhinemutu pā in Rotorua, and the Te Arawa troops moved out of the fortified pā to attack him. Te Waharoa then moved his camp into the grounds of the Rotorua mission house at Te Koutū outside the pā. The mission house was highly compromised as Te Waharoa attacked Rotorua and then withdrew. The two young missionaries in the mission house, Samuel Knight and Henry Pilley, panicked:

> two of the enemy came up and demanded admittance; alleging, as their reason, a desire to search whether any of their enemies were secreted there. . . . They would not believe me; . . . I walked through the house, through such a scene as beggars all description: every room was filled with naked savages, armed, their countenances lighted up with an infernal expression of rage and exultation, horrifying; and many, most of them, sprinkled with blood, warm from the bodies of their enemies.[34]

Knight was pulled around a room in the station, but then he was rescued by 'a young Chief of Waikato', perhaps Tarapīpipi or Ngākuku.[35] Pilley for his part resisted by force:

> the Natives . . . threw him down and stamped upon him. One struck him with the butt-end of his musket, and threatened to shoot him: another struck him under the ear with his fist, the mark of which I afterward saw.[36]

The Te Arawa people subsequently seized the mission station and torched it.[37] Chapman, the senior missionary, who had been absent in Matamata, returned a fortnight after the sacking along with John Wilson, and they reported that all that remained was a chimney.[38]

Brown conceded that 'the stripping on the part of the Waikato natives was not a premeditated act', and another missionary saw the burning as a Te Arawa attempt to ensure that Ngāti Hauā did not use it again as a base.[39] Still both tribes had shown no respect to the neutrality of the mission station. Nothing like this had ever happened in the Bay of Islands since the attack on Wesleydale at Whangaroa in 1827.

Māori believers subsequently warned the missionaries that the Matamata station was under threat and the junior missionaries left there unwisely decided that they would evacuate before their station too was sacked. A group of friendly Māori were the first group to evacuate to Pūriri. While this party were making their way through the swamps, Ngākuku's daughter Tārore was killed by Te Arawa raiders. The beheading and cutting out of the heart of the little girl were peculiarly ruthless, and arguably an indirect attack on the mission.[40] The remnants of that group of evacuees, led by John Flatt and Ngākuku, fled back to Matamata.

Local Māori had moved into the Matamata pā, meanwhile, in expectation of a Te Arawa attack. The mission station was outside the walls, and as a further precaution Morgan began transferring goods out of the mission station. In the absence of Te Waharoa he felt that 'we were left, under God, upon our own resources'.[41] In doing so they undercut the tapu (sacred restriction) which Te Waharoa had imposed over the station for its protection.[42] Members of Te Waharoa's own tribe of Ngāti Hauā on 13 September 1836 sacked the station, breaking open the packages, stealing and scattering the contents.[43] The missionaries tried but failed to evict the marauders, although the missionaries experienced no violence.[44] Stokes has suggested that local people were acting on the assumption that the missionaries had abandoned the station.[45]

Initially Te Waharoa was thought to be behind the sacking. Morgan heard a rumour that the chief had suggested the raid, although he subsequently concluded that this was not Te Waharoa's intention.[46] There were bitter conversations between the missionaries and the chief. Brown demanded an explanation but Te Waharoa argued that the local people had betrayed his instructions and could no longer be trusted.[47] When the compensation demanded by the missionaries was not forthcoming, the missionary committee decided that the station should be closed.[48] Meanwhile most of the missionary force returned to Paihia for their safety and only gradually returned.[49]

The role of the missionaries in the crisis

The missionaries initially hoped that they would be immune in the war, even after Philip Tapsell, the local European trader, was manhandled at Maketū. In the north the missionaries had enjoyed the protection of a tapu, but it was less effective in the south.[50] Brown and Robert Maunsell demanded that Te Waharoa's taua (war party) keep away from the Tauranga station after the Maketū attack.[51] The missionaries felt that the promises given to them had been broken, and Brown accused Te Waharoa of inciting the violent reprisals in Rotorua.[52]

The events of 1836 were very troubling to the missionaries. They had thought that the mission was making rapid progress, and they believed that they had strong support from local Māori. They had enjoyed some respect as they accompanied the war parties of both sides as negotiators. The missionaries refused to greet Haerehuka whose murder of Te Hunga had started the war. John Wilson and William Wade interceded with Te Waharoa before the Maketū attack. Thomas Chapman and Wilson went to Rotorua 'to soften, if possible, the feelings of the chiefs; also to accompany them to whatever place the first assault is to be made'.[53]

Mission work could make no progress in this environment. Brown observed the dramatic decline of numbers attending services from a high of 500 as fears grew of a Te Arawa attack.[54]

> Our work in the settlement seems almost at a stand. Even the school boys desert their houses at dusk and go either into the Pa to sleep or secrete themselves in the Bush, lest they should be surprised in the night by the fight [i.e. fighting party] which they are expecting from Rotorua as payment for the Chiefs killed at Maketu.[55]

He commented elsewhere, 'they seem too much engrossed with the Rotorua affair to attend to the message of mercy and peace'.[56] Brown analysed the problem thus:

> Neither the promises nor the threatenings of God's holy word seem at all to affect them, while the prophecy of their lying God that the Pa will be attacked on Friday next, is the absorbing theme of their conversation. Waharoa was more

> inclined to listen than he usually is, although . . . he said that he wished I would not speak to him about our sacred things for two or three years, at the expiration of which time he meant to believe. I was obliged to tell him that before that period arrived he might probably be in a place where repentance and faith would be unavailing.[57]

As far as the missionaries were concerned the destruction of the station was critical. Wilson was not impressed with the evasiveness of the Rotorua perpetrators of the sacking, but the conditions he set for the mission to remain at Rotorua were met, and the stolen property returned. Wilson was hopeful that the mission could return to Rotorua:

> Through our united efforts we now expect the place will again be built and once more be occupied by our good brother. At present he is much cast down, and no wonder! Yet he still holds his ground in the respect and confidence of the natives. Our way, dear Anne, just now is toilsome and strewed with a few sharp thorns, but come what may, there shall be peace at the last that will more than suffice, and in which all the troubles of the present shall be forgotten, or if remembered, will only increase our joy.[58]

In Matamata the conditions were not met and that is why the missionaries did not return.[59] The mission had been commenced on the basis of a promise of peace and protection which had failed.

Te Waharoa and the crisis

The missionaries misunderstood Te Waharoa. His responsibility was to preserve tribal mana (prestige, authority, influence) against Te Arawa. His welcome to the missionaries was part of his strategy but his first priority was tribal status. Te Waharoa told John Wilson in March 1836 that when the war was over, then 'I wish that my tribe and myself may stand before God'.[60] After the destruction Te Waharoa continued to express the intention of believing once the muru was completed.[61] His prior commitment was to the pursuit of utu but after that the God of peace might be invoked. Te Waharoa was proud of his muru even though the missionaries viewed it as barbaric.[62] He willingly defended cannibalism to Brown.[63] The brutality of the war did not concern him, despite a blunt exchange with Brown in which the missionary warned him that he was destined to go 'to that place of torment which was reserved for persons who . . . would not close with offers of salvation made in His name. The old man looked rather thoughtful, but his heart is now too fully bent on revenge and murder, to pay much attention to a Gospel of love, mercy and peace.'[64]

Yet Te Waharoa had repeatedly warned the missionaries that they were vulnerable in the war. He suggested that movables at Tauranga station be placed on the mission ship, the *Columbine.* He undertook to protect the mission station at Rotorua and placed a tapu over the Matamata station.[65] He also sought to protect the missionaries, and urged them to evacuate their wives after news of the Rotorua sacking.[66] Melvin has argued that Te Waharoa was surprisingly tolerant of missionary breaches of tapu and suggests that Brown expected far too much of someone who was not a convert.[67]

When Te Waharoa died three years later, Brown commented: 'Waharoa was a remarkable character; fierce, bloody, cruel, vindictive, cunning, brave; and yet, from whatever motive, the friend of the Mission.'[68] It was a limited tribute but it contained much truth.

Combining preaching and peacemaking

The missionaries were clearly shaped by a public theology as well as an evangelistic motive. When William Fairburn confronted Koinake, a young chief, at Kopu near Thames in August 1835, he lectured him on the morals of war:

> He seemed to take great pride in two double-barrelled guns. . . . I told him that it was men like him who brought whole tribes into trouble; that . . . most of the Chiefs he was connected with were disposed for peace; but that as long as such men as he . . . were seeking for blood, peace could never be established. . . . I then told him that New Zealand was a land deeply stained with the blood of revenge and [it] was a crying sin before God, and his vengeance hung over the heads of all those persons who committed [murder].[69]

Fairburn's approach to peace negotiations between Te Waharoa and his opponents was to give a sermon on the Prince of Peace.[70] Brown emphasised that the Christian message was one of mercy and peace. Warfare flourished in its absence, and the missionaries felt that the slaughter during the 1836 war was divine judgement on the unrepentant tribes. He felt that Te Waharoa had experienced God's just wrath for not making peace with Rotorua and commented that 'perhaps God was displaying his anger towards them for their sins by cutting off their allies and that they ought to look upon it as a sign to make peace with Rotorua'.[71]

The missionaries believed that Christianity would best be protected by the decline of Māori traditions of revenge and 'the fostering & protecting care of a well-regulated Government'.[72] Certainly Brown saw evidence of 'retributive providence' in the counter-attacks of Te Waharoa against Rotorua, but he considered that the iron law of utu made peace unobtainable.[73]

Missionary magazines went into some detail in their descriptions of the brutality of the war and the resort to cannibalism by warriors on both sides.[74] The extent and scale of the violence also shocked some members of the local tribes, and provoked renewed interest in Christianity in the late 1830s. While at the time it seemed that the Southern Station was an unmitigated disaster, with two stations destroyed and others abandoned and the missionaries forced back to the Bay of Islands, change was afoot.[75] Te Waharoa complained to Brown in 1837 that 'his sons would not listen to him as they used to do formerly—but were always urging him to make peace & he attributed their change of conduct to the Karakia & our Sacred Books'.[76] Missionary peacemaking may have failed at the time, but in the long run the search for peace led many Māori to adopt Christianity.

Christian converts embrace peace

So, while most of the missionaries were absent, a significant group of younger tribal leaders felt the missionaries had been right.[77] They slowly emerged as a Christian party. A key figure was Ngākuku, nephew of Te Waharoa and father of Tārore, who had been deeply impressed by Brown at Matamata in 1835, along with another chief, whom Brown calls Ngataha.[78] By late 1835 Ngākuku was accompanying Brown on his preaching tours.[79]

Tarapīpipi, son of Te Waharoa, had been taught to read by the missionaries and he became another key advocate of peace.[80] After the war he became intensely interested in the Christian message, sought native teachers to remain at the pā when the missionaries withdrew, and then wanted to accompany them to the Bay of Islands.[81] He acted as eyes and ears for the missionaries. When Te Waharoa died, Brown reflected: 'This will be a trying season for his son. May he be kept faithful in his profession, and hold the beginning of his confidence steadfast unto the end!'[82] He was baptised Wiremu Tāmihana on 23 June 1839 at Tauranga, while Ngākuku was baptised a little later.

The would-be converts sensed that the killing of Tārore was specifically targeting the Christian party. They had observed how quick the missionaries were to defend their interests, for the missionaries were very aware that if they were not tough their property would all be pilfered. Ngākuku, however, abjured revenge for his daughter's death.

> There lies my child: she has been murdered, as a payment for your bad conduct, but do not you rise to seek a payment for her. God will do that. Let this be the finishing of the war with Rotorua. Now, let peace be made.[83]

Targeting of the 'professing party' continued, including the murder of six Matamata believers at Horotiu in September 1838 by a Thames war party.[84] This provoked further debate that 'unless they were permitted to get up and defend themselves from these unprovoked assaults, they would all soon be cut off'.[85]

Gradually utu was curtailed by converts. The advocacy of Ngākuku after the death of his daughter was significant. When the murderer, Uita, professed repentance and asked to join the catechists at the Christian pā at Pātetere, he first sought reconciliation with Ngākuku. Ngākuku was willing to embrace

Wiremu Tāmihana Tarapīpipi Te Waharoa, son of Te Waharoa, was one of the most influential Māori Christian leaders connected with the southern CMS mission. An advocate for peace, his mana was central to the formation of new experimental polities, including Christian villages and the Kīngitanga movement. Source: MS-Papers-1491-09/1-3-03, Alexander Turnbull Library, Wellington.

him and Uita was admitted to the pā, although he was later expelled for a period for adultery. At Kuranui in 1849 Brown observed Uita and Ngākuku together at a prayer meeting, evidently friendly towards each other, and commented 'who but the Christian loves his enemy?'[86] This model of a different way to resolve differences was important for the Māori believers, as they sought to interact with unconverted members of their tribe and show that the Christian path could be implemented, although reconciliation was rarely without difficulties.

Such an approach was difficult when other members of tribes continued to embrace utu. Some early converts tentatively created a Christian village adjacent to the Tauranga mission house.[87] In Matamata, the abandonment of the mission station forced the professing party to develop a more independent strategy. They began to separate themselves from the rest of Ngāti Hauā, 'lest they should be partakers of their sins and receivers of their plagues'. In 1839 William Williams observed that their pā at Aongatete contained 300 people.[88] Wiremu Tāmihana (Tarapīpipi Te Waharoa) later established the Christian marae at Pēria where he sought to establish a purified Māori culture. In the absence of a resident missionary he developed his own version of faith. This aspect of the background to the Kīngitanga has rarely been appreciated.[89]

Conclusion

The CMS had held back from commencing the mission in New Zealand while the situation was unstable, but by 1833 they were confident that they could expect a commitment to peace when entering new territory, although they were convinced that only when Māori adopted Christianity would they abandon traditions of violent revenge. But their southern strategy collapsed after Te Waharoa's war, and they were forced to be more cautious in the location of their stations.

Evangelism proved more effective than pledges in bringing peace. The converts among Ngāti Hauā were attracted to the peaceful implications of Christianity, and found ways to embrace reconciliation and communities committed to the rejection of violent utu. The Māori Christian villages were very important in the development of Wiremu Tāmihana's vision of the need for a king movement. The Kīngitanga arose in part as an expression of the introduction of Christian principles to the tribal communities. It was intended to be a Māori Christian peace movement based on scriptural principles. As in the Old Testament, the king was anointed to bring peace between the tribes. The Kīngitanga was criticised by the missionaries and by Bishop Selwyn as antithetical to the peace of the land, but it was in origin a Māori Christian version of the missionary demand for peace. Te Waharoa's war led the missionaries to leave Matamata because the pledges of peace had failed, but this left scope for the converts to develop their own distinctive vision of how to bring the Christian peace. And in the New Zealand peace tradition, this explains the profoundly Christian strands in the Māori effort for peace in the face of Pākehā incursions.

4

Te Mānihera, Kereopa and Christian Peacemaking among Māori

Stuart Lange

Early in 1847 two Christian Māori from Ngāti Ruanui in south Taranaki, Te Mānihera Poutama and Kereopa Hemi Patene, travelled up to the Taupō region to preach Christianity among Ngāti Tūwharetoa, their tribal enemies. The two men were ambushed near Tokaanu and slain. They have often subsequently been regarded as New Zealand's first Christian martyrs. In the two years following their deaths, peace between Ngāti Ruanui and Ngāti Tūwharetoa was made, and the leading killer and his people built a church and accepted a Christian teacher.

The story of Te Mānihera and Kereopa provokes a number of questions. Was their motivation proselytising, or peacemaking? Why were they killed? How were these events interpreted at the time, and since? Is this a martyrdom story, or is it more a Christian mission story, illustrative of the great vigour and expansiveness of early Māori Christianity? If so, how well was the original missionary aim of Te Mānihera and Kereopa fulfilled? Or is this primarily a peace story, demonstrating the pervasive emphasis on peace among both missionaries and Christian Māori? Was peace achieved by utu (reciprocity, payback), or by Christian peacemaking? To what extent did the peacemaking also tap into existing Māori protocols of reconciliation, and possibly reflect some pragmatism on the part of Ngāti Tūwharetoa? What does this story tell us about Christian peacemaking?

Answers to such questions begin to emerge from a study of the sources. The principal primary sources come from the Church Missionary Society (CMS) missionary the Reverend Richard Taylor, who was personally involved in the Te Mānihera story at several key points, and especially in the peacemaking phase. He knew all the other main players, and was tireless in keeping a detailed daily journal.[1] Another significant source is the memories captured in the tribal histories of Ngāti Ruanui and Ngāti Tūwharetoa.[2]

The background to the killings

Ngāti Ruanui, whose rohe (area) was south and south-east of Mount Taranaki, had received Christianity from the late 1830s through former slaves released by Ngāpuhi, especially Wiremu Nēra Ngatai. They then helped take Christianity to tribes further south, Ngā Rauru of Waitōtara and Te Āti Haunui-a-Pāpārangi of Whanganui, and made peace with them. After missionaries arrived in the early 1840s, Ngāti Ruanui related to both Wesleyan missionaries, based at New Plymouth, and CMS missionaries, based at Pūtiki (Whanganui). Taylor was at Pūtiki from 1843.

Ngāti Ruanui and Ngāti Tūwharetoa had long been enemies. In the mid-1830s, Ngāti Ruanui had raided the upper Whanganui River area.[3] In August 1840, a 130-strong Ngāti Tūwharetoa taua (war party) had been soundly defeated in battle at Pātoka Pā near Waitōtara.[4] Several chiefs were slain, most notably the rangatira Tauteka II. Despite the protests of CMS missionary Richard Matthews, a number of Ngāti Tūwharetoa prisoners were then killed by a party of Ngāti Ruanui. Taylor recounted how 'this act was never forgotten. The Taupos said, after they had shaken hands with their prisoners, and fed them, they [Ngāti Ruanui] killed them in cold blood, and, therefore, they [Ngāti Tūwharetoa] determined to murder the first they could meet with from that tribe, as a satisfaction for the blood then shed'.[5] Significantly, however, Tauteka's son Te Herekiekie was spared, possibly because of his rank and tribal connections.[6]

Intent on utu, a large taua of Ngāti Tūwharetoa returned in March 1841, led by paramount chief Mananui Te Heuheu Tukino II (known as Te Heuheu). Local tribes declined to fight, on the basis they were now Christian, and retreated up the coast to Patea. Te Heuheu killed a couple of people, and went home with Tauteka's bones.[7] In January 1845 he came back again with 300 warriors, causing great alarm among local Māori, missionaries and settlers. Taylor met him, and tried to negotiate peace.[8] Local Māori left him gifts of kumara, tobacco and fish, and a message that they felt no enmity. Captain Robertson of the warship *Hazard* warned him he would take military action if he did not leave. Te Heuheu decided to go. He acknowledged the influence of the missionaries in making peace, and that of a son who was Christian.[9] While Te Heuheu was personally contemptuous of Christianity,[10] Christian peacemaking had nevertheless helped avert war.

The following year, 1846, a calamitous landslide swept through Te Heuheu's kainga (settlement) at Te Rapa (Waihi). He and sixty others (including his eight wives) died. To build relationships, Taylor went on an arduous mid-winter trip up to Lake Taupō, taking two weeks each way.[11] He took others with him, including his head teacher at Whanganui, William Te Tauri, who was himself Ngāti Tūwharetoa.[12] Taylor's visit was appreciated. He spent time with two key chiefs: Iwikau Te Heuheu Tukino III, the new paramount chief (known as Te Iwikau, he was Te Heuheu's son and successor), and Te Herekiekie, the leading chief at Tokaanu. Both of them subsequently visited Taylor in Whanganui.[13]

In the 1840s, Christianity was only lightly established among Ngāti Tūwharetoa. Although some Ngāti Tūwharetoa had associations, nominal or otherwise, with Catholic, Wesleyan or CMS forms of Christianity,[14] the tribe generally 'looked askance' at the Christian faith.[15] Visits by CMS missionaries were rare. CMS 'native teachers' were few, or 'very indifferent'.[16] There had briefly been a CMS mission at Motutere on the south-eastern shore, but the missionary (Seymour Spencer) lived at Rotorua. Alfred Brown assessed the state of Christianity among the Taupō people as 'very low'.[17] Taylor referred to some 'Christian villages', including Waimarino (Korohe);[18] it appears, however, that the hapū (sub-tribes) on the western side of the lake (Ngāti Te Aho at Tokaanu, Ngāti Pehi at Pūkawa and Ngāti Waewae at Rotoaira) were rather less Christianised. It was that element of Ngāti Tūwharetoa which had been at war with Ngāti Ruanui. Some of them remained eager for utu. Among those was Te Kahurangi II, the aggrieved widow of the rangatira Tauteka.

By contrast, the mood among many Ngāti Ruanui had become enthusiastically Christian. For several days over Christmas, in 1846, large numbers of Māori Christians gathered at Pūtiki for prayer and church services, marked by 'much fervour'.[19] On Christmas Day more than 2000 were present. Taylor noted that they were from several tribes 'who but a few years ago could not have been induced to meet together on any terms' but now 'sat quietly by each other's side as brethren'. The same day he baptised eighty-eight adults.[20]

Te Mānihera and Kereopa and their missionary call

The next day, at a prayer meeting with Taylor's native teachers, of whom he had 150, Te Mānihera and Kereopa proposed their dramatic missionary trip.[21] Taylor wrote:

> The duty of aiding those still sitting in heathen darkness was alluded to, when Manihera arose, and said, they had received the Christian faith from the distant country of England, and if we had left our native land, in obedience to the Lord's command, 'To go unto all the world, and preach the Gospel', surely it was theirs also to do the same amongst their own benighted countrymen. For his part, he willingly offered himself as a Missionary to go to his enemies, the Taupo natives, who were still heathen.[22]

The primary motivation, then, was evangelistic. But it must also have appealed to Te Mānihera to take the gospel to enemies in particular, in response to biblical injunctions to love your enemies and do good to those who hate you.[23]

Te Mānihera (Maunsell) Poutama, a middle-aged Ngāti Ruanui chief, was head native teacher for the CMS work at Waokena, on the coastal clifftop near Hawera. Kereopa (Cleopas) Hemi Patene was head teacher at Awetokotoko. Te Mānihera had an intriguing history. In his youth he had been captured by Waikato, then a second time by Ngāpuhi. Off Cape Brett, for the price of some biscuits he had been taken on board a passing Wesleyan mission schooner and spent time with the Wesleyans in Tonga and Norfolk Island.[24] Taylor had 'full confidence' in the 'spiritual state' of both men, and had particularly high regard for Te Mānihera. He wrote: 'love for

God and man beamed in his very countenance, and was manifest in all his actions', and 'he was always conspicuous for piety and attention to his duties, and instead of his first love growing cold, his appeared to increase with time'. Taylor felt that Te Mānihera strikingly demonstrated 'the wonderful effect and power of the Gospel on the mind'.[25]

A number of people warned the two men of the great danger of going into Ngāti Tūwharetoa territory. They were advised not to go, or to delay.[26] Te Mānihera insisted, however, that they were 'tapu to the Lord' and must press on. Taylor felt 'their zeal overcame their prudence'.[27] On 6 February 1847 the two men set out on their mission. They first went south to Porou-ta-whao, in the Manawatū, to urge the anti-government chief Te Rangihaeata to commit to peace.[28] Te Rangihaeata joined those who were predicting their demise. From there they crossed over to the East Coast.[29] Some weeks later they arrived in the Rotorua district, where they spent time at the CMS missions at Te Ngae and Tarawera, and preached at both. Two years later, a Māori at the Te Ngae mission told Taylor that 'we all loved him [Te Mānihera] for his manifest love of God'.[30]

Once at Lake Taupō, the two men proceeded for some days down the south-eastern shore. At Motutere, as elsewhere, they preached. They were warned that the tribe they wished to go among was 'a very wicked one', where the people would not listen but would instead probably kill them. Te Mānihera responded that the reason they were being told they should go no further was the very reason they should: their kaupapa (purpose) was to preach the Gospel to the wicked.[31] From there they continued to Waimarino, which Taylor described as 'a Christian pa').[32] Evidently bypassing Waitahanui at the mouth of the Tongariro River, they arrived at Te Waiariki, north-east of Tokaanu. Again, Te Mānihera preached.

The killings

In the morning, 12 March 1847, Te Mānihera expressed a presentiment of impending death: during the night he had dreamed he had been 'in the Reinga, and met many of his deceased friends, who told him he should soon be with them'.[33]

Accompanied by about ten unarmed young men, from what Taylor called 'the Christian party' of the Taupō people, they set off on the trail towards Tokaanu.[34] Their coming was anticipated.[35] The widow of Tauteka, who lived at Tokaanu, had persuaded Huiatahi of Rotoaira to kill the two Ngāti Ruanui men, as utu.[36] The fact that they were envoys of Christianity was probably of no relevance. A party of about thirty hid in the scrub until the escorting party had filed past. Kereopa was killed outright, by musket fire. Huiatahi, an old man, repeatedly tomahawked Te Mānihera, who was blinded but survived for some hours. Before Te Mānihera died he was able to speak and pray, and to hand to one of the escorting party both his New Testament and a journal which Taylor had requested him to keep.[37] Both Ngāti Ruanui and Ngāti Tūwharetoa retained versions of Te Mānihera's purported waiata poroporoaki (farewell song), in which among other things he voiced his love to his wife Hārata.[38]

Reactions to the deaths

The young men carried the bodies back to Te Waiariki and buried them near their pā (fortified settlement). Outraged, they sent messages to all the 'Christian' villages urging them to 'take up arms and avenge the deaths'.[39] They also wrote to Taylor. Ten days later, Taylor received the news. 'We were all', he writes, 'deeply affected'.[40] At a special prayer meeting the next day with local Christian Māori, Taylor preached that 'the Almighty would over-rule this sad event for good', and that 'the blood of the Saints is the seed of the Church'. Just as Saul, who consented to Stephen's death, later became 'the chiefest of all apostles', so too 'may this tribe which has consented to and joined in this cruel murder hereafter become eminent in its love for God'.[41] Taylor also wrote back to the Taupō Christians, urging them not to seek revenge.[42]

A week later, hundreds attended a second meeting at Pūtiki.[43] Ngāti Ruanui expressed great sorrow and indignation, and at least one speaker urged revenge. Letters from relatives and friends of Te Mānihera and Kereopa, however, 'all breathed a very Christian spirit'.[44] William Te Tauri, Taylor's head teacher

The graves of Te Mānihera and Kereopa at Wareroa Waiariki (1849), as sketched by CMS missionary the Reverend Richard Taylor. Source: E-296-q-015-5, Alexander Turnbull Library, Wellington.

Gathering at the graves of Te Mānihera and Kereopa. Source: Richard Taylor, *The Past and Present of New Zealand with its Prospects for the Future* (1868), 48.

at Pūtiki, suggested the analogy that when the parent kahikatea tree falls, a thick grove of young seedlings then sprouts up. One speaker proposed that further Māori missionaries be sent, two by two, until such time as Ngāti Tūwharetoa converted. The Christian commitment to non-retaliation prevailed, and Taylor was commissioned to go and make peace on behalf of Ngāti Ruanui.[45]

The first peace mission of Te Teira and Te Tauri

On 6 April, Taylor, Te Tauri, Tahana and Aperaniko left Whanganui on their peace mission, by way of the Whanganui River. At several places en route, they were told of rumours that they were seeking revenge.[46] After seventeen days, they arrived at Pūkawa, to be welcomed by Te Iwikau, the new paramount chief. Te Iwikau declared: 'my brother, my child, my father Te Teira [Taylor], welcome!'[47] Taylor replied that they came 'not to avenge, but to make peace'—judgement they left with God. Peace must now be made, and it had been purchased with the blood recently shed.[48] Interestingly, Taylor was not appealing to Christianity as the means of peace, but to the cultural practice of utu. In doing so, he was invoking utu against itself, and thus subverting it; instead of provoking further utu, utu could now secure the cessation of utu. Also, with his language of purchase and shed blood, Taylor was possibly associating utu with at least a tinge of the biblical concepts of sacrificial, redemptive death.

The meeting at Tokaanu the following day, face to face with the killers of Te Mānihera and Kereopa, was much more difficult. The atmosphere in the Tokaanu meeting was extremely tense. Most of the people came in carrying their guns. There was no tangi, the ritual crying when friends meet. For a full fifteen minutes, no one said a thing. At last Te Hemapo, Te Herekiekie's brother, broke the silence. He regretted the lack of the usual welcome. Tahana (one of Taylor's party) reciprocated by saying that for now they were not willing to shake hands. A local speaker avowed that the Tokaanu people were of one mind, and were not at all sorry for the murders. Huiatahi, the chief who had hatcheted Te Mānihera to death, said that his heart was 'not at all dark' for what he had done, as he had killed in accordance with ritenga (custom).[49]

Taylor's co-worker William Te Tauri spoke. The fact that he was Ngāti Tūwharetoa may have helped Te Tauri gain a hearing. Taylor then rose. He declared that they had come 'not to avenge, but to avoid further shedding of blood', and that they left vengeance to the Lord. On the one hand, his party hoped the Tokaanu people would 'see the enormity of their crime, and repent of it'. On the other hand, they accepted that the Tokaanu people had killed Te Mānihera and Kereopa 'in accordance with their ancient customs'. Taylor appealed for an end to killing: 'sufficient blood had been shed'. He explained that they wished the blood of Te Mānihera and Kereopa to be 'the price of a permanent peace between their tribes, that henceforth love might prevail'. Taylor thus set out the basis of abandoning enmity, and embracing peace. He also proposed a process: if Ngāti Tūwharetoa agreed, one of their chiefs should go back and make peace with Ngāti Ruanui. Aperaniko confirmed Taylor's authority to speak for Ngāti Ruanui.[50]

The pivotal response to Taylor was by Te Herekiekie, the leading Tokaanu chief. Te Herekiekie was the son of Tauteka (the rangatira whose slaying in 1840 was the key provocation) and his mother was Te Kahurangi II (the primary instigator of the recent utu). Te Herekiekie said he did not agree with the killings, and would have prevented them if he had been at home. He then declared that he agreed with the proposal for peace, and that Ngāti Ruanui would now be welcome at his pā.[51]

Te Herekiekie's speech had no apparent Christian motivation or content. Nevertheless he did appear to want peace. Pragmatic considerations may have played a part: if peace was refused there was a risk of war; further fighting would mean further loss of life; hapū in the western Taupō area could be outnumbered by the combined forces of Ngāti Ruanui and other 'Christian' tribes; there was a possibility that the Governor might apply the law and send soldiers against the killers, notwithstanding their isolation in the mountainous hinterland. For any of those reasons, Te Herekiekie may have considered it expedient to accept the offer of peace, especially since it was being offered at no cost. The Ngāti Tūwharetoa tribal historian, John Te Herekiekie Grace, gave a different reason: Te Herekiekie, he argued, was always grateful for having been spared from the carnage back at Pātoka in 1840, and thus he favoured peace.[52] Grace, a great-great-grandson of Te Herekiekie, attributed the decisive peacemaking role to his own tupuna (ancestor): 'After a speech full of emotion, the proud chief sat down, and so brought to a close the feuds that had existed for so long.'[53] Te Herekiekie's support for peace was certainly necessary. The crucial initiative for peace, however, was the Christian peacemaking mission by Taylor and his party on behalf of Ngāti Ruanui.

Taylor saw himself as central to the peace offer: he wrote that Te Herekiekie 'fully agreed to my proposal'.[54] It is likely, however, that Taylor had closely collaborated with Te Tauri, Tahana and Aperaniko, and earlier with Ngāti Ruanui, in formulating the peace proposal. Taylor noted his thankfulness to God that he had been 'instrumental in putting an end to what had threatened to bring on a general war', a comment that reflected his fears (partially confirmed in the following days) that some Taupō, Te Arawa and Waikato tribes could easily have risen up against the killers of Te Mānihera and Kereopa.[55]

The uneasy meeting concluded. Taylor and his party, still declining to shake hands or accept food, left for a time of mourning and prayer at the graves of Te Mānihera and Kereopa. They prayed that 'their precious blood . . . might not fall into the ground in vain, but be blessed to the conversion of those by whom it was shed, and become the means of dispelling the darkness of this tribe to spiritual things'.[56]

At Waimarino and Motutere, the party found Māori Christians still very angry about the killings, and deeply sceptical about the sincerity of any peace agreed to by the people at Tokaanu. Taylor was asked why he had come. 'Was it to see the Church trampled underfoot, and the servants of God slain?' 'Was I content to see my beloved children murdered with impunity?' Several spoke 'in the same strain, brandishing their hatchets, and strongly recommending war'. Taylor urged them to keep the peace, and wrote along similar lines to the native teachers at Rotorua.[57] A few days later, while travelling north,

Taylor heard the view that now all the tribes were 'one in Xt [Christ]', they formed a 'mass . . . strong enough to seize the murderer and put him to death'.[58]

In keeping with the agreement at Tokaanu, some chiefs from Ngāti Tūwharetoa subsequently visited Ngāti Ruanui. They 'made peace', were 'hospitably received', and the 'long feud . . . was terminated'. 'Here then', reflected Taylor, were 'the first fruits of Manihera's death': it had 'caused peace'.[59]

The second peace mission

The sealing of the peace, however, required a reciprocating visit by Ngāti Ruanui to Ngāti Tūwharetoa. The young Ngāti Ruanui chief chosen to go was Piripi Wiremu Hanataua, Te Mānihera's successor as head teacher at Waokena.[60] Ngāti Ruanui would not allow him to go, however, unless Taylor went with him.[61] Taylor was able to begin the trip in February 1849, accompanied by Piripi, Tahana, Wiremu Kingi and Hāre Purumera.[62]

At Tokaanu, their reception was very different from what it had been two years earlier. After the karanga (call), Te Herekiekie welcomed them as 'friends and relatives': 'Piripi, friend of Manihera, welcome. Te Teira [Taylor], the object of your journey is good, and as messengers of peace you are all welcome.' Huiatahi, the principal murderer of Te Mānihera and Kereopa, added his welcome to Taylor and Piripi. Piripi said he came 'to cement the peace' and 'to prove that his tribe entertained no enmity'. Others spoke, including Wiremu Kingi and Taylor. They all shook hands, and shared in a feast prepared in their honour.[63]

At Taylor's request, everyone then went and gathered at the graves of Te Mānihera and Kereopa. Those who had carried out the murders pointed out the places where various things had taken place, but Taylor sensed a lack of remorse. To a large crowd, Taylor read the account of Stephen's death (Acts 7), and preached.[64] 'The sight was affecting', he later recalled: 'there were the memorials of the deed before us, and there were the perpetrators of it, with down-cast heads, listening to that Gospel which Manihera and his companion came to proclaim'.[65] Taylor assured the people that he and his party had nothing but love for them. He urged them to repent so that God may forgive them, and prayed for the murderers.[66]

Back at the Tokaanu pā, Huiatahi proposed that a missionary be sent to his kainga at Poutū (Rotoaira), and that there he would give land and construct a church and mission house. Also, many people came forward asking to be instructed as candidates for baptism.[67] Taylor felt 'this was indeed a great and wonderful change, and . . . evidently the Lord's doing'.[68] The following day he preached again, and went on his way. At the request of the chiefs, Taylor left Piripi to stay longer.[69]

As always, there were ambiguities. Taylor was disturbed about the growing 'pikopo' (Catholic) influence in Tokaanu.[70] He had concerns about Te Herekiekie and his wife; he believed the latter was complicit in the murders.[71]

Taylor's third visit, and aftermath

When the church at Poutū had been completed, Taylor and some of his teachers returned to open it, and were 'received with every demonstration of joy'. He received about thirty candidates for baptism, whom he saw as 'fruits of Manihera's death'. He appointed Te Hemapo, who was already baptised (and the brother of Te Herekiekie), as teacher for the new church. When Taylor preached again the next day, he felt 'overpowered' and unable to continue. When he left, 'the entire congregation followed me for nearly a mile, and with many tears bade me farewell. Thus terminated the Mission of Manihera and Kereopa.'[72] This experience contrasted with his previous feeling, that the 'chief possessors' of Rotoaira were 'heathenism and popery'.[73]

Taylor left Taupō 'with the conviction that those gloomy hills of darkness would soon be made light by the bright beams of the Gospel'.[74] However, despite the encouraging responses in 1849 at Rotoaira and Tokaanu, the overall response to Protestant Christianity in the western district appears to have been something of a disappointment. Te Iwikau and Te Herekiekie did not become Christian. It was Te Iwikau who cynically told a visiting CMS missionary (Alfred Brown) that 'When you are in Taupo I am a Churchman. When the Wesleyan missionary is here, I belong to him. When the R.C. priest calls, I am a Papist, and when no

European is here, I am a Heathen.'[75] Two years after T. S. Grace established a CMS mission at Pūkawa in 1854, he reported congregations of 100 but felt that the 'the spiritual condition of the Taupo Maories is far from encouraging. . . . Their belief in witchcraft, and their fear of "tapu", I think could never have been stronger than at present.' Grace noted, however, that peace had been maintained: many disputes which would once have led to war were now settled in a 'Christian manner'.[76] Because of the Hauhau movement, the mission was abandoned in 1862.

How has the story of Te Mānihera and Kereopa subsequently been regarded?

Some earlier treatments emphasised the theme of martyrdom. These included a devout 1854 volume of sixty-two pages of verse:

> Foreseen but yet not fear'd; two fatal balls
> Their destin'd objects reach. Kereopa dies
> Without a sigh; while Manihera gasps
> Within the arms of agonizing death;
> A brother Christian's hand receives from his
> That blessed Book which daily fed his faith,
> While 'mid convulsive throes, his gushing words
> Proclaim its great unutterable worth.[77]

In 1916, Archdeacon George MacMurray wrote a colourful martyrdom piece, published on the front page of the *New Zealand Herald*. His article was factually incorrect in almost every respect (except perhaps that both men were killed). The heart of his re-telling was:

> The devoted teachers were led to the place of execution on a little ridge outside the pa. They asked for time to pray which was given, and after robing themselves in their white garments (surplices) they knelt and prayed fervently, using the prayer of St. Stephen, and uttering words of love and forgiveness to their murderers. Both fell wounded at the first volley, and one (Te Manihera) rose to a sitting posture, still praying, and after being struck with a tomahawk he carefully arranged his white robe over his body and gave up his heroic spirit.[78]

As a later author commented, MacMurray's piece 'bears the mark of fanciful additions'.[79]

Much more subtly, the martyrdom motif was picked up in a restrained narrative in the appendices of the *New Zealand Prayer Book*.[80] A similar approach was taken with the Te Mānihera and Kereopa memorial gravestones outside St Paul's Anglican Church in Tokaanu: the inscriptions do not claim the men were 'martyrs', but 'messengers of Christ' who 'loved not their lives unto death' (Revelation 12:11).[81] A diocesan history summed up the issue of whether or not this is a martyrdom story: 'Although they were not killed for their faith they were there as Christian missionaries and the Maori church has in them its martyrs'.[82]

In 1935, and in a broadly secular way, James Cowan presented it as an example of a *hero* story. Cowan asserted 'that the missionaries who were the chief figures in the story were Maoris themselves heightens the value of their devotion to a noble ideal and their self-sacrifice in the cause of intertribal peace'.[83] Cowan provided no evidence, however, to corroborate his tale about how the men were killed as a human sacrifice for Te Herekiekie's new meeting house.

A. S. Thomson's 1857 early general history included a rudimentary and rather muddled version of the story.[84] William Williams' account (1867) appears derived from Taylor, as was that of Sarah Tucker.[85] In more recent times various parts of the story have been narrated in three published tribal histories and in Keith Newman's *Bible and Treaty*.[86] A careful, brief account is given in Allan Davidson's *Christianity in Aotearoa*.[87] The story does not appear to have been mentioned, however, in recent general histories.

Interpretation

So how should we understand the story of Te Mānihera and Kereopa?

In the first place, this is clearly still something of a martyrdom story. There is something intrinsically evocative about people being put to death for their faith, or—as in this case—being killed as a result of following their sensed call from God despite extreme danger. The story is best told simply as it happened, without embellishments.

Secondly, this is a story about Christian mission—by Māori, and to Māori—in the dynamic years of Māori Christianity in the 1830s and 1840s. The story of Te Mānihera and Kereopa highlights the great vitality of Māori Christianity in the south Taranaki and Whanganui areas in the early to mid-1840s. The story is another example of Māori initiative and agency in disseminating Christianity, in this case across tribal barriers. Along the way, the story illustrates other recurring aspects of the missionaries' work in this period: the missionaries' dependence upon 'native teachers', their teamwork with them, the vast amount of arduous travel, the frequent stopovers in remote Māori communities and the efforts put into building relationships with chiefs. The story demonstrates how the results of Christian mission among Māori in this period could sometimes be spectacular, but also often ambiguous and disappointing.

Thirdly, and perhaps most importantly, this is a story about Christian peacemaking among Māori. Although such earlier peacemaking is often overlooked in writings about the modern New Zealand peace movement,[88] the story of Te Mānihera and Kereopa underscores the immense emphasis in this period, among both missionaries and Christian Māori, on making and keeping peace. It was that preoccupation with peace which inspired Te Mānihera and Kereopa, while assembled at Pūtiki with their former tribal enemies, to hear a call to take the Christian faith to their current tribal enemies. In responding to their murders, many Christian Māori showed themselves willing to operate within the new Christian paradigm of forgiveness, reconciliation and peace. It was the Christian commitment to peace that successfully averted retaliation, and instead inspired a strenuous new round of Christian peacemaking.

In Taylor's speech in 1847 at Tokaanu, numerous elements of Christian peacemaking among Māori can be discerned: the repudiation of retaliation, leaving judgement to God, a call for repentance, a call for no further bloodshed, the appeal to utu as having paid the price of a permanent peace, commending the way of love and sealing the peace with reciprocal hospitality. Taylor's peacemaking, which presumably reflected considerable previous discussion with Māori co-workers, was significantly contextualised within Māori culture: Taylor recognised the cultural imperative of utu, he appealed to the recent utu as a way of now ending utu, and the process he suggested for sealing the peace reflected one of the traditional Māori customs of peacemaking. While Taylor included in his speech some specifically Christian concepts, such as repentance and judgement, his pitch for peace did not depend upon his Māori hearers becoming Christian: they were free to accept peace, for whatever reasons they might have, without committing to Christianity. Taylor no doubt hoped, though, that if they accepted peace their receptivity to Christian faith would also increase. The reality was that the embrace of peace and the acceptance of Christianity—in either order—were often linked. Huiatahi exemplified that linkage when two years later he offered to build a church and host a Christian teacher.

The story of Te Mānihera and Kereopa shows how Christian peacemaking helped build a new mood among Māori for peace. The Christian emphasis on peace assisted both Christian and non-Christian Māori to abrogate utu and make peace. The story of Te Mānihera and Kereopa exemplifies the general truth of what a chief at Rotoaira declared to Taylor in 1849, that wherever the faith of Christ went, 'it brought peace with it'.[89]

5

A Peaceable Puritan? Rutherford Waddell and God's Own Country

John Stenhouse

In 1888, the Reverend Rutherford Waddell, a young Presbyterian minister from the north of Ireland, made national headlines by leading a campaign against sweated labour in Dunedin. Over the next four decades, Waddell spoke out on most of the great issues that significantly shaped society and politics during this formative period of New Zealand history: workers' rights, women's suffrage, drink, Sabbath observance, Bible-in-Schools, gambling, church-state relations, race and immigration, international affairs, the Anglo-Boer War and the First World War. Striking testimony to his popularity came from *New Zealand Truth*, the country's best-selling newspaper, which normally ridiculed 'wowser' parsons. In 1927, *Truth* praised Waddell as 'a scholarly, broad-minded man . . . idolized by all, who dedicated his life to elevate, to live justly and to help the fallen.'[1]

Today, Waddell tends to be remembered, if at all, for the anti-sweating campaign. The first section of this essay explores the peacemaking dimensions of Waddell's reforming activities during the 1880s and 1890s. Focusing on his campaigns against sweating and for women's suffrage, prohibition and Sabbath observance, I argue that Waddell and his allies aimed to build a cohesive, well-integrated and peaceable society that left behind, as far as possible, class conflict, sectarian strife and domestic violence. They wanted to build God's Own Country along puritan lines. That was the problem, according to critics. Despite Waddell's collegial style, he and his supporters sometimes clashed with Anglicans and Roman Catholics, especially over drink, suffrage and the Sabbath. Even peaceable puritans brought a sword as well as peace.

A second section focuses on Waddell during the Anglo-Boer and First World Wars. Existing research, influenced by a powerful anti-war literary tradition emerging out of the horrors of the Western Front, has tended to lump together the major Protestant churches as crusaders for nation and empire.[2] Presbyterians appear in this literature, much like their Anglican and Methodist counterparts, as just war patriots if not holy warriors, largely indifferent or hostile to the few pacifists and conscientious objectors who refused military service.[3] Yet Waddell was too critical of war in general, and the Anglo-Boer War in particular, to fit this Protestant crusader image. By the same token, he does not neatly fit the pacifist resister either, as the Great War illustrates. I argue for a more nuanced approach to Christian thinking about war and peace that opens up space between the polarised images of patriotic crusader versus pacifist resister.

Northern Irish origins

Readers unfamiliar with Waddell may find some biographical background helpful. Born in Ballyroney, County Down, around 1850,[4] Waddell grew up in Antrim and Down, the heartland of rural Irish Presbyterianism. His mother died when he was young. His father, a busy minister, rarely appears in Waddell's autobiographical reminiscences.[5] Brought up by an aunt, strict, kindly and devout, Waddell credited his mother, as he called her, with saving him from ruin. At an Irish national primary school, a one-armed Roman Catholic teacher beat him and other pupils with a wooden ruler, knocking the stuffing out of a sensitive boy. Often playing truant, Waddell took years to recover. Retreating to books and his imagination, he became an omnivorous reader. From the age of 14, he worked long and hard for little pay for four years as a draper's apprentice at Banbridge, a centre of the Irish linen industry. A typical preacher's kid, he sat through too many boring sermons on hard pews to like church much. During his teenage years, he focused on enjoying himself. At the age of 18, a passionate sermon by an earnest preacher in a country church sparked a spiritual crisis. He studied English at Queen's College, Belfast, and—following family tradition and the inspiring example of his older brother Hugh—studied for the ministry at the Presbyterian Theological College.

Already Waddell had developed a capacity to sympathise with outsiders, the suffering, the exploited and those at or beyond the borders of the church. When a pious fellow student denounced the poet Robbie Burns, a lover of whisky and women, as a drunken sot, Waddell defended the Bard, insisting that he drank at deeper wells of inspiration than drink, and hung a picture of Burns in his college room. He leaned for a time toward Unitarianism, attracted by the learning, moral stature and literary talents of its leaders, but eventually wrestled his way to orthodox Christian convictions, centered on Christ.

After being rejected by an Irish congregation and then for missionary service, Waddell sailed south with his new wife, Kathleen, in 1877.[6] After two busy years in the parish of Lincoln-Prebbleton near Christchurch, Waddell preached such a riveting trial sermon at St Andrew's in Dunedin that the congregation issued a call on the spot. His new parish included some of the city's poorest areas, including a triangle bounded by Princes, Maitland and Maclaggan Streets that locals called the Devil's Half Acre. Containing cottages, hovels, grog shops and brothels, it included many of the city's Lebanese and Chinese as well as some Irish Catholics. St Andrew's also included some of the city's leading citizens, living in big houses in and around upper High Street.

Peace: building bridges

Having analysed Waddell's role in anti-sweating previously, I simply summarise it here.[7] After launching the campaign in October 1888, Waddell worked closely for the next few months with Presbyterian women and men from St Andrew's and Knox Churches.[8] When Silas Spragg's *Otago Daily Times* reports confirmed Waddell's claims about the exploitation of women workers in the clothing industry, concern spread round the country. In Dunedin, anti-sweating won strong support from working-class leaders such as William Hutchison, a Presbyterian unionist and labour politician, Harriet Morison, a Bible Christian preacher and unionist, and Henry Smith Fish, a populist Anglican city councillor and politician. Middle-class, politically liberal Protestants from the evangelical (non-Anglican Protestant) churches joined them.[9] Encouraged by the Reverend L. M. Isitt, the Wesleyan Conference condemned sweating and called for better pay and conditions for women workers. So did Jewish businessmen such as Bendix Hallenstein and George Joachim, the Irish Catholic bishop of Dunedin, Patrick Moran, and Robert Stout, the city's leading freethinker. The campaign won strong support from all classes and creeds, with Anglicans, roughly a third of the city's population, a partial exception.

Like the Reverend D. M. Stuart, the widely loved minister of Knox Church, Waddell built bridges across boundaries of class, church, creed and nationality. Networking skills helped him not only to build a large and loyal congregation but also to mobilise broadly based reform coalitions.

Convinced that capitalism tended to exploit workers, he championed the welfare of working people. As well as leading the anti-sweating campaign, supporting unions and serving as honorary president of the country's first female union, the Tailoresses' Union, Waddell fought from 1894 as founding editor of the *Christian Outlook*, a Presbyterian weekly, to preserve a godly Sabbath. He did so not only because he believed that Christians ought to honour God by obeying the Fourth Commandment but also because he believed that capitalists would force employees to work on Sundays unless prevented from doing so by law.[10] When defending workers, Waddell could sound radical, warning the Presbyterian Synod in 1888, for example, that the working classes were loath to attend church because churchgoers 'prayed for' the poor on Sundays and 'preyed on' them the rest of the week.[11] By quoting this saying from Presbyterian unionist William Hutchison, Waddell aimed to goad comfortable Christians into action. He aimed ultimately to reduce, not exacerbate, class conflict.

Determined also to reduce sectarian strife, Waddell often worked with, and partly for, Roman Catholics. During the early 1880s, after another Irish famine, Waddell served with Patrick Moran, the Irish Catholic bishop of Dunedin, on a committee of Protestants, Catholics and Jews that raised funds to relieve the suffering.[12] Moran respected Waddell's literary talents and concern for the poor, and strongly supported him throughout the anti-sweating campaign.[13] Plenty of working-class Irish Catholics benefited from Waddell's efforts. In 1894, Waddell publicised the plight of Miss White, a Roman Catholic teacher rejected by the Protestant-dominated Moa Flat School Committee, urging 'right-hearted' *Outlook* readers to 'reject religious intolerance of this sort'.[14]

Waddell forged strong relationships with transplanted dissenters, often speaking at Baptist, Methodist and Congregationalist churches around the south. In the *Outlook*, he frequently stood up for dissenters against the powers-that-be, making the *Outlook*, in part, an organ of the Nonconformist conscience. In 1894, for example, he condemned the Dunedin City Council's attempts to pass a bylaw to prevent the Salvation Army from meeting in public.[15]

Waddell's sympathy and respect for those beyond the church served him well in a culture where popular suspicion of the 'unco guid' (the rigidly righteous) and sympathy for the underdog flourished. He often lectured on George Eliot's novels and the poetry of Robbie Burns, whose kirk satires exposed churchgoing hypocrites. He worked closely with Robert Stout on anti-sweating, prohibition and suffrage. Battling sweating with Bendix Hallenstein and George Joachim, Waddell also worked with Mark Cohen, another Jewish community leader, to establish the country's first free kindergarten, named after Rachel Reynolds of St Andrew's.[16]

In his Synod report for 1885, Waddell urged the churches to do more for Māori, praised the heroism of local Māori who rescued a minister's wife from drowning, and presented each with a Māori Bible.[17] He often defended the Chinese, on whom Alexander Don, Presbyterian missionary to the Chinese, kept him informed. No Otago Chinese, Waddell reported in the *Outlook*, had 'ever been accused at the Bankruptcy Court, or at the Police Court', or 'been a beggar at the Charitable Aid Board'. Anti-Chinese agitators indulged in 'ways that are dark and tricks that are vain'.[18]

In all these ways, then, Waddell stood up for workers, women and children, non-whites and outsiders. He did so partly because he never forgot being abused and exploited in Ireland. Moreover, in a city dominated by Scots and English, he never entirely lost the sense of being an outsider.[19]

The sword: prohibition and suffrage

Yet some of Waddell's causes sparked conflict. To understand why this peaceable puritan brought a sword as well as peace, we must understand the challenges he faced. By using charged language to prick consciences, he hoped to mobilise support for reform. But this had dangers. An angry prophet who laid on the lash too heavily might divide his flock, alienate supporters and weaken reform movements.

In 1892, Waddell was one of several leading Dunedin prohibitionists who strongly supported votes for women. His motives for doing so were similar to those that inspired his anti-sweating campaign. Pastoral visits in his socially mixed parish convinced him that heavy drinking reduced household budgets, sometimes led to domestic violence, and hit poorer families, especially women and children, hard. Although he did not consider drink intrinsically evil, he found the country's drinking culture troubling enough to urge Christians voluntarily to sacrifice a legitimate pleasure to enhance the common good. Convinced that too many male politicians were too friendly with the liquor industry and the drinker vote to deal with the problem, he believed that female voters would force politicians to be more attentive to the welfare of women, children and families. Prohibition and suffrage would, he hoped, lead to happier families, safer communities and a more responsible society.[20]

Southern anti-sweating leaders who joined the prohibition and suffrage campaigns in 1892–94 came mostly from Scottish Presbyterian (especially Free Church) and English Nonconformist backgrounds. The Dunedin Women's Christian Temperance Union (WCTU) supported all of Waddell's causes.[21] Several Catholic and Anglican leaders prominent in anti-sweating, by contrast, rejected prohibition and suffrage. Bishop Moran's *Tablet* had from the beginning carried extensive advertising from Irish Catholic hoteliers. Catholics were not about to be dictated to.[22]

Formidable opposition came from a group of men with strong ties to the Licensed Victuallers' Association (a powerful lobby group), Speight's Brewery, the City Council and variable links to the Anglican Church. Henry Fish, the populist politician who had supported anti-sweating, occasionally accompanied his wife and children to church. As chief parliamentary spokesman for the liquor trade, Fish pilloried prohibitionists and denounced votes for women as 'worse than giving children razor-blades and revolvers to play with'.[23] Fish's main allies included William Dawson, Charles Speight and Charles Greenslade of Speight's Brewery, the latter a pillar of St Paul's Cathedral, and R. L. Stanford, a lawyer who had been vicar of All Saints Anglican Church. These men led Dunedin's self-styled 'Moderate' party against Waddell's 'Temperance' party. Fish's friend Sam Lister, editor of the *Otago Workman* newspaper and a lapsed Presbyterian, also attacked the 'male women' and 'female men' campaigning for prohibition and suffrage.[24]

In Wellington, too, the main parliamentary opponents of prohibition were Anglicans such as Fish, William Pember Reeves and Richard Seddon, the Premier. As chief architect of the Alcoholic Liquors Sale Control Act of 1893, Reeves insisted that 60% of voters in any electorate must vote for prohibition before it could go dry. This angered many 'dry' evangelicals, to whom this Act symbolised the old Anglican establishment arrogance their forebears had battled in the United Kingdom. To them, the 60% clause turned them into second-class citizens whose votes counted for less than those of (mostly Anglican and Catholic) 'wets'. Trampling on direct local democracy, this Act symbolised to evangelical prohibitionists the kind of Old World evil that God's Own Country was supposed to leave behind. The energy of the prohibition movement was fuelled, in part, by evangelical demands for equal citizenship.

A tumultuous public meeting in Dunedin's Town Hall in 1892 illustrates how deep ran divisions between Waddell's Temperance party and its Moderate opponents. Since both sides tended to see themselves as fighting the good fight against a dictatorial

Other, each tended to seize the high moral ground and denounce the enemy. In these culture wars, mutual understanding and common ground became hard to find, even for those such as Waddell, who tried.

John Jago, Congregationalist editor of *The Prohibitionist*, urged the vast audience packing the Town Hall to reject government compensation for those who lost liquor licences.[25] John Carroll, an ex-publican who became the city's first Catholic mayor in 1890, dismissed Jago's 'claptrap', called compensation 'fair and just', and said that he could respect prohibitionists were they not so 'aggressive and dishonest'. Once the hisses died down, Maurice Joel, a Jewish brewer, extolled the 'British nation' for its 'liberal ideas' on 'justice for all' before complaining that the prohibitionists had already cost him ten to fifteen thousand pounds in lost revenue. This perhaps inauspicious admission sparked uproar. The Reverend William Ready, Bible Christian founder of the Methodist City Mission in Stafford Street (near St Andrew's), regularly attracted congregations of well over a thousand to Sunday services in the Garrison Hall. He exhorted 'the people' to 'throw off the shackles of the divine right of brewers' and refuse to be 'oppressed by publicans'. We 'have been fighting for the protection of property too much, and not enough for men and women'. Laughter as well as jeers greeted Ready's conclusion that 'all who believe in the grand old Book [the Bible], should compensate the publicans for all the empty coffins, pawnbroker's tickets and drafts on the bank of hell'. Supporters then called for Waddell, who got drowned out five times before he could speak. He felt 'a good deal of pain' in 'opposing gentlemen whom he respected', including several 'intimate friends'. But the interests of 'a large number of citizens' harmed by drink had convinced him about prohibition. Why should government compensate liquor sellers when nobody considered compensating workers forced out of their jobs by industrial machines? Supporters applauded and critics hissed so loudly that, after trying for several minutes to continue, Waddell gave up and sat down. The meeting voted to reject compensation. The evangelical campaign to build happier homes and a responsible society by banning drink kept old theopolitical tensions bubbling.

The *Christian Outlook*: promoting peace

Appointed founding editor of the Presbyterian weekly *Christian Outlook* in 1894, Waddell poured enormous time and energy into what many saw as a vital arm of the church's ministry to its own people and its outreach to the wider society. George Fenwick's *Otago Daily Times* provided sponsorship and support. Waddell solicited advertisers, attracted new subscribers and wrote editorials and articles giving readers an informed Christian perspective on church affairs, theology, literature, science, history, and local, national and international politics.

In August of 1897, he drew readers' attention to the slaughter of Armenians by Turks in the decaying Ottoman Empire. Although 'stirred', most British and European citizens were too preoccupied with their own 'business' and 'pleasure' to display 'active sympathy with those outside' their 'immediate circle'. Such 'indifference to the suffering of others', reflecting 'ingrained cruelty', might lead to 'national extinction', Waddell warned.[26] As ever, his charged language aimed to awaken readers to a sense of global civic responsibility.

In February of 1899 Waddell highlighted the intensifying arms and naval race among European imperial powers, whose rivalries were spreading round the globe, especially in Africa. He urged *Outlook* readers to support the peace proposals of the Russian Orthodox Tsar Nicholas II and the English radical journalist W. T. Stead, a Congregationalist. These included a 'truce of God' for five to ten years; no more armaments; and international arbitration to resolve disputes between nations. A 'hideous evil', war cost vast sums, killed thousands, impoverished the masses and ruined 'vast multitudes' of young men. For Christian nations 'armed to the teeth' to claim 'to worship the Prince of Peace' constituted a 'hideous contradiction'. Urging 'all who believe in Christ' to support peace, Waddell warned that unless European nations stopped the arms race they would drag everyone into 'the red gates of a world-wide war'.[27]

The Anglo-Boer War, 1899–1902

The Second Anglo-Boer War broke out on 12 October 1899. As with the Great War, the home front has received less attention from historians than the battlefront.[28] Yet debates over the justice of the war divided southern churches. Two weeks before Britain declared war, New Zealand's Premier Richard Seddon, an English-born Anglican, offered a contingent of mounted rifles to the imperial government. New Zealanders had a duty 'as Englishmen', he told parliament, to support Britain.[29] When Seddon's proposal passed by an overwhelming majority, members sang 'God Save the Queen' and gave three cheers for Queen Victoria.[30] In Dunedin, too, English-born Anglicans took the lead in drawing citizens together in loyalty to Queen and empire.[31]

Several evangelical churchmen, by contrast, questioned the British position. In a sermon at First Church widely reported in the press, the Reverend James Gibb, a Scottish-born Presbyterian, declared it 'impossible, in the face of conflicting evidence, to say' who was responsible. Although 'it is for the good of South Africa that Britain should be the supreme power in that region', since 'no great Power in the world today' is 'so just and upright and generous', Gibb was 'not so sure of the righteousness of her motives'.[32]

Writing to the *Otago Daily Times*, 'Fair Play' rebuked Gibb for blaming the war on Cecil Rhodes, head of the British South Africa Company, and the British Colonial Secretary, Joseph Chamberlain. Gibb had been led astray by the 'insinuations' of the Reverend William Robertson Nicoll, a Scottish Free Church minister and journalist who founded the *British Weekly*, suggested the writer. Under Nicoll's editorship, this journal became a key link between the Scottish Free Church and English Nonconformists. Far from being self-contained, New Zealand debates were part of a global British world, in which Nonconformists were among the most outspoken critics of British domestic and foreign policy.[33] Via the *British Weekly* and the *Christian Outlook*, the Nonconformist conscience, keeping a critical eye on the English establishment, reached Australasia.

Prominent Presbyterian minister and social reformer the Reverend Rutherford Waddell, c. 1900. Waddell was an outspoken critic of the Anglo-Boer War and proponent of peace, though he was not an absolutist pacifist. Source: P-S-15-22, Presbyterian Archives Research Centre, Dunedin.

Waddell was unambiguous in his opinion. In late October, he told *Outlook* readers that Chamberlain had 'jockeyed the nation into an unnecessary war'. Quoting Nicoll's *British Weekly* articles, Waddell claimed that 'public opinion' in Britain was already 'rising against' Chamberlain. He also condemned the 'public odium' heaped on the few New Zealand politicians courageous enough to criticise the war. Refusing to demonise the Boers, Waddell insisted they were fighting for the 'Liberty' which 'fired the best of our race', and would resist freedom's 'despoilers with the last drop of their blood'. Waddell also criticised Captain William Russell, Anglican leader of New Zealand's parliamentary opposition, who said that 'as an Englishman' it was 'no part of his duty to inquire deeply into the cause of the trouble'. In Waddell's view, this amounted to the 'pernicious principle', all too popular in modern nations, of 'Our country, right or wrong'. The 'free citizens of free States' must not shirk their duty to protest if they think their country 'about to act unjustly' or if 'public opinion seems . . . to be taking an evil direction'.[34]

A week later Waddell amplified his position. War might be a 'stern necessity' to defend 'home and altar' from an aggressor, but only when all peaceful means of resolving disputes were exhausted and the war was transparently just. Waddell accepted traditional Christian just war teaching in principle. In practice, however, he claimed that 'history does not disclose to us any such course'; no actual war had been just. Behind 'our Chinese wars' of the mid-nineteenth century lay the lucrative but immoral 'opium trade' of the British East India Company 'and the lies furbished up' by supporters to justify them. Similarly, at the siege of Mafeking in October of 1899, English commander Colonel Robert Baden-Powell, an Anglican, feigned a retreat to lure Boer soldiers over lyddite mines that killed 1500 men. On the 'hideous maxim' that 'everything is fair in war', wrote Waddell, such 'atrocious conduct' was 'excellent strategy'. It 'irks us terribly to say that we can see no good or sufficient reason for the disastrous step' the British took in South Africa. Aware of the dangers of appearing one-sidedly pro-Boer, Waddell took care to empathise with readers' British loyalties. Though holding 'no brief for the Boers', and preferring to 'stand by our own kith and kin', Waddell identified 'the insatiable greed and lust for power of the South African Chartered Company, as represented publicly by Cecil Rhodes and privily by Mr Joseph Chamberlain', as largely responsible.[35]

In the same issue, Waddell urged Presbyterians to sustain their traditional commitment to 'political breadth and popular well-being' in the face of growing pressures to embrace a narrowly conservative patriotism. The Scottish Covenanters of the seventeenth century, often 'misrepresented' as 'narrow and intolerant', were 'the only liberal politicians of their age', resisting 'kingly tyranny and every form of wrong and oppression'. Waddell quoted from *Lex, Rex* (1644) by the Reverend Samuel Rutherford, the Scottish Covenanter from whom he descended and after whom he was named. A leading Calvinist theologian and devotional writer, Rutherford wove together Scripture, natural law, Scottish law, and reason to argue for the rule of law and against royal absolutism. After the restoration of Charles II and the Anglican establishment in 1660, English authorities condemned Rutherford for high treason, but he died before they could kill him. In 1683, they burned *Lex, Rex* at Oxford University, in England's last official book burning.[36] Covenanting clergy such as Rutherford, concluded Waddell, had excited the 'inquisitive and democratic spirit' of the people as the 'only effectual guarantee' against the tyranny of 'kings and nobles'.[37] Waddell was pressing Scottish Presbyterian history into the service of a liberal and dissenting theopolitical tradition coming under pressure during the war.

Despite Waddell's attempts to respect readers' British loyalties, some responded angrily. A political liberal committed to free speech, Waddell published their views. The correspondent 'Veritas' (Truth), for example, complained that Waddell's 'extreme' views, overly influenced by Nicoll and Stead, sparked 'strong indignation' among *Outlook* readers. Waddell politely stuck to his guns.[38] Debate erupted in the Presbyterian Synod of Otago and Southland when, early in November, the Reverend Dr James Copland, a conservative Calvinist theologian and physician from Gore, moved that the Synod publicly 'regret' the *Outlook*'s 'damaging reflections' on the 'Imperial Government'. The Synod must vindicate its 'loyalty to the Throne and Empire' against statements made in its official publication. The Reverend William Hewitson, minister of Knox Church, responded by moving an amendment declaring the Synod's 'appreciation of the independence of opinion on public questions—sometimes unpopular public questions' displayed by Waddell, and of 'the fullness and prominence he has always given to the opinions of those differing from him'. Criticising Copland's attempt to 'censure' Waddell, Hewitson insisted that 'there were some things which were done by the British Government which they all condemned in the severest terms'. For the Synod to 'pester' and 'worry' Waddell, for whom Hewitson felt 'great reverence', would be 'very ungracious'. James Gibb argued that for the Synod to allow 'attacks of this kind' would make the position of the *Outlook* editor 'intolerable'. The Reverend Johnston said he regarded Waddell as an 'ideal minister and an ideal gentleman' and hoped that Copland would feel 'ashamed' of his motion. Hewitson's amendment, supporting Waddell and editorial freedom, defeated Copland's motion by 73 votes to 18.[39] If this debate was any indication, southern Presbyterians were determined to make up their own minds about British wars. The Synod was a sometimes unreliable ally of empire.

This vote reflected the strength of moderate and liberal Presbyterians committed to freedom of speech and conscience. Probably some of those who supported Hewitson's amendment did not necessarily agree with Waddell's views on the war, and voted largely to defend the editor's liberty of conscience. The vote also reflected Waddell's popularity and the relative unpopularity of Copland, whose uncompromising personality and combative style had often sparked criticism within and beyond Presbyterian circles during the 1870s and '80s.[40]

Waddell restated his position on 4 November: 'We disapprove of the war.' But he took care to applaud the 'patriotism' of the colonies and to honour the 'brave' men who volunteered. Here, as usual, Waddell tried to avoid alienating those who did not see things his way. The wisest course now was to 'close the ranks' and end the discussion.[41] Doing so also made practical sense. Having poured enormous time and energy into building up the *Outlook*'s readership and financial viability since 1894, Waddell did not want to perpetuate a debate that might lose subscribers and undermine years of work.

In August 1901, Waddell's health, never robust, broke down from overwork. His congregation sent him overseas to recover. After the Reverend James Chisholm stood in briefly, Dunedin Presbytery invited William Hutchison, an experienced journalist, unionist, politician and elder at Knox Church, to serve as acting editor. Waddell may have recommended Hutchison for the job, because they had worked together against sweating. Hutchison served as vice-president of Dunedin's Fabian Society, which progressive Presbyterians such as Waddell, Gibb and Frederick Barclay, who taught law at the University of Otago, also supported.[42]

Hutchison sustained Waddell's pacific editorial stance. Alerting readers to rising tensions between Britain and Germany late in December 1901, Hutchison challenged Joseph Chamberlain's claim that the British in South Africa committed fewer 'cruelties' than the Germans during the Franco-Prussian War of 1870. Urging readers not to abandon the 'mighty truth' that 'God has made of one blood all nations of men to dwell on the face of the earth', Hutchison criticised the 'miserable attempt' of New Zealand journalists and politicians, including Premier Seddon, to 'belittle' Australia's Premier for refusing to send more troops to South Africa.[43]

In early January, Hutchison sharpened his critique. The South African war cost the British taxpayer £1.25 million a week, destroyed thousands of 'precious lives', devastated a beautiful land and embittered 'every animosity'. Urging *Outlook* readers to understand the Boers, Hutchison wrote that they were 'fighting for what they believe to be a good cause—for their countries, their families, their all'. Disease and 'pestilence' were killing more Boers than the sword, especially in the 'concentration camps', where 'in three months 3245 children have died on our hands'. Hutchison then quoted the Anglo-Catholic theologian Charles Gore, Canon of Westminster, who called the camps 'a stain which we shall not be able to obliterate' that should outrage 'the whole Christian conscience of the country'. Predictably, wrote Hutchison, William Knox-Little, Canon of Worcester Cathedral, poured 'the usual vituperation' on Gore, which led the Prime Minister, Lord Salisbury, to appoint Knox-Little Bishop of Worcester, with royal approval. The Anglican establishment closed ranks against internal critics.[44]

A correspondent signing himself 'Albion', probably to indicate English origins and sympathies, attacked Hutchison's views. All 'unprejudiced persons' supported 'Britain's objects in the war', because South Africa needed 'strong government' to secure 'justice for the natives . . . equal rights for all white men in the country' and 'the prevention of militarism and foreign intervention'. The war would cure 'racial hatred', since we don't 'hear much of the animosity of the Maoris, the natives of India, or the French Canadian'. The 'mismanagement' of the 'concentration camps' had 'hardly been established', concluded Albion.[45] In Nelson, the office-bearers of St John's Methodist Church unanimously protested the *Outlook*'s 'pro-Boer' articles.[46] Dunedin Presbytery censured Hutchison. He graciously resigned. A committee appointed by Presbytery took over the *Outlook*, and, refusing to comment further, ended the controversy.[47]

Several factors explain Hutchison's fall. He did not always display the pastoral sensitivity to readers' British loyalties that Waddell took care to express. Secondly, Hutchison did not have the web of personal connections with clergy and laity that enabled Waddell to fend off Copland's attack in 1899. Thirdly, Waddell, out of the country, could not defend Hutchison. By 1901, moreover, popular patriotism and intolerance of dissent had hardened. Nevertheless, the Hutchison controversy showed that some Presbyterians condemned the Anglo-Boer War more strongly than Waddell. Hutchison's fate, when contrasted with Waddell's, suggested that style as well as content mattered when promoting peace. Waddell's willingness to understand and identify with pro-British readers made him a less zealous and perhaps more effective pacifist than Hutchison.

The First World War

Having admired Waddell's courageous stance before and during the Anglo-Boer War, I hoped when beginning research on the Great War that he would continue to dissent. Now, however, he took a more circumspect line. By 1914 he was in his early sixties. Celebrating his thirty-fifth anniversary at St Andrew's in April 1914, he told his congregation that his ministry was coming to an end; many hearts 'were near to tenderness', reported the *Evening Star*.[48] Secondly, having always been a believer in just war in principle, he considered this war met the key criteria better than previous British wars. As he told a Dunedin Council of Churches war intercession service at Moray Place Congregational Church in December, German science, philosophy and politics 'denied God and derided the Church', while the 'creed of the German war lords had deluged the world in blood'.[49] That such a courageous critic of earlier British wars should consider this one just illustrates how appalled most English-speaking Christians were by German militarism and war crimes in Belgium. New Zealand Christians were more united, at least initially, over the First World War than over the New Zealand wars or the Anglo-Boer War.

Even so, Waddell did not simply abandon his previous pacific convictions to become a jingoistic holy warrior. He continued to see war as a terrible thing and courageously to defend freedom of conscience. Historian Peter Lineham has noted that, after coming together in 1914, cracks soon opened up between the churches, especially during 1916.[50] When the government introduced the Military Service Bill in June, transplanted Nonconformists were conspicuous among politicians defending freedom of conscience. The Reverend L. M. Isitt, a Christchurch Methodist and prohibitionist who supported Waddell's anti-sweating and temperance campaigns, urged the House of Representatives to recognise conscientious objectors. Those such as Quakers whose religious convictions prevented them from fighting—Isitt guessed they numbered around one thousand in all—should be allowed to undertake alternative non-combatant service. Although he could not understand objectors' 'mental attitude', he knew they were genuine, and urged the Minister of Defence, James Allen, a pillar of Dunedin's All Saints Anglican Church, to 'make this concession to genuine cases'. J. T. Paul, a Dunedin Methodist labour leader, expressed similar views in the Legislative Council.[51]

Writing his weekly column in the *Otago Daily Times* under the pseudonym 'Civis', the Reverend Alfred Robertson Fitchett, vicar of All Saints and Dean of St Paul's, sneered at Isitt and Paul for imploring the government 'with tears' to exempt Quakers. Accepting that 'two or three score' Quaker men of military age should qualify, Fitchett insisted that any other objector was 'worthy of the utmost contempt, and nothing else'. He complained that a 'conscientious objector' in Dunedin Presbytery, possibly Waddell, had even objected to the 'unchristian sentiment' of the Battle Hymn of the Empire. Thankfully, he was 'sung down and drowned out by the more energetic voices of the rest'.[52]

On Saturday 17 June, the Reverend W. Arthur Hay of Trinity Methodist Church and the Honourable George Russell, Minister of Internal Affairs and Public Health, addressed a large crowd assembled on the steps of Dunedin's Town Hall. By now, many Methodists had become ultra-patriotic, much as they had during the New Zealand wars of the 1860s. The Methodist Annual Conference in 1915, supporting the war, identified the 'British empire, with all its defects' as the 'largest instalment of the Kingdom of God that has yet arisen among men'.[53] Hay claimed that every man 'with conscientious scruples' had already gone to the Front because 'their scruples would not allow them to stay at home'. Those who 'now developed conscientious scruples' were 'conscientious humbugs' trying to avoid doing their duty. Applause greeted Hay's conclusion that 'every man' must 'go and fight' to 'remove the enemy standing in the way of the world's progress'.[54]

The Reverend J. J. North, a Christchurch Baptist minister, protested in a letter to the *Otago Daily Times*. Raised in Dunedin, where his father was minister of the Hanover Street Baptist Church, North was educated at the Presbyterian Theological Hall and the University of Otago, and maintained strong links with Dunedin, where Baptists were much more numerous than their national average. The Military Service Bill, he wrote, 'dooms Quakers, who refuse service, to rot for four years in gaol' and fines anyone daring to employ them £100. It forces the Quaker either to 'make the Parliament of New Zealand his God' or, if convinced that God forbade 'armed resistance to evil', to endure all manner of 'pains and penalties'. Although North, echoing Isitt, did not agree with the 'Quaker conscience' on this issue, he could not stand to see a Methodist minister such as Hay, 'whose ancestors had queer consciences and suffered for them, to the world's great good', support the 'bludgeoning' of others' consciences. New Zealanders must not 'coerce the religious conscience in order to uphold the State'. Unless the Legislative Council stepped in, said North, 'some of the gentlest and purest Christians in our land' would end up 'working in our quarries with thieves and blackguards, because in conscience they cannot consent, at the bidding of the modern State, to do what they believe is against the mind of Christ'.[55]

Hay accused North of lapsing into 'hysterics' over the Quakers.[56] Waddell sprang to their defence. Recognising the difficulty of making exemptions, Waddell said that the Quakers took a position 'wholly different from the sporadic honest or dishonest conscientious objectors who are but of yesterday and will be gone tomorrow'. Thanks to their 'noble and beautiful character', Quakers had long made an 'immeasurable' contribution to British 'national righteousness'. Waddell considered that to persecute such people was 'contrary to the very principles for which we are fighting'. Political wisdom must allow objectors alternative service without provoking a 'collision between conscience and the bayonet'. The 'bayonet may win the battle', concluded Waddell, 'but it loses the war'.[57]

The following evening, Waddell addressed the first united intercessory service organised by the Dunedin Council of Churches at Trinity Methodist Church. The press reported a 'large attendance'. They ought not to come 'primarily to pray for victory and the end of this horrible carnage', said Waddell, refusing to glorify war. The 'one purpose' that brought them together was 'to know God's will, and to ask not for what we wanted, but for what He wanted'. Since worldliness—'business as usual, pleasure as usual, gambling as usual, drinking as usual'—was waxing, an Allied victory would 'ruin us' by confirming us 'in the old ways'. Contrasting the 'vast and splendid efforts' in 'labor and money and life for the sake of the Empire' during the war with the 'paltry efforts' devoted to extending 'the

Kingdom of God', Waddell concluded that 'God was waiting for the churches to make an absolute surrender' to His will, the result of which would prove 'astonishing'. Even in a war he considered just, Waddell did not identify the kingdom of God with the British Empire.[58] As Allan Davidson and Peter Lineham have shown, some other major churches and church leaders did. Amongst Presbyterians, James Gibb acted as a virtual recruiting sergeant before turning to pacifism in 1917, while the Church's leading theologian, the Reverend Professor John Dickie, became a fierce anti-German patriot. Waddell remained on the pacific end of the Presbyterian just war spectrum.[59]

Critics noticed. 'Civis' congratulated the Reverend Hay for speaking what should have been the 'last word' on conscientious objectors. Unfortunately, North and Waddell had protested against 'bludgeoning' Quaker consciences. Waddell, 'of a charity that is proverbial', praised Quaker contributions to 'national righteousness' as springing from a 'noble and beautiful character'. Here Civis assumed that the Presbyterian was referring to George Fox, the seventeenth-century founder of the Quakers (Society of Friends). Waddell could hardly have chosen a 'happier illustration of the vagaries, caprices, whimsies' and 'absurdities, that shelter under the name of "conscience"', sneered Civis. He went on to ridicule Fox—and Waddell—by repeating the famous English historian Lord Macaulay's hostile caricature of Fox.[60]

Alfred Robertson Fitchett had succeeded his brother, Frederick, as writer of the weekly 'Civis' column around 1900. Frederick, a lawyer-politician, had clashed with Waddell over sweating in 1889, ridiculing the 'feverish enthusiasm' with which 'idealists' made 'vain' proposals to regulate wages by 'act of Parliament.'[61] This incident probably informed Civis's sneer at Waddell's 'proverbial charity'. A. R. Fitchett's All Saints congregation included pillars of the nation such as Sir James Allen, the Minister of Defence. Fitchett joined Bishop Samuel Nevill in enthusiastically sanctioning both the Anglo-Boer War and the First World War.

Correspondents to Dunedin newspapers tended to support Civis. 'Britisher' insisted that no special provision be made for Quakers. Since 'Scripture tells us' that the '"powers that be"

Waddell standing at the pulpit of St Andrew's Presbyterian Church, Dunedin, in 1917, marking 38 years of ministry in St Andrew's parish. Among his many sermons preached from this pulpit, none was more famous or influential than 'The Sin of Cheapness', in which he attacked the evils of sweated labour in 1888. Source: P-S6-35, Presbyterian Archives Research Centre, Dunedin.

are appointed of God' in Romans 13, this patriot reasoned that government must 'use all the persons necessary' to 'protect ourselves' and could see 'no legitimate excuse for conscientious objectors'. John J. Ramsay, a doughty controversialist from Hyde, ridiculed the 'academic platitudes' of 'reverend correspondents' who defended any man's right to 'fail in his duty to the British Empire in its stress'. He had 'sent a lad to the front', like many parents, because it was 'imperatively necessary for liberty'. Inhabitants of the Empire 'should do their duty to the flag or get out from under its protection'. The Quaker 'who cannot see that . . . needs the whip' and has no more right to object 'than any other shirker'.[62]

Waddell respectfully corrected Civis's assumption that he was praising George Fox as the 'noble and beautiful character' inspiring Quaker contributions to British 'righteousness'. Criticising Macaulay's hostile portrait of Fox, Waddell quoted T. H. Huxley's *Life and Letters*, where Darwin's bulldog praised Fox for inspiring 'a vast body of devoted followers, whose patient endurance of persecution is a marvel'. Fox moved the world, said Huxley, far more than Benjamin Franklin. 'We can all laugh' at the 'eccentricities' of such spiritual leaders, concluded Waddell, 'but few can imitate their genius.'[63]

Conclusion

Striking testimony to the respect Waddell inspired even among old foes came in 1918, when the City Council decided to rename some city streets. Old ethno-religious tensions resurfaced. The Early Settlers Association, dominated by descendants of the Scottish Presbyterian 'Old Identities' who founded Otago, insisted on retaining the Edinburgh street names in the original City block. Councillor John Carroll, son of the city's first Irish Catholic mayor (who arrived with the 'New Iniquity' of the 1860s), had little time for what he called the 'Old Nonentities Association'. His father, Mayor John Carroll, an ex-publican, had clashed publicly over drink with Waddell's Temperance party in 1892. Yet Councillor Carroll suggested that Walker Street, site of St Andrew's Church, should be renamed Waddell Street.[64]

This incident captures the breadth of respect Waddell inspired in the wider community. His wartime columns in Dunedin's *Evening Star* newspaper became so popular that readers requested he publish them. *Until the Day Dawn: A Message of Comfort for War Time* appeared in 1915 followed by *Killed in Action* in 1919; all proceeds from the latter Waddell donated to the wives and children of deceased soldiers.[65] Letters sent to him by soldiers and their families showed that many were wrestling with hard questions about God and death, and considered Waddell sufficiently open-minded to consult. Several asked about the fate of men killed in action who liked drinking, cursing and womanising more than church. Were they damned to hell? Behind the 'scornful exterior' such men assumed 'in order to shock feminine piety', observed Waddell, lay many a 'true and unselfish' soul.[66] Many who made 'no profession of religion' looked unselfishly, even heroically, out for their mates. We 'can leave them with strong confidence' to Him 'who died for all of us on Calvary', Waddell reassured readers.[67]

Peter Lineham has argued that the New Zealand churches emerged from the war with their reputations seriously damaged, especially among soldiers.[68] Although he has not convincingly substantiated this claim, nor engaged with recent British revisionist scholarship critical of such interpretations, he has identified an important issue for future research. In answering this question, historians must include church leaders such as Waddell who remained popular as well as those that did not.

Waddell retired in 1919. By then, the First World War had turned his old friend James Gibb, the leading Presbyterian statesman of his generation, from patriot into pacifist. By 1920, Gibb was campaigning to 'open the eyes of the Church and the community to the horrors and wickedness of war' and establish a League of Nations Union in New Zealand. Taking plenty of criticism, he received complete support from Waddell, writing from his home in Broad Bay. Gibb described Waddell's letter as 'a draught of clear hill water to a thirsty soul'.[69]

Waddell was always too critical of war and militarism to fit the prevailing picture of the Protestant crusader. Yet he was no absolute pacifist either. If 'lumping' people into binary categories of patriotic crusader or pacifist resister has dominated the historiography of religion and war in New Zealand, as elsewhere, then 'splitting' may open up space for understanding those, possibly many, who fit neatly into neither category. Such an approach may be particularly important in the case of peaceable puritans such as Waddell who, far from backing Britain right or wrong, assessed the justice of war differently in different cases. Finally, many New Zealand historians have hammered puritans, especially since the 1950s.[70] I have argued here that Waddell's social crusades aimed to build a responsible, cohesive and peaceable society as free as possible of class, religious, and domestic conflict and violence. Perhaps it is time to rescue our puritan ancestors, warts and all, from the condescension of posterity.

6

Comrades in Arms: Germany, the *War Cry* and the Salvation Army during the Great War[1]

Harold Hill

On 16 January 1915, the New Zealand *War Cry* carried a surprising news report, reprinted from *Der Kriegsruf*, its German counterpart. This included an illustration showing a German in military uniform preaching to a group of soldiers; it was headed, 'German Salvationist speaks of God's grace to his comrades at the Front'. The Salvationist was Lieutenant Robert Treite, serving with the German Army in France. On the same page, a report from Switzerland mentioned that eight German

Lieutenant Treite conducting a service. Source: *War Cry*, 16 January 1915, 3.

officers serving in Switzerland 'had been called up for service in the Fatherland'.[2] Given prevailing attitudes within New Zealand, what on earth were New Zealand Salvationists doing relaying stories that appeared sympathetic to German soldiers—much less reprinting from *Der Kriegsruf*, whose masthead in 1915 carried the legend 'Mit Gott für Kaiser und Reich'?

New Zealand was, at this time, in the grip of anti-German hysteria. As early as 1 September 1914, the *New Zealand Herald* carried four separate articles expressing such feeling under the evocative headlines: 'Brutal Treatment of Refugees in Germany', 'Unspeakable German Outrages at Louvain', 'Cowardly Germans' and 'Atrocities in Belgium'. Anti-German vigilante committees were formed in many New Zealand towns, devoted to hounding people of German descent or with German-sounding names out of their jobs and, if possible, out of the country. Mrs Ida Boeufve declared to the Women's Anti-German League at a 1916 rally in Napier that, 'To be truly British we must be anti-German'.[3] Over 300 German people were interned in New Zealand during the war period; a number of them were subsequently deported to Germany after the war.[4] Being a naturalised New Zealander and British subject was no defence under the Revocation of Naturalisation Act 1917. In an infamous case, Parliament passed the 1915 Alien Enemy Teachers Act specifically to deprive George William Edward Ernest von Zedlitz of his post as Professor of Modern Languages at Victoria University College because the College Council refused to dismiss him.[5]

Given this background, we might wonder at the apparently counter-cultural character of the *War Cry* report. Why did such reporting appear? How exceptional was it? What kind of backlash did it provoke? Were sellers of the *War Cry* abused in hotel bars, or their Citadels' windows broken? In fact, the 1915 report was far from unique—there were many other stories like it. Perhaps surprisingly, such accounts also appear to have elicited little reaction. There were no complaints from Mrs Boeufve, and daily newspapers even occasionally reprinted the reports. This chapter examines the reporting of the *War Cry* during the First World War, focusing on ways that Germany appeared. It seeks to account for the presence of sympathetic reporting and benign sentiments within the newspaper's pages, and to explore the significance of this material in terms of attitudes to war within the Salvation Army.

News from behind enemy lines

Apparently sympathetic reporting about Germany in the *War Cry* took a number of forms, ranging from the benign to the laudatory. Three in particular predominated. First, some articles simply provided updates on what was happening in Germany. This reporting revealed a wide range of spiritual and practical activity by the Army as a whole, as well as recounting news of individuals' efforts. For example, in November 1914 a report headed 'Salvation in the German Army' recounted the experiences of German Salvationists in the forces, including Captain Soinicksen, a crew-member of *U15* who survived when this vessel was sunk by HMS *Birmingham*. A letter from Captain P. Schmidt, wounded while fighting as a sergeant in Alsace, described the horrors of warfare and his efforts to pray with dying soldiers. Staff-Captain Grüner, editor of *Der Kriegsruf*, had been made a regimental scribe, Ensign Claudi a medical orderly, and Ensign Witzled a chaplain. Adjutant Tebbe, director of Salvationist social work in Cologne, had been appointed back to that city and given permission to carry on with his Salvation Army work in addition to his military duties.[6]

The following month, another article described social relief work in Germany. It indicated that Salvation Army Halls had been converted into relief centres and children's homes. Nearly 1000 hungry people were being fed daily in Hamburg and there were similar programmes in other large cities. Letters from German soldiers, Heinrich Keienburg and Sergeant Ludwig, were quoted, and stories were told of Sergeant Gratz and Band-Secretary H. Boldt, both wounded. Women Salvationists in Essen were busy knitting warm socks for the troops.[7] The following January the *War Cry* included Germany amongst other nations in a brief synopsis of Salvation Army work in the war zone, mentioning that many of its buildings were now in use as hospitals and that 100 German Salvation Army officers were 'on the firing line'.[8]

An article in February 1915 claimed that despite the difficulties of the war, the 'purely spiritual work in the 150 Corps [churches] throughout the Territory is not greatly interfered with. . . . At Magdeburg, a hundred souls have been saved in eight weeks. . . . A new Corps has sprung into being at Altona, near Hamburg.' A liberal response was reported to an appeal for assistance for the thousands of refugees from East Prussia arriving in the west. A War Auxiliary League had been set up to care for the wives of soldiers, and women officers of the Salvation Army were assisting with this. Extracts from letters from Brother Franz Rensch of Charlottenburg (since killed in action) and Penitent-Form Sergeant Ebert of Altona were also included.[9] When Staff-Captain Fuchs, formerly Divisional Commander in Hanover and a holder of the Iron Cross, was killed in action near Ypres, the *War Cry* noted the loss of one of the Salvation Army's 'most valiant German Officers'.[10]

A second form of reporting focused on stories of 'good' Germans, obviously intended to counter the picture of brutality common in the press. General Bramwell Booth cited one such example in an article reprinted from the British *War Cry*, describing two Uhlans stopping for food outside a Belgian inn. Some children were passing and one of the 'grim soldiers' removed his 'terrible helmet', sat a child on his knee and kissed her. 'Ah, my God, I have five of my own at home', he said, tears running down his cheek.[11] The usual reports of Germans in Belgium at this time told tales of butchery and rape. In another article, Booth quoted correspondence from Adjutant Somers, an English Salvation Army officer nurse still working in a German military hospital in Strasburg, describing the support she received from the German chief surgeon.[12] Her story was expanded upon in a later number, and reprinted in the *Otago Daily Times*.[13]

A February 1915 number reprinted from the British *War Cry* two stories told by 'Brother Moore, of the 1st East Lancs [Lancashire] Regiment', recovering at home from wounds received in the first battle of Ypres. In the first he described fetching water for a wounded German; in the second it was another wounded German who struggled out of his own greatcoat and flung it over a shivering, almost naked and evidently dying British soldier at an Allied dressing station.[14]

'Good Germans' were often Salvationists, exemplifying Christian virtues. One story concerned the kindness shown by a senior German officer who also happened to be a Salvationist. This involved an Alsatian Salvationist, Adjutant Müller, stationed in Paris on the outbreak of war but called up to the German forces, his wife returning to Alsace. Serving on the Eastern Front, Müller asked for compassionate leave on hearing that one of his children had died. This was initially denied, but the officer commanding his Brigade recognised Müller's name and acceded to the request. Mrs Müller then took up an appointment in Switzerland where their second child also died. Although leave to a neutral country was unheard-of, the Brigade commander stood surety for his comrade and he was able to attend the funeral.[15]

The German officer in this story was not named, but the *War Cry* did describe the circumstances of his conversion in 1912. He had mistaken the time for a lecture he planned to attend at the Circus Busch and found himself in a Salvation Army meeting being addressed by Bramwell Booth. Realising his error and rising to leave, he had been directed to the enquiry room, engaged by a counsellor and converted. His obituary, giving the circumstances of his conversion and reprinted in the *Evening Post* from the *War Cry* in 1930, identified him as Colonel Ferdinand Peterssen of the Prussian Guard. Apparently fellow officers had complained to the War Office about his membership of the Salvation Army and Kaiser William II himself had responded that 'he did not consider it a slight to the dignity of his Prussian officers' corps that one of its members should belong to the Salvation Army or wear the uniform of that organisation'. After the war, Peterssen served as a prison chaplain at the Plötzensee penitentiary.[16]

A third form of *War Cry* article evidently intended to emphasise the common humanity, and especially the common Salvationism, of British and Germans. One of these articles was headed 'Salvationists Meet in Bayonet Charge'. Salvationist John Coombs of the 1st Gloucester Regiment wrote home to his wife of the aftermath of a bayonet charge in which he found a wounded German trying to reach his water bottle. This proving empty, Coombs gave the German water from his own bottle. Seeing a Salvation Army badge on Coombs' uniform, the German whispered, 'Salvation Army; I am also a Salvation Army soldier'. Indeed, he was also wearing a Salvation Army badge. Coombs carried the dying German to an ambulance and heard his last words, 'Jesus, safe with Jesus'.[17]

Interestingly, a similar, yet even more poignant story was printed in several papers, although not in the *War Cry*:

> A gruesome coincidence is recorded in the meeting of a German soldier who is a member of the Salvation Army and a British soldier who also belongs to the Salvation Army. The Germans were charging the British trenches with the bayonet and the German Salvationist, as he drove his bayonet into the British Salvationist, found that he had killed the man at whose house he had been a guest for some weeks during the International Congress of the Salvation Army which was held in London in May last.[18]

It was not uncommon for British and European Salvationists in the forces to wear under their military tunic their red Salvation Army guernsey (jersey) embroidered with a Salvationist emblem or the words 'Salvation Army'. One story reprinted from *The Social Gazette*, a British review of Salvation Army social work, was told by a member of a British burial party during a lull in the fighting. In this, another soldier called out to him: 'One of your lot here, old man.' Through the unbuttoned tunic of a dead German showed the red guernsey. The writer was able to recite words of committal and write to the widow, whose address in Cologne was with the dead man's effects.[19]

There were fewer references to German Salvationists in the *War Cry* as the war progressed. In the last four months of 1914, there were eleven such articles; in 1915, a total of fourteen; in 1916, only six; for 1917 just two references; in 1918, three. This change could have been due to the increasing difficulty of obtaining information; a 1918 article commented that 'only occasionally does there come through to us tidings of the work which is being carried on by our . . . comrades in Germany'.[20]

Whispered in broken English, 'I also am a Salvation Soldier.'

Source: *War Cry*, 2 January 1915, 3.

Both international and local New Zealand factors in the Salvation Army lay behind such reports. It is possible to interpret this material as evidence of wartime stirring for peace, for there were deep-seated internationalist and anti-war impulses within the Salvation Army, based in part upon institutional, theological, and evangelistic imperatives. These had a significant influence on its official policies, yet the movement was not distinctly pacifist, and, like other Christian churches and organisations, found itself drawn in competing directions.

International editorial policy

Reports similar to those mentioned here were also found in Salvation Army publications in Australia, Canada and other countries—although not in the United States, where different attitudes prevailed. The Army's American leader, Evangeline Booth, threw her influence totally behind the war effort, and her 'doughnut girls' became famous with American troops. She was not infrequently at odds with her brother, the General, and her *War Cry* happily spoke ill of the enemy.[21] Setting aside the North American difference, what lay behind such relatively benevolent reporting? Several strands may be teased out.

Firstly, the Army's International Headquarters editorial department functioned like an international press agency for Salvationist publications. It is possible that the stories were run on instruction from London—certainly the General's articles would be—though the New Zealand *War Cry*, habitually referring to 'Home' and the 'Motherland', probably needed no such editorial direction. Like the Catholic Church, but unlike most other churches, the Salvation Army had no independent national jurisdictions. It was an international organisation, not a national church. That unity was evidently not maintained without difficulty, however, even before the war. The masthead legend on *Der Kriegsruf*, 'Mit Gott für Kaiser und Reich', indicated a significant and deliberate identification with German patriotism within Die Heilsarmee (The Salvation Army). There were also tensions concerning the extent of British Salvation Army leadership in Die Heilsarmee, as indicated in 'Terms and Conditions to the General from the German Salvation Army', dated 9 July 1915.[22] The Salvation Army in the area controlled by the Central Powers was largely cut off from contact with International Headquarters, though two years into the war Bramwell Booth was able to meet with the acting-Territorial Commander for Germany, Lieutenant Colonel Treite, in Sweden.[23]

Beyond that, Rebecca Carter-Chand suggests of the Salvation Army that:

> it was not the ideals of cultural internationalism (i.e., the hope that international identities and international contact would lead to a more peaceful world order) that carried it through dark times. Its internationalist identity was based on a multi-national structure (i.e., it existed globally as one international organization, divided along national lines but

> reporting to the International Headquarters in London). This multi-national structure was inspired by British imperialism, and later celebrated as evidence of the flowering of cultural internationalism.[24]

The New Zealand *War Cry* would have been unable to comment on tensions between European assertions of nationalism and autonomy, and the control of the Army's International Headquarters in London, but it did try to keep the peace by stressing transnationalism and accentuating values held in common. Although the *War Cry* supported the local war effort in raising funds for soldiers' 'comforts', for example, it largely refrained from denouncing the enemy. The Army's keenness to safeguard its international unity in time of war perhaps distinguished the *War Cry* from most other local denominational papers.

Secondly, there was some theological and philosophical rationale to the Salvation Army's position, and the *War Cry* had a didactic purpose in this regard. This purpose related not only to the Army's commitment to the universality of the Christian gospel, but also to the somewhat naïve triumphalism of its eschatology. While officially espousing no particular end-times doctrine, the Army's post-millennialist optimism, as well as its internationalism, was reflected in its popular culture and especially in its hymnody.

> This world shall be set free,
> This is our rallying cry, From land to land, from sea to sea
> Our colours we will fly.
> Advance, advance,
> The bugle sounds advance.[25]

Further, and ironically, given that he founded an 'Army', William Booth and most of his family, the majority of whom held senior positions in the organisation, were pacifists to varying degrees—although not pacifists for pacifism's sake, unalloyed. His biographer, Harold Begbie, recalled Booth's priorities. In short, war was a distraction from saving souls:

> It was not only the dreadful and inhuman hatreds roused by war which distressed William Booth. The moral earnestness

> which it occasions always seemed to him a waste of the human spirit. He saw with bewilderment and pain a nation which tolerates sin and suffering in its own midst roused by war to an almost incredible condition of moral energy and spiritual enthusiasm. Why, he asked himself, would not people give to the war against evil—which is the root cause of poverty and pain—something of this same energy and enthusiasm?[26]

Thus, the first issue of the private magazine for officers in 1893 laid down its editorial policy: 'No bloody war spirit, no pandering to the brutal craving for wholesale slaughter, has polluted our pages. We hate war, and all its paraphernalia. . . . Let us beware, even in our illustrations, lest we pander to, or tolerate, the cruel taste for blood.'[27] On the outbreak of the Second Anglo-Boer War in 1899 William Booth had written, 'No matter who wins . . . I lose, for there are Salvationists fighting on both sides.'[28] His instructions to Salvationists at that time were reprinted in the *War Cry* of 5 August 1916: 'Live in the spirit of intercession. Plead for a speedy termination of the horrid strife. Pray for your comrades . . . on the British side, and pray also for your comrades, the Salvationists, who are on the other.'[29]

Bramwell Booth, who had succeeded his father as General in 1912, made a similar appeal in 1914.[30] He forbade Salvation Army officers to enlist as combatants unless they were compelled by law to do so.[31] On the basis of this directive, twenty New Zealand Salvation Army officers resigned or took leave to enlist. Although Booth did not always succeed in maintaining strict neutrality in his public statements, he forbade the use of the word 'enemy' in Salvation Army publications and echoed Tertullian in his 1915 Christmas message claim that 'Every land is my Fatherland for all lands are my Father's!'[32] Florence Booth, the General's wife, wrote that to pray for victory was not an option open to Christians since 'victory must equally mean defeat for others'.[33]

The nearest the New Zealand *War Cry* came to explaining its editorial policy was in response to criticism by the *Maoriland Worker*, the Labour paper opposed to conscription, of an article headed, 'To the Shirker'. Charles Rixon, the editor of the *War Cry* through the whole of the war period, responded that if the critic had read the article he would have found that it was about the war against sin and was intended to encourage Salvationists to be whole-hearted in their Salvationism, rather than to denounce 'shirkers' from military duty. He pointed out that the Salvation Army was:

> AGAINST WAR, believing it to be of the devil. But seeing that the horror is upon us, our duty is to . . . utilise our organisation to serve every combatant possible on whichever side he may be fighting, irrespective of creed; to visit the wounded of each Army, and to minister to the bereaved and suffering of every nation. The *War Cry* has carefully avoided matter and illustrations calculated to encourage the military spirit, and has only reproduced those which would call forth the best qualities in our readers, and make the abhorrence of war greater, thus making for a lasting peace.

The *Maoriland Worker* graciously printed Rixon's letter along with a retraction.[34]

Nevertheless, there was a degree of ambiguity about the Army's position—both with respect to war itself, and in its relationship with Germany. While refusing to apportion blame for the South African War, William Booth had initiated welfare services amongst British troops serving there, under the direction of Staff-Captain Mary Murray—herself the daughter of a British Army General. Similar support was provided from 1914, along with military chaplaincies. Perhaps cannily reading the likely response of his troops, Bramwell Booth did not attempt to bind upon Salvationists his own pacifism, rejecting any suggestion that he should forbid Soldiers of the Salvation Army to take up arms or proclaim that all war was murder.

It is true that the *War Cry* apparently made no explicit effort to counter the victimisation of people of German descent in New Zealand, though one reprinted British report described the successful efforts made by a Salvationist to have German workers—dismissed because of their nationality—reinstated in their positions in a British factory.[35]

The Salvationist war effort

We do not know for sure how far their leaders' transnationalism or pacifism was adopted by individual New Zealand Salvationists. Local sentiment, individual as well as official, would also have been involved in their responses to 'the Empire's call'. By the early twentieth century the once radical and counter-cultural Salvation Army was becoming part of the New Zealand establishment, both in how it was seen by others and in how Salvationists saw themselves. This was partly because of its growing social work and partly because of a second-generation sectarian tendency to assimilate to prevailing social norms and become more conformist. For many young Salvationist men, then, there would have been no doubts about enlisting.

An exception was 79921 William Charles Frederick Hill of St Albans, Christchurch, who attested 'Salvation Army' on 15 November 1917. He was arrested upon failure to comply with his call-up and was sentenced by Court Martial to 'Imprisonment with Hard Labour for two years' in May 1918. It was noted on the record that 'This man is a Conscientious Objector'.[36] Hill did not feature in the *War Cry*, unlike many Salvationists who joined up. One such, also from St Albans, was 7/2149 William Sheward who enlisted in October 1915.[37] After more than three years at war, Sheward returned to New Zealand with a diagnosis of 'Exhaustion Psychosis' and was discharged from the Army to the Seacliff Mental Hospital in April 1919.[38] Knowing men like Sheward, other Salvationists at St Albans may have been less than sympathetic to Hill's cause. The relevant Minute Book is missing so we have no evidence, but conviction and imprisonment would in any case have meant his being suspended or removed from the Salvation Army Corps Roll.

The *New Zealand Tablet*'s James Kelly, however, thought that Salvationists, along with Congregationalists and Plymouth Brethren, were shirkers and should triple their contributions to the forces.[39] It is not clear how many Salvationists actually enlisted, since military attestations did not always record denominations accurately. Nevertheless, the numbers which can be traced certainly fall below the proportion of eligible men which might have been expected from a movement comprising nearly 1% of the census population, so Kelly may have been right.

In early October 1916, the Anglican Archbishop Alfred Averill, perhaps responding to an MP's contentious enquiry, released percentages for denominations enlisted, ranging from 53% Anglicans down to Congregationalists at 0.5%. Salvationists came in at '1% (less than)'.[40] A Return presented to Parliament the following year included just 272 Salvationists in the 70,445 soldiers who had gone overseas with the Expeditionary Force up to and including the 25th Reinforcement in April 1917—just 0.38% of the total.[41] Whether the Salvation Army 'pulled its weight' in this respect was therefore a controversial point for some. If the Army had contributed almost 1% of the total, as Archbishop Averill had averred, that would have meant almost 1000 soldiers by the end of the war. We do not know of anything like that many.

According to military records checked, at least 263 men attested as Salvationists, 234 of these being also mentioned in the *War Cry*. A further forty men were described in the *War Cry* as Salvationists or were otherwise known as Salvationists even though attested as belonging to other denominations. Another seventy-eight men were mentioned in the *War Cry* as being Salvationists in the forces, but have not yet been traced in military records. Together these numbers tell us of at least 380 Salvationists enlisted and there may have been others not yet traced. The *War Cry* also mentioned a further forty-nine servicemen who were friends, children, siblings or spouses of Salvationists, but may or may not have been Salvationists themselves.

Does that mean that the official figures underplayed the Salvationist contribution? A degree of guesswork and assumption is sometimes necessary in assigning names to such categories. Even an exhaustive examination of 100,000 military records would not necessarily provide a more complete picture because of the vagaries of attestation. There were complaints from other denominations about this—even a Methodist minister being entered, despite his protests, as Anglican.[42] Although there will have been others not identified, the figures obtained still amount to only half of the number that might have enlisted proportionate to the eligible population. Given that conscription would have gathered in the less willing from 1917 onwards, it is possible that Salvation Army ranks included a disproportionate number of the unfit, or of women, or of men below and above the liable age range—none of which seem entirely plausible demographic explanations for the discrepancy. Either attestations were even less accurate than suggested or some Salvationists were indeed reluctant to enlist.

Some of those who enlisted may have sublimated such anti-war sentiments as they harboured. It would appear that possibly 10 to 12% of enlisted Salvationists served in the Medical Corps, compared with 3.6% of all New Zealand soldiers. With perhaps a third of enlisted Salvationists being bandsmen before the war, however, the fact that military bandsmen doubled as stretcher-bearers in the early years of the war may have been a contributory factor here. That practice was discontinued when the high casualty rate amongst those so engaged endangered the viability of military bands, which were considered essential for maintaining morale.[43]

In one respect the Salvation Army contributed generously. Only 0.38% of the New Zealand forces officially attested as Salvationists, but the Salvation Army provided 6% of New Zealand chaplains overseas; eight chaplains went with the troops, while two officer-couples provided welfare services at base camps in France. This disproportionately high number of Salvationist chaplains may have resulted from military leaders' regard for Padre Alfred ('Buckshee') Greene. A further ten officers provided chaplaincy services in training camps at home, as well as an unknown number of non-officer employees staffing recreation huts.[44] The Army supported the combatants, if not the combat.

Salvationists marching as to war

New Zealand Salvationists were not immune to the 'holy war' crusade ideology that influenced their contemporaries. Although the *War Cry* refrained from encouraging or promoting such views, there were sufficient hints of patriotic bellicosity elsewhere. Shaw Clifton notes that the Salvation Army overseas, especially in the United States, though to a lesser extent in Australia and even less again in New Zealand, failed to adhere strictly to the International Headquarters' policy of neutrality.[45] For example, a public meeting, chaired by the Canterbury Divisional Commander, was called in Lyttelton to pass a Declaration Day resolution:

> That on this anniversary of the declaration of a righteous war, this meeting of the citizens of Lyttleton records its inflexible determination to continue to a victorious end the struggle in maintenance of those ideals of liberty and justice which are the solemn and sacred cause of the Allies. . . . Prayers will be offered . . . for the success of Great Britain and her Allies.[46]

Florence Booth would not have been impressed. Of a similar meeting reported in Wellington, the *Maoriland Worker* noted that German Salvationists were no doubt praying that God would help defeat the Allies, and asked would 'the *War Cry* please explain which of the two sections is right?'[47]

Bandmaster Henry Goffin, of the Wellington City Corps, celebrated the sinking of the SMS *Blücher* by HMS *New Zealand* in the Battle of Dogger Bank in 1915 by publishing a song, the chorus of which ended, 'They'll sink the Kaiser's dreadnoughts, manned by cowardly German Huns.'[48] Salvation Army bands often provided musical accompaniment for soldiers marching to wharfs to embark on troopships, and turned out at railway stations to greet parties of men returning home. Commissioner Henry C. Hodder, Territorial Commander of the Salvation Army in New Zealand, who had two sons serving in the Canadian forces, frequently spoke along patriotic lines, especially when fundraising for soldiers' 'comforts' during the war years. In his 1919 Report on the Army's War Services, he could not resist stating his conviction that Germany had 'forced war upon the world', and that the 'Salvation Army flag followed the Union Jack'.[49] The *War Cry* reprinted British comment by Arthur Mee justifying the 'punishment' of the Peace Treaty on the grounds of Germany's 'crime'.[50]

Apart from such fragments, we have little to go on in trying to discern the average Salvationists' views on the war, whether for or against participation. The Army's adherents tended to be working people, not greatly given to journaling, and few letters or diaries are known to have survived.[51] People did not identify as Salvationists in public debate on such matters, and the *War Cry* recorded those who went to war rather than any who may have refused to go. The *War Cry*'s content was vetted by the Army's leadership and it did not feature readers' correspondence. Nor did the Salvation Army's polity include any representative organs, conferences or assemblies where dissenting—or even supporting—voices might have been raised. Its soldiers' opinions were not recorded and they could vote only, in Lenin's apt and contemporary phrase, with their feet. But they do not appear to have done so; their numbers declined relative to the population but not absolutely. In the 1916 census, there were 10,004 registered Salvationists, or 0.94% of the population. In 1921, there were 11,591 Salvationists, or 0.87%.

Soldiers of peace

Had the Salvation Army's pacifist genes quite succumbed to a dominant patriotism? If Bramwell Booth's pacifism was ambivalent, and Evangeline Booth's long discarded, another of their siblings, Herbert, remained faithful to the cause and he was well regarded by New Zealand Salvationists.[52] During the war, Herbert Booth, who had resigned from the command of the Salvation Army in Australasia in 1902, launched his non-denominational 'Christian Confederacy', one of whose tenets was pacifism.[53] Article X of the Covenant of the Confederacy promised that 'I will refuse to shed the blood of any fellow-man in defense [sic] of any earthly realm'. In 1918, Herbert rebuked his sister Evangeline, Commander of the Salvation Army in the United States (1904–1934), for identifying the Army there too closely with American war aims. He outlined his pacifist beliefs in *The Saint and the Sword*, which was written during the war though not published until 1923.[54] The Christian Confederacy received no Salvation Army encouragement—rather the reverse, since Herbert was viewed officially as a renegade. He did retain the affection and loyalty of some Salvationists in Australia and New Zealand, however, so his views may have influenced some individuals, although it is not clear how much should be read into this.

A decade later, in 1927, the Salvation Army was represented, along with Anglican, Roman Catholic, Presbyterian, Methodist, Baptist, Church of Christ, and Congregational Churches, and the Society of Friends, on the Reverend Dr James Gibb's United Peace Committee in Wellington.[55] The Army's Chief Secretary, Colonel Charles Knott, and the Field Secretary, Lieutenant Colonel David Gunn, were amongst the official church representatives and were signatories to the committee's unanimously adopted Manifesto.[56] Both men had wartime military experience. Knott had been engaged in welfare work with British troops in Egypt and the Middle East during the war; Gunn had been one of the first four Salvation Army territorial chaplains appointed in 1913—he had served as a chaplain in training camps in New Zealand, although not overseas. Knott was an Englishman, but Gunn had been one of Herbert Booth's officers.

The Peace Committee's Manifesto denounced war as an instrument of policy, and urged support for the League of Nations and disarmament as a means of ensuring peace. The next step was to ask each of the churches concerned to approve the document and officially endorse it. For most other churches this would have involved referring it to church courts for debate, but the Salvation Army had no such representative or policy-making bodies so we do not know how far this initiative was of interest to Salvationists in general. Presumably it was not even considered necessary that they should be informed, as the *War Cry* did not mention either the Conference or the Manifesto.

There does not appear to have been any direct link between Booth's Christian Confederacy and Gibb's 1927 Committee. Both, along with support for local branches of the League of Nations Association, were evidently reactions to the awfulness of 'total war'. Those who had been most involved in the war were sickened by it. Former Salvation Army chaplain, Brigadier Charles Walls MC, was later reported as saying in an Anzac Day address at the Cenotaph in Wellington that:

> [O]ur losses, the wreckage of war; the wastage, misery and suffering consequent upon war, all urge the utter futility of

> war as a means to idealism. . . . War victims are all about silently, yet eloquently, calling upon us who are in full possession of health and faculties to see the abhorrent misery which is the result, and the calamity of such practices, and to live and move that history will never again repeat itself in such a diabolical setting. Once again, on this day, let it be reaffirmed that war is hell, that hostilities cannot be relied upon to settle national differences. . . .[57]

Already it was clear that the lesson had not been learned. Walls went on to express dismay that while the Motherland had shown commendable selflessness in forgiving war debts, she had recently been spending £200 a minute on armaments and 2½d in the same time for peace.[58]

Neither Dr Gibb's proposals nor speeches like that of Walls led to any further action and international events gradually eroded churches' support for the strategies proposed. Salvationists, like everyone else, were war-weary but most had not become pacifist in consequence. A later exception was evidently the unidentified but uniformed Salvationist who appears in a photograph of those attending the 1940 Conference of the Christian Pacifist Society.[59] But in 1914–1918, all that lay far in the future.

Conclusion

In accounting for the presence of apparently sympathetic reporting of German stories in the New Zealand *War Cry*, this chapter has identified a number of significant factors—international and local, institutional and personal, some relatively well documented and others more speculative. Editorial policy reflected aspects of the Salvation Army's internationalism, its evangelical imperatives, and vestigial pacifism, along with a general theological universalism which maintained that in Christ there was neither German nor Briton. These convictions were evidently shared and upheld by individual New Zealand Salvationists, though to significantly varying degrees. Further, whatever the ambivalent internationalism and the attenuated pacifist tendencies of the organisation, its desire to be of use, to be involved, and to be recognised, along with its soldiers' willingness to enlist, led to its becoming deeply embedded in the war effort. That was probably the case on both sides of the conflict.

We might conclude that during the Great War the New Zealand Salvationist saints did stir for peace, but fairly gently, and largely in ways that avoided local confrontations. They were not pro-German, but at least by representing Germans with humanity, as fellow Christians and comrade Salvationists, the *War Cry* tried to counter the inhumanity of the times and protect the integrity of the Salvation Army as an international movement.

7

Under the Surface: Archibald Baxter's Christian Faith

David Tombs

Archibald Baxter is New Zealand's most famous war resister. His story is well known for a number of reasons, not least because of the mistreatment he experienced during the war of 1914–1918.[1] Baxter has become the most prominent of fourteen conscientious objectors sent from New Zealand to England in 1917, and subsequently to the Front, where he and three others were subjected to 'Field Punishment No. 1'. Baxter told the story in his own autobiographic account, *We Will Not Cease*, which was first published in 1939.[2] In more recent times, it has been retold in a variety of places and in different media, including the paintings of Bob Kerr,[3] and a powerful television film, *Field Punishment No. 1*.[4] Moreover, as the father of New Zealand's most celebrated poet James K. Baxter, who also wrote about him, Archibald has attracted further interest and a high profile.

Religious conviction has been previously recognised as a factor in Baxter's opposition to war. For example, David Grant identified Baxter as a Christian socialist who 'made the decision to resist on his own, for reasons both socialist and religious';[5] the Ministry of Culture and Heritage also lists Baxter and his five brothers among those who objected to war on religious grounds.[6] Yet, as his wife Millicent noted in 1978, the depth and centrality of Baxter's religious commitment has not been well understood—in large part because he was reluctant to share his beliefs, even with her.[7] This has led to very different interpretations of Baxter's relationship to religion. Frank McKay states: 'His belief was not based on religious grounds, since he belonged to no organised religion, but on his own understanding of Christ's command, "Thou shalt love thy neighbour as thyself"'.[8] He adds: 'Archie was a humanist, though he believed in God and prayed to Him.'[9] Penny Griffith has recently suggested Baxter was a 'Quaker at heart' even though he never joined the Religious Society of Friends.[10] Griffith cites Paul Oestreicher, the famous Anglican priest and Quaker pacifist, who knew Baxter some years later and described him as 'a humanist who had no specific belief in God'. Oestreicher suggests that Baxter was sympathetic to the Quakers but had 'too much integrity to join a religious society when he did not feel religious'.[11]

So what can be known about Baxter's religiosity and personal beliefs in the years 1917–1918, and why was he so reticent about making them known? As shown below, the authorities had particular trouble understanding his religious stance in this period. At different points they identified him as agnostic, Catholic, Plymouth Brethren and eventually as simply 'a Believer'. The fact that Baxter never joined the Quakers is undisputed, but was this because he was essentially secular, or is this to misunderstand him?

This chapter provides the first detailed account of Baxter's religion as it relates to his opposition to war, drawing primarily upon Baxter's own writings. Whilst acknowledging the difficulty his reticence creates in a number of passages, it suggests that there is clear enough evidence that he had strong religious beliefs, though not in a conventional denominational way. It is possible that he had had contact with Plymouth Brethren as a child, but if so this had ended long before he was a conscientious objector. In 1917 he was not a member of any other church or sect, but nor was he an agnostic or a non-believer. Baxter's faith at this time is best understood as an example of unaffiliated 'practical Christianity'. His public reticence should not be read as stemming from a lack of belief, but from his conviction that religion was something to be acted upon rather than talked about, and that public ostentation should be avoided at all cost.

Background and biography

Archibald McColl Learmond Baxter was born on 13 December 1881 in a small sod house at Scrogg's Hill near Brighton, about twelve miles from Dunedin.[12] His maternal and paternal grandparents had all migrated to Otago from Scotland. Archibald's paternal grandfather, John Baxter, was from the Western Highlands and had left Scotland in 1860. He arrived at Port Chalmers, Otago, in 1861 along with his wife, Mary, and their three children: Archibald, John (father to Archibald) and Isabel. His maternal grandfather, Archibald McColl, was a Gaelic-speaking Scot from the Western Highlands, and had arrived in Port Chalmers in 1859, with his wife Margaret and their five sons and two daughters, including the nine-month-old baby Mary McColl (mother to Archibald).[13] John Baxter married Mary McColl in 1879; they had eight children (seven sons and one daughter), of whom Archibald was the second-born. John Baxter worked hard as a farm labourer, but also spent quite freely, especially on drink. The family never had much money, and John's drinking made it hard to build any capital or purchase property.

Archibald left school when he was twelve years old, taking different jobs including work as a seasonal farmhand in Central Otago. In 1898, he won a small plot of land on Scrogg's Hill in a land lottery, and was able to start his own farm.[14] During the Second Anglo-Boer War (1899–1902), the British recruited troops in New Zealand to help their war efforts. Archibald apparently considered joining up, in part because enlistment would have brought some financial security. A speech by a Dunedin lawyer and Member of the House of Representatives dissuaded him, however, having convinced him of the injustice of war.[15] Baxter thereafter became a staunch advocate of pacifism—from his early twenties until his death. His religious convictions played an important role in this stance, as did his socialism, though authorities repeatedly mistook and misunderstood his religious identity.[16]

With the outbreak of war in August 1914, it seemed that there might be widespread resistance to military recruitment in New Zealand. In response, a National Register in 1915 required all men of military age to confirm whether they would undertake military service. The result indicated that, of 187,593 respondents aged 19–45, 109,683 were willing to serve overseas; 43,425 expressed willingness to serve at home in a civil capacity, while 34,386 stated they would not volunteer for either.[17] Six of the seven Baxter brothers signalled their refusal to fight.

Archibald Baxter at Gladbrook Station, c.1900. Baxter is standing in the middle, fifth from the right, with upturned hat. Source: MS-0975/227, Hocken Collections, Uare Taoka o Hākena, University of Otago (image enhanced).

The Military Service Act 1916, which introduced military conscription, passed into law in August, with balloting commencing on 16 November. Baxter was one of the first arrested under the provisions of the Act, in late February 1917—even before receiving his call-up papers, or therefore formally refusing them.[18] A clause allowed that men in families where no member had gone to war could be called up without first being selected by ballot. Even so, Baxter had expected a period of three weeks between notification of this and subsequent arrest. He believed that he was picked out because of his well-known opposition to the war.

Following his arrest, Baxter was taken to Dunedin, and then sent to Trentham Military Camp in the Upper Hutt District near Wellington. At Trentham, he refused to obey orders or wear a uniform and consequently was sentenced to eighty-four days of hard labour in Wellington Terrace civil prison.[19] Since he still refused to obey orders at the end of this time, the military authorities decided to make an example of him in order to deter others. In July 1917, Archibald and thirteen other conscientious objectors—including his brothers Jack and Sandy—were placed on the troop ship *Waitemata* to be transported to England. An outbreak of measles led the ship to stop en route in Cape Town until November. He arrived in Plymouth on 26 December 1917.[20]

In England, Baxter spent time in detention at Sling Camp on Salisbury Plain before being sent on to Folkestone, and then across the Channel to Boulogne. From there he was sent to Étaples, and subsequently to Abeele on the border of France and Belgium.[21] When Baxter still refused to follow military orders, Lieutenant-Colonel George Mitchell sentenced him to twenty-eight days of Field Punishment No. 1.[22] When soldiers at the nearby compound at Oudredoum refused to carry out this punishment, Baxter was moved to another compound near Dickebusch, known as Mud Farm.[23] There, he was subjected to a prolonged period of Field Punishment in February–March 1918.[24]

Since Baxter persevered in his resistance, he was then sent to the Front, on 5 March, where he was beaten and forced to remain in an area exposed to enemy shelling at Ypres.[25] Eventually, on 1 April 1918, he was taken to a hospital in Boulogne and subsequently diagnosed with a mental disorder. After a few further months in a British hospital, he was sent home in August 1918, arriving back on 21 September 1918. His military record lists his service as lasting from 1 March 1917 to 5 December 1918 (1 year and 280 days), and his decorations as British War Medal and Victory Medal. It states that he was discharged because he was no longer physically fit.

Of the fourteen conscientious objectors on the *Waitemata*, Archibald Baxter and Mark Briggs were the only two who managed to maintain their refusal to accept any form of war service or obey military orders, despite all the mistreatment.[26] A Labour MP, Henry Edmund (Harry) Holland, collected testimonies from Baxter and other prominent objectors and published them in 1919 in *Armageddon or Calvary: The Conscientious Objectors of New Zealand and 'The Process of Their Conversion'*. Holland hoped that publicising their experiences would influence the New Zealand General Election in November that year.

Meanwhile, Baxter rejoined his family near Brighton, picking up his work as a seasonal labourer, despite having to overcome discrimination and resentment from some in the community who, with no apparent irony, saw his refusal to fight as a form of cowardice. In February 1921 he married Millicent Macmillan Brown, eldest daughter of the prominent university professor and administrator John Macmillan Brown and Helen Connon. Millicent and Archibald had two children, Terence Baxter (23 May 1922) and James Keir Baxter (29 June 1926), both born in Dunedin. In 1936, the family moved to Wanganui, where Terence and James enrolled at the Quaker St John's Hill School. In 1937, the Baxter family travelled to England. There, with Millicent's encouragement and assistance, Baxter wrote down his experiences in *We Will Not Cease*, which Victor Gollancz published in London in 1939—the year after the family returned to New Zealand.[27] The Baxters remained outspoken pacifists—Terence was a conscientious objector during the Second World War. Later in life, Archibald and Millicent followed the example of their son James, who had converted to Catholicism in 1958. They received instruction from Father Stuart Sellar and their earlier reservations on the Church's commitment to peace found some reassurance in *Pacem in Terris*, the encyclical on peace published by Pope John XXIII in 1963.[28] They were received into the Catholic Church at St Peter Chanel in Green Island in 1965.

Archibald Baxter's religious faith

There is no doubt about the importance of Baxter's church membership to him after his conversion to Catholicism.[29] But his earlier religious commitments, particularly as they related to his wartime experiences, are less obvious. There is some external, independent evidence of his views, to which I will return. The main sources come, however, from his own writing. Three key sources are relevant, and are examined here in chronological order: first, his letter to his parents (1918); then, his testimony presented to Harry Holland (1919); and finally, his account in *We Will Not Cease* (1939).[30] A careful reading of these show that he was clearly familiar with Christian faith, but he said very little about his own beliefs, and his own religious identity was repeatedly misunderstood and miscategorised by the authorities and others.

The earliest evidence from Baxter's own hand comes from a letter written to his parents from France on 5 March 1918, just before being sent up to the Front.[31] This letter was copied and subsequently circulated amongst supporters in New Zealand. Millicent Baxter (then Millicent Brown) read it in early winter (probably June 1918) and described its impact on her outlook as life-changing.[32] Two years later, during a period of residence in Dunedin, it prompted her to seek out the author in person. They married six months later.

In this letter, Baxter explained that he had been treated as a soldier who disobeyed and was accordingly subjected to No. 1 Field Punishment. He wanted to reassure his parents that he would never accept military work or military orders. He told them that if they ever heard he had served in the Army, or taken his own life, they should not believe that 'I did it in my sound mind'.[33] He also promised that his family's prayers for him were not in vain, and that 'I will pray for you all to the last'.[34] Towards the end he wrote: 'I know that we will meet again. Oh what a bright morning that will be whether in this world or the next.'[35]

A slightly shortened version of this letter also appears in *We Will Not Cease*. Significantly, the comments on prayer, and meeting in the next world, are both omitted in that later account.[36] This gives the book version a much less explicitly religious tone. It is not clear why this change was made. One possibility is that the book was intended for a public audience, and that Baxter was more concerned in that context for privacy around religious matters. Another possibility is that, since the book was written shortly before the outbreak of the Second World War, the explicit religious references were downplayed to give it a wider appeal amongst those opposed to war. A third possibility is that Millicent, who assisted her husband in writing the book, placed less importance on the religious element. Regardless of what the reason might be, the consequence is that one of Baxter's clearest expressions of his own faith is missing from his best known work.

Baxter's testimony in Holland's collection, *Armageddon or Calvary*, opens with a statement on the underlying principles of his pacifism. In this he first explains that his intention is not to publicly 'parade my opinions or principles', but simply to 'make a plain statement of facts'.[37] He then addresses his objections to war:

> I am against war on this ground, and I wonder that any sane person who knows the destruction, the degradation, the misery, and the sorrow caused by war, can regard it as anything else than diabolical in the extreme.[38]

This passage does not draw attention to the religious foundation of his pacificism but it does not exclude it. A more explicitly religious concern is evident in subsequent comments:

> I believe that a man should seek to bring his life and actions into agreement with his truest sense of duty towards God and Man. I believe that the Soul of Man is not, and cannot be, subject to any earthly State, for no earthly State is perfect.[39]

Baxter then cites three reasons for his opposition to war that do not foreground his religious outlook but are compatible with it. First, his belief that 'passive resistance to evil is the power which will conquer the world'. Second, his rejection of the militarist principle that 'Man is merely the property of Man'. Third, his stance for universal brotherhood and his view of all men as 'comrades and brothers in different stages of moral, intellectual, and spiritual development'.[40]

On the same page, Baxter refers to chains and fetters forged on the 'anvils of hell'.[41] He later comments:

> I know that far above all earthly States is to be found the awakened Soul of Man struggling onward and upward, away from long cherished delusions towards that universal harmony which to know in its fullness would be perfect comprehension, freedom, and love.[42]

Towards the end of his statement Baxter also remarks on comments made about him in the *Otago Daily Times*, which claimed that he had set his will against the will of the community. He responds:

> it was not a matter of me setting up my will against the public, but of doing what I believed to be right, and refusing to do what I believed to be wrong. . . . All that I need to say in conclusion is that, although it was said that I appealed as a Religious Objector, as a matter of fact I did not appeal before a board on any ground at all, although I sent in a notice of appeal in which I stated that I would not act against my belief, and that by the help of God I would not do violence to any man.[43]

The authorities, and Baxter's contemporaries, found his position hard to understand, but Baxter evidently preferred to be misunderstood than to explain his beliefs in more detail. The fact that he did not appeal on religious grounds is not strange, since he would not have been successful, as he noted in *We Will Not Cease*. Nonetheless, it is interesting that he wished to set the record straight and correct the view that he appealed as a Religious Objector.

Baxter's Attestation for General Service, completed in 1916, supports his claim about not seeking exemption. This indicates that he answered most questions, but left question 26—the crucial question asking about willingness to serve in the New Zealand Expeditionary Force—blank.[44] He neither confirmed nor denied that he was willing to serve; but a handwritten note at the top of the record reads: 'Refuses to be attested'.

We Will Not Cease, 1939

The main source for our understanding of Baxter's religion comes from *We Will Not Cease*, the title of which references William Blake's poem 'Jerusalem' (1808), with its vision of Christian persistence in building a 'new Jerusalem' on English soil.[45] The relevant verse is included on the inside title page of the book's 1968 edition. Yet the references to Christian beliefs in the book are notably enigmatic about Baxter's own views.

In his Foreword to the 2003 and later editions, Michael King asserts that Baxter 'argued his case for exemption from service on the grounds of the teachings of Christ ("Thou shalt not kill"; "Turn the other cheek"; "Do good to them that hate you")'.[46] King does not provide references to these words in Baxter's writing. Although Baxter would most likely have shared these sentiments, the quote marks are potentially misleading: the words are from the Sermon on the Mount, rather than from Baxter.[47] The verses indicate what Baxter probably believed but King's suggestion that Baxter sought exemption on these grounds is also misleading. In the book Baxter repeats the point he made to Holland that he did not apply for exemption on religious or other grounds, knowing that he had 'no hope for it'. Indeed, he described the appeal boards as farcical, and rejected their right to judge a person's sincerity.[48]

A key factor in Baxter's grim appraisal of his prospects for exemption relates to his lack of formal religious affiliation. The regulations to permit conscientious objection were drawn very tightly, limited to a small group of recognised members of religious bodies who viewed armed service as contrary to divine revelation.[49] Furthermore, any objector had to demonstrate that he had been a member of such a group on 4 August 1914, and to have remained a member in good standing since that time. The conscientious objectors this religious exception most clearly applied to were the Quakers, Christadelphians, and Seventh-day Adventists, but members of other denominations, including Plymouth Brethren, also applied. Baxter, however, emphasised that: 'I belonged to no organised church and did not base my beliefs on the teaching of any sect.'[50]

Lack of church affiliation as an adult should not be assumed to indicate a lack of Christian conviction, however, nor the absence of a significant church background as a child. Given the very high rates of Sunday school attendance in Otago in the late nineteenth century, it is likely though not certain that Archibald and his siblings attended.[51] Working-class families often sent their children to Sunday school even if they did not participate in church themselves. Boys and girls attended Sunday school in reasonably even numbers; it was typically after adolescence that male working-class church involvement declined. Whether or not he attended Sunday school, lack of church membership as a young adult male is not especially unusual. For various reasons, limited working-class participation was common in many areas, especially for males.[52]

In the first lines of *We Will Not Cease*, Baxter makes no explicit mention of the role of Christian values in his opposition to war. He simply states: 'Many years before the war of 1914–18, I had reached the point of view that war—all war—was wrong, futile, and destructive alike to victor and vanquished.'[53] These words on the destructiveness and futility of war are consistent with his testimony to Holland, but are even more reticent on his religious convictions. At different points in the book he nevertheless demonstrates familiarity with scripture and offers astute comments on its significance. His description of the Dunedin speaker who convinced him on the merits of pacifism as 'a voice crying in the Wilderness' is an example of this.[54] Later, he uses the analogy of 'sheep and goats' (from a parable of judgement in Matt. 25:31–46) to describe the separation of two religious objectors from their religious comrades in the Trentham barracks.[55] He clearly understands the meaning of this biblical passage, and links it to the inferior status of goats vis-à-vis sheep, as seen in their perception of prisoners like Baxter as goats rather than sheep.

This use of biblical language is also significant because it points to the importance of practical action in Christian faith. In one of the relatively few explicit statements that Baxter makes about Christianity, he places great significance on the practical and social element in its teaching:

> To me, Christianity is based on the commandment: 'Thou shalt love thy neighbour as yourself.' I do not profess to live up to this ideal, but one can at least go so far along the road as to try and treat other people as one would wish to be treated by them, and war cuts this position at its very roots.[56]

This practical, social element was also a significant factor for Keir Hardie, the Scottish socialist who served as the first Labour Member of Parliament at Westminster. Hardie was known for his religious convictions, and served as a lay preacher. He visited New Zealand in 1912, and Baxter mentions this briefly.[57] Archibald's admiration for Hardie is demonstrated in the naming of his younger son, James Keir Baxter, but Baxter does not discuss Hardie at any length.[58]

In his conversations with various chaplains at Sling Camp, Baxter also argued for the practical consequences of Christian teaching but gave little detail on his own beliefs. To one chaplain who suggests that Baxter could not avoid taking part in the war, Baxter responds:

> I object to government forcing the people of a country under conscription to murder the people of another country. I am making my protest in the best way that I can. War is an evil thing, should be done away with, and I believe can be done away with. It seems right to me to stand out against it, no matter what I suffer, even if they kill me.[59]

In response to another apparently more sympathetic chaplain, he says: 'I told him he did not need to be sorry for me. I was standing on my convictions and trying to practice what he preached from the New Testament.' He stresses his willingness to accept the consequences of his convictions rather than escape them: 'I said I was not concerned with consequences, but with making my stand against what I believed to be wrong. What I had suffered and probably would suffer had nothing to do with it.'[60]

Further on, Baxter reports a conversation with Colonel Mitchell in France, during which Mitchell asked if he had religious views:

> I said I did not belong to any organised church, but that it seemed to me that the teaching of Christ was entirely against war or taking part in it. But even if that had not been so I would still consider I was right in taking my present attitude.[61]

This response reflects Baxter's persistent reluctance to be drawn into giving a clear statement of his own views, or to debate the religious basis to his convictions. It also illustrates his deft ability to avoid giving a direct answer to a seemingly straightforward question. When another chaplain asked if Baxter based his objection on religious grounds, Baxter replied: 'I base it on the fact that war is evil. It is murder and I object to murder and to people being forced into doing it.'[62]

There is, however, a vivid exception to this in his account of Field Punishment No. 1. In this, Baxter describes how, early in his punishment, he started to feel overwhelmed by the pain he would have to endure.[63]

> I began to think of the length of my sentence and it rose up like a mountain. The pain grew steadily worse until after half an hour it seemed absolutely unendurable. Between my set teeth I said, 'Oh God, this is too much. I can't bear it.' . . . At the very worst, strength came to me and I knew I would not surrender. The battle was won and though the suffering increased rather than decreased as the days wore on, I never had to fight it again.[64]

At this low point, Baxter says he called out to God and soon afterwards found a new strength. This passage is the clearest evidence of his own faith in the book, and it shows that his faith was a critical element in sustaining him in the face of suffering.

It is particularly intriguing that these comments come in the context of a punishment that soldiers referred to as 'crucifixion'. If he had wished, Baxter could have described his experiences of No. 1 Field Punishment as crucifixion, thereby aligning with Christ's suffering. Contemporary churches and newspapers were full of references to patriotic military service in such terms.[65] War rhetoric and imagery, such as James Clark's painting *The Great Sacrifice* (1914) and George Hillyard Swinstead's *The White Comrade* (1915), explicitly linked soldiers' deaths to the suffering and sacrifice of Christ.[66] Baxter's experience offered a more direct and immediate link to Christ's suffering, and a ready illustration of what Holland recognised as Calvary. Yet Baxter says little about his suffering as crucifixion, and if anything understates the connection. He merely acknowledges that Field Punishment No. 1 was known as crucifixion.[67]

Baxter's restraint is even more striking because the question of field punishment as 'crucifixion' had become highly contentious in Britain in the wake of an article by Robert Blatchford, a former army sergeant turned journalist, entitled

Archibald Baxter, c.1940s, around the time that *We Will Not Cease* (1939) was first published. Source: 1/2-037732-F. Alexander Turnbull Library, Wellington.

'Why "Crucify" Tommy?', which described the punishment in graphic detail.[68] This followed an earlier storm in the British press over claims that German soldiers had crucified a Canadian soldier at Ypres in 1915. Baxter's letter to his parents does not mention the term crucifixion at all, perhaps partly because it would have attracted the censor's attention.[69] He may simply have been unwilling to appear arrogant by comparing himself with Christ—even if privately Christ's suffering and compassion was meaningful for him.

Baxter's reserve about crucifixion, and more generally on his religious commitments, cohered with widespread contemporary views about the privacy of religion. Such sentiment may have been heightened for the independently minded Baxter, particularly given the climate of controversy over issues such as religious exemption. Crucially, his reticence also reflected a remarkable degree of personal reserve that is evident elsewhere in his writing. For example, when he returned to New Zealand, Baxter was interviewed by Sir James Allen, who asked him whether he knew anything about No. 1 Field Punishment. Baxter's reply, 'Not much', was an extraordinary understatement.[70] In the same conversation, Baxter was similarly plainspoken, yet muted, on whether he was a 'conscientious objector': 'I answered that I was called one in the Army, but did not call myself by any name. He said: "Why did you object to military service?" and I replied, "Because I am against war."'[71]

External evidence on Baxter's religious beliefs

In addition to Baxter's own written work, his military records and an interview by Michael King with Millicent Baxter are useful additional sources that provide evidence about his religious belief. Each in its own way provides further indications of his outlook, the influences upon him and the way that others perceived his religious commitments.

Michael King's unpublished interview with Millicent Baxter was conducted as part of King's research on James K. Baxter. In one particularly revealing question, King asked: 'Would you say that your home life at the time that Jim was a boy, was of a distinctively Christian kind—were you . . . ?' To this, Millicent answered: 'Well, it wasn't . . . I think it was really fundamentally Christian but though the boys said their prayers at night and that sort of thing, we didn't call it Christian. It was really fundamentally Christian, I mean, my husband was . . . .'[72] Millicent starts by answering that the family wasn't distinctively Christian, but then says the family was 'really fundamentally Christian', and this is sufficiently important for her to repeat almost immediately. It appears that although the family were fundamentally Christian in their practices, they did not think of this as particularly distinctive in the culture of the day, and did not call themselves a Christian family.

Millicent mentions that she and Archibald admired the Quakers and had hoped that James and Terence might become Quakers in their time at Wanganui. However, 'there were certain things about them that would have been impossible for us to join them, but all the same we did admire them'.[73] This admiration may help to explain Ostreicher's belief that Baxter was essentially Quaker, but it would have been long after the war.

Millicent goes on to recount Archibald's experience at the Wellington jail. In *We Will Not Cease*, Archibald records that he was moved to a better room in the prison after a bout of severe sickness. He noticed that his name card listed him as an 'agnostic'. He objected to this, and told the warder: 'I said I didn't belong to any organised church. That's not to say I'm an agnostic. I'm not, and you can take that down.'[74] Baxter adds that, to his surprise, the card was taken down. Shortly afterwards he was ordered to join the Catholic prisoners on their way to service, and had to object that he was not Catholic either.[75] He had been moved into a cell which previously held a Catholic prisoner, and taken an interest in the hymn book and prayer book that his predecessor left behind. The authorities apparently noticed this and decided to complete his newly blank affiliation card by assuming he must be Catholic.

Millicent's account of the agnosticism incident strengthens Archibald's response, and adds the detail that he claimed to be 'a believer', which is not included in *We Will Not Cease*. According to Millicent, 'he found he was put down as an agnostic and he was very annoyed at this. He said "I am not an agnostic, take that out. I don't belong to any Church but I am not an agnostic, certainly not—I am a believer".'[76]

Many years later, Millicent managed to get Archibald's medical file from 1918. She comments on a phrase in the record that states Baxter 'was very fond of religion', which she rightly says 'is a funny way to put it'.[77] Millicent notes: 'He said he was a believer. Well I think that it shows that it's sort of under the surface all the time, all through that book.'[78] In Millicent's view, this reserve meant that most people did not see the Christian dimension of *We Will Not Cease*:

> I mean he wasn't explicit about it and that was the peculiar thing about his spiritual side, that even I who knew him best of any . . . better than anyone else could, I didn't get into that at all hardly. He was so reserved on it.[79]

Millicent returns to this later in the interview:

> Well it's difficult to know because I didn't really know what his spiritual feelings were—spiritually he was terribly reticent . . . he could rise to heights I couldn't, and in some ways he was a mystic.[80]

Father Sellar, who prepared them both for entry into the Catholic Church, also described Arichbald as a 'genuine mystic'.[81] To what extent Baxter's outlook during the war years was also marked by a mystical streak is unclear, but if it was it would probably have reinforced his reluctance to explain his beliefs.

His reticence was hard for the authorities of his day to appreciate, and Baxter's designation as first agnostic and then Catholic reflects the confusion, and miscategorisation. More intriguingly, Baxter's military records also identify him as Plymouth Brethren.[82] The designation is strange, for there is no mention of any relationship with the Brethren in Baxter's writing, or in any comments from his family. The affiliation may simply have been applied by the authorities, who recognised his religious commitment but were otherwise at a loss to describe his lack of affiliation. An alternative possiblity is that the affiliation related to his childhood. Baxter's military record was originally written in black ink, and just states his religion as 'Ply Bren'.

Subsequently, it appears, someone added in red ink the word 'Otago' above this, and the numbers '3.12.82' beneath. If this date is 3 December 1882, Baxter would have been just short of his first birthday.

John Baxter, Archibald's father, was a deeply religious man. Despite potential disapproval from the Presbyterians, who were predominant in the area, he went to hear Plymouth Brethren preachers when they visited Brighton.[83] Their impact was so powerful that he apparently gave up drinking for thirteen years (though other extravagances ensured that the family's financial position scarcely changed).[84] Some Brethren did practice infant baptism,[85] and it is possible that John and Mary had Archibald baptised in 1882. In this case, the military record may accurately preserve a childhood affiliation that was no longer active for Baxter as an adult.

If Archibald had been a member of the Plymouth Brethren as a child, it is likely that his brothers would have been as well. There is some evidence to support this in the Report of the Religious Advisory Board (RAB) from 1919. The RAB investigated 273 men who had been court-martialled for refusing military service, to judge the merits of their case to determine who should not be included on the forthcoming list of military defaulters. The Report features Archibald's brothers Donald and Hugh, who had both been sentenced to hard labour for eleven months on 21 August 1917.[86] It notes that neither Donald nor Hugh presented themselves at their RAB hearing, and determines that both came under Schedule 5, indicating an absence of *bona fide* religious grounds as defined in Section 9 of the New Zealand Expeditionary Forces Amendment Act 1918. Even so, later in the report under the details of hearings, Donald's religious background is identified as 'Plymouth Brethren'. The RAB lists other Plymouth Brethren objectors who they recommend as satisfying the religious objection critieria. Failure to make this recommendation for Donald suggests that, as with Archibald, any previous affiliation had since ceased. It seems odd that the column on religious adherence is blank for Hugh, but this may be because he had already been released by the time of his RAB hearing, whereas Donald was still in prison.[87]

Another later entry in Archibald's military record, the 'Medical Case Sheet' from his examination in April 1918, lists yet another description of his religion. This recognises Baxter's religious disposition but describes it more generically: 'says he will still continue to resist all military ideas—he does not believe in war. He was always fond of religion & is "a Believer". He belongs to no denomination.'[88] This is the medical note that Millicent referred to in conversation with Michael King. The term 'Believer' is given in inverted commas and may originate with Baxter himself, or it may reflect the doctor's uncertainty on how to categorise him more precisely. Here as elsewhere, Baxter's commitment to faith is acknowledged but immediately qualified with the statement that he did not belong to a denomination. This is probably the best categorisation of his Christian identity in this period of his life. In the terminology later made popular by British sociologist of religion Grace Davie, Baxter evidently believed, but did not belong.[89]

In light of the evidence in his own writing and from what Millicent says, Baxter's faith at the time he was a conscientious objector is probably best understood in terms of 'practical Christianity', which hung loosely to institutional forms, was often anti-doctrinal and held belief to be personal and private. What matters is not so much what you say, but what you do, and it is often better to say very little.

Baxter's Scottish heritage

One final factor worth considering in relation to Baxter's religiosity is his ancestral Scottish heritage. While the precise nature of this influence must remain somewhat speculative, Baxter's pride in his Scottish heritage is well attested, as exemplified in his love of the poetry of Robert Burns.[90] Aspects of this heritage, including that mediated through Presbyterianism, may help to explain aspects of his religious and moral outlook, and his reluctance to speak of it publicly. For example, the criticism of religious ostentation and hypocrisy in the poetry of Robert Burns may have further encouraged Baxter's inclination to say little about his own personal beliefs.

Scottish Presbyterianism formed a significant part of Baxter's family and cultural milieu, and was shaped by a significant tradition of principled political defiance going back to the seventeenth-century Covenanter movement and beyond. In that tradition, institutional conformity and political obedience were considered secondary to the demands of conscience and integrity. This contributed to a long history of division and conflict with political authorities, and also within the church itself. Notably, the Free Church of Scotland split from the established Church of Scotland in the Disruption of May 1843 over the right of patrons, under parliamentary law, to determine the appointment of church ministers. The Otago Association was founded in 1845 by Free Church members, who rejected patrons' power. Dunedin was established as a Free Church settlement in 1848 just five years after the Disruption, and the influence of this legacy was profound.

This heritage of dissent did not lead to wholesale Presbyterian opposition to war, however. Indeed, during the First World War, the Presbyterian Church in New Zealand generally supported the military cause. According to the 1915 National Registration survey, people in the Otago-Southland stronghold of Presbyterianism and Scotland-born New Zealanders were also disproportionately prepared to volunteer.[91] Nevertheless, the Presbyterian tradition authorised religious conscience standing up to political power, and such opposition had a kind of mythological status. If Baxter's understated manner reflected a strain of practical, unostentatious Scottish Presbyterianism, his deeply embedded moral confidence also aligned with the values of its dissenting tradition. It supported a Christian obligation to stand fast to what he believed was right, despite the criticism and suffering to which he was subjected. The sense of individual religious conscience as the foundation of his convictions comes through consistently in Baxter's writing. As he said to Colonel Mitchell at Abeele: 'I was sure of the ground on which I stood.'[92]

Baxter's opposition to war may also have been strengthened by his sense of being Scottish rather than English. Scottish identity within wider British identity was not straightforward. Baxter was aware that at times his ancestors had fought both for and against the Crown. During his time in Cape Town on the voyage to England, as Baxter recovered from sickness, a doctor suggested that as a good Highlander Baxter would soon be fighting for his King. To this, Baxter replied: 'Yes, they fought for the king, except when they were fighting against him. I'm fighting too, only I'm on a different tack. I'm fighting against the war.'[93]

Conclusion

Baxter's Christian faith was neither conventional nor transparent. He eschewed church membership until later in life, and was reticent about his own beliefs when writing for the public. *We Will Not Cease* refers to religion in a number of passages but offers little explicit discussion on his own faith, or its importance to his pacifism. In some places the book seems to downplay or omit references to religion which are clearer in his other writing; when religion is mentioned, Baxter is usually more explicit on what he was not than what he was, and in many places his writing is open to different interpretations. He never unambiguously offered his religious beliefs as the basis for his objection to war. It is therefore understandable that some have suggested that Baxter did not have a personal faith or believe in God. However, despite the inevitable challenges his writing creates for understanding his beliefs, there is sufficent evidence to conclude that his belief in God and Christian faith was a significant factor in his moral outlook and opposition to war. Three key pieces of evidence support this interpretation. First, his own words in a letter to his parents in 1918, which record his belief in prayer and a fairly conventional Christian expectation of an afterlife. Second, the words of his wife Millicent in a 1978 interview with Michael King, which describe him as much misunderstood but 'essentially Christian' with a faith that was always 'under the surface'. Third, his own description of his suffering during Field Punishment No. 1 and the strength he says he derived from God at this time.

In a denominational age, when denominational affiliation was often considered integral to Christian identity, Baxter's unwillingness to align with particular institutions made him hard to place. If the mystical streak that characterised his later years had also been significant during the war years it would have complicated things even further. It is little wonder that the authorities were repeatedly confused by Baxter's religious convictions, identifying him at different times in prison as agnostic and then Catholic, and listing him as Plymouth Brethren on his military record. The 1918 military medical record that identified him more generically as 'a believer' seems to have finally got it right, and may be a quote from his own words. This does not preclude the possibility that the Baxter family had earlier been involved with Plymouth Brethren, and Archibald may have been baptised as an infant, but he was not a member as an adult.

Christian traditions reached beyond denominational boundaries in early twentieth-century New Zealand, as Christian ideas, language and moral imagination shaped the broader culture. Such forms of unaffiliated Christian commitment are not easily traced and analysed, but occupy an important place in New Zealand's anti-war traditions. Baxter's reserve about his faith should not be interpreted as evidence that it was of little importance to him. Millicent makes clear that the opposite was the case. He saw faith as a private matter with practical implications. His sense of integrity and personal privacy prevented a more public statement of his convictions, and he was determined to avoid 'parading' his beliefs. He was reticent precisely because he took his faith so seriously.

8

Compulsion or Conscience: Alun Richards and Opposition to Compulsory Military Training, 1927–1930

Allan K. Davidson

In June 1927, Alun Morgan Richards, a twenty-year-old university student, was charged in the Magistrate's Court in Auckland with failing to attend compulsory military training (CMT). He 'pleaded not guilty and applied for exemption on conscientious grounds'. When it was pointed out that the previous year when he was at Hamilton High School he had 'sought non-commissioned rank in the school cadets', Richards declared he had 'absolutely no intention to drill, now or any other time'. As a son of the manse, preparing to enter the Presbyterian ministry, Richards was questioned about his Church's attitude towards CMT. He responded that the General Assembly had called for its abolition. The Magistrate, W. R. McKean, pointed out, however, that the Legislature had not given exemption for CMT to members of the Presbyterian Church. Richards responded that 'he believed it was his Christian duty to do all he could to make war impossible', taking his stand 'by my own conscience'. The magistrate replied that he hoped Richard's 'conscience will point out that you owe a duty to the State' and refused to grant him exemption, imposing a fine of twenty shillings.[1] Over the next two and a half years, Alun Richards' name figured prominently in the Magistrate's Court, public debates over CMT, the Presbyterian Church's deliberations about peace, appeals to the government and interactions between the government and the opposition over the repeal or continuance of CMT.

The extent of support Richards gained from the Presbyterian Church highlights the way in which the Church at this time was sometimes a very effective pressure group, in this case contributing to the national debates about peace and peacemaking. At the same time the Church also had to deal with contending voices within its own body. While not a pacifist church, some of its leaders in the post-war environment of the 1920s sought peaceful alternatives to the devastating impact of the Great War.[2] Richards' stand proved to be both an irritant and a rallying point within the Church and wider society, raising questions about the right of conscience over compulsion, the duty of the individual to the State and the approach of New Zealand to preparing for war in a time of peace.

Compulsory military training in New Zealand

The implementation of CMT in New Zealand was raised at various times in the nineteenth century, but it was not until the Defence Act 1909 that a 'universal obligation to be trained' in cadet forces was imposed on male youths aged twelve to twenty-one years.[3] The same Act also revised previous legislation about the liability of all males up to the age of fifty-five (with some exceptions, including ministers of religion) to serve in the Militia in time of war if a Proclamation was duly issued by the Governor.[4] This Act was amended in 1912 and provided for exemption if a magistrate was 'satisfied that the applicant objects in good faith to such training and service on the ground that it is contrary to his religious belief'. Those exempted were 'liable to perform as an equivalent to such service and training such non-combatant duties as are prescribed by the Governor-in-Council'.[5] No provision was made for conscientious objectors appealing on non-religious grounds. There was vigorous opposition to the implementation of CMT from Christian groups, peace activists, anti-militarists, individuals and trade unions, particularly to the imprisonment of defaulters.[6]

The First World War sharpened the debates over the rights of conscience and exemption from military service on religious and conscientious grounds. Initially, the soldiers who served overseas were volunteers. Faced with the continuing need to raise and maintain reinforcements during the war, the government introduced conscription by ballot in November 1916. Military Service Boards were set up to hear appeals against serving. The only ground available for appeal was if the appellant had been a member since 4 August 1914 (the day before New Zealand declared war):

> of a religious body the tenets and doctrines of which religious body declare the bearing of arms and the performance of any combatant service to be contrary to Divine revelation, and also that according to his own conscientious religious belief the bearing of arms and the performance of any combatant service is unlawful by reason of being contrary to Divine revelation.[7]

Three small denominations were recognised as opposed to war under this narrow definition: Christadelphians, Seventh-day Adventists and the Society of Friends.

For other religious bodies there was no automatic exemption from conscription, including their clergy; they and their members could not appeal to conscientious objection. Churches protested over the conscription of clergy. For Methodists and Baptists, their major concern was over manpower and the supply of sufficient ministers to meet the needs of the church and military chaplaincy.[8] Anglican leaders supported clergy going overseas as chaplains but opposed their enlistment as soldiers, with A. W. Averill, the Anglican Bishop of Auckland, 'requesting the Clergy to stick to the Spiritual work to which God has called them'.[9] For Catholics, their objection was based on the vows taken by priests that precluded them from military service. Presbyterians, under the forceful leadership of Dr James Gibb, minister at St John's, Wellington, who was very pro-war, passed a motion with substantial support, 'That military exemption should be sought for no minister called to service whose place can in any way be filled.'[10]

Church delegations to the Minister of Defence, James Allen, resulted in a messy *modus vivendi*. Allen assured their representatives that certificates would be available on application

A young Alun Richards, photographed during his training for the Presbyterian ministry. Source: A-S12-46 23-23, Presbyterian Archives Research Centre, Dunedin.

for clergy who had been conscripted and that these certificates could be submitted to Appeal Boards who would grant exemption.[11] Confusion over the status of theological students and teaching brothers, and criticism of the special status given to the churches, in effect exempting clergy from conscription, inflamed both sectarian and anti-church sentiment. By January 1918 it was agreed that appeals by Marist Brothers would be dealt with in the same way as clergy.[12]

The grounds for exclusion from conscription during the First World War were so narrowly defined and applied so strictly that only seventy-three objectors were offered exemption. New Zealand gained a reputation for the harsh treatment of objectors, particularly through the punishment of fourteen dissidents sent to Europe and most notably in the callous treatment of Archibald Baxter and Mark Briggs, who refused the forced attempts to make them support the war. The last of the defaulters were not released from prison in New Zealand until November 1920, with a number deprived of their civil rights for ten years, including their right to vote and work for the government.[13]

A reduced form of CMT continued after the First World War with an obligatory requirement for those aged nineteen to twenty-two to attend annually eight half-day parades and twelve drill sessions, as well as spend a fortnight in camp.[14] This training was conducted against the background of a growing anti-war, pro-peace sentiment. In the Presbyterian Church, Dr Gibb changed from his militant endorsement of war to recruiting support in the churches and community for the League of Nations as an instrument for resolving conflict. Gibb was also at the forefront of moves to work with other churches, including Catholics, in repudiating war altogether and drawing up an ecumenical peace manifesto.[15] In 1924, the Church's League of Nations Committee became a standing committee of the General Assembly. Two years later, the Church appointed representatives to an ecumenical 'committee for the propagation of the principles of peace'.[16] At the same Assembly, Gibb, as convenor of the Presbyterian Public Questions Committee, raised an issue originating from the Auckland Council of Christian

Congregations: the abolition of CMT and its replacement by a volunteer system.[17] The Church's resolution called for the reduction of military activities in New Zealand and steps to be taken to abolish CMT.[18]

Alun Richards and protest against compulsory military training

Before his first appearance in court on 15 June 1927 for failing to undertake CMT, Alun Richards had written to the Auckland Presbytery, a regional Presbyterian body, indicating that his refusal was largely influenced 'by the utterances of several of yourselves, and especially the Assembly's resolution on the matter'. The Presbytery, which met the day before Richards' court appearance, pointed out that he was going beyond what the Assembly had decided. Morgan Richards, Alun's father and minister at Takapuna, mistakenly, as it turned out, thought that 'there was a conscience clause . . . which his son could plead'. Alun, who was present at the meeting, told the Presbytery: 'He still felt that the Assembly's resolution [on CMT], if carried out to its logical conclusion, did support his attitude.'[19] As noted above, the magistrate refused to grant Richards exemption.

Richards' personal protest against CMT was part of a much wider public debate over the continued use of compulsion to enforce military training. The Labour Party, from its formation in 1916, was opposed to compulsion in military recruiting and training. John A. Lee, the Labour politician and First World War veteran, introduced into Parliament on 14 July 1927 the first of three attempts by Labour representatives to repeal CMT. In introducing the second reading, Lee referred to 'the great conscientious objector', Jesus, 'who delivered the Sermon on the Mount and then had to choose between nails and his opinion'. For Lee, 'the world is ready for a naval and military holiday' and called for CMT to be taken out of the law. The United and Reform party members, who had strong imperial and military sympathies, however, defeated the Bill by forty votes to eleven.[20]

When Richards' case was heard a second time in September 1927 he gave three reasons for his non-attendance at military drill. First, because war was 'wholesale murder at the bidding of politicians' and others, and preparations for it were unchristian;

it was therefore his duty as a Christian 'to take no part in them'. Second, as a Presbyterian he took his Church's stand that military training was 'wrong in principle' as a reason why he should not 'take any part in it'. Finally, he believed it was his 'Christian duty to do all I can to help make war impossible' and therefore to encourage 'others to do likewise'.[21]

The Magistrate, E. C. Cutten, imposed a fine of £10 on Richards, telling him: 'There is no help for you. I cannot grant you exemption. Why cannot you make up your mind to obey the laws of your country?'[22] He suggested Richards 'could play some useful part such as cleaning out latrines'.[23] Cutten's judgement drew a critical response from six leading Presbyterian ministers, including David Herron, who served as a chaplain, and James Thomson, who was a stretcher-bearer during the war. In their view, Richards' treatment was 'extraordinary' considering he had made his claim for exemption on religious grounds. The correspondents protested against the Magistrate's 'truculent attitude' and 'ungentlemanly language'.[24] Herron, who declared that he was not a pacifist, spoke several weeks later to the Auckland Council of Christian Congregations opposing CMT, and pointed to other parts of the British Empire, including Britain, where it had been abolished in favour of a voluntary system. With a mixture of Christian idealism and prudery he concluded: 'we will not have our boys at their most critical age taken out of the clean, healthy atmosphere of Christian homes and for three months exposed to the spirit of war and to the moral dangers of a military camp'.[25]

Support for protests over compulsory military training

A deputation from the Presbyterian Public Questions Committee took up Richards' case with F. J. Rolleston, the Minister of Justice. They argued that Richards was entitled to exemption as someone who was 'absolutely genuine'. While his stand differed from that of the Church on CMT, they 'would assuredly stand to the last in defence of the rights of conscience'. It was also pointed out that some individuals, including Duncan Hercus, another candidate for the Presbyterian ministry, were granted exemption by a Christchurch magistrate on religious grounds. Rolleston, however, defended the Court's refusal of Richards' claim for exemption, the magistrate having applied 'the principle which had already been followed'.[26]

The issues arising from Richards' objection to CMT were debated widely in correspondence to the newspapers, and they were taken up by other churches. The Baptist Union at its Conference in 1927, for example, urged upon the government 'the desirability of the abolition of compulsory training in favour of a system of physical training unassociated with war'.[27] A long report was presented to the Presbyterian Assembly by its Public Questions Committee, leading to the reaffirmation of the Church's position on CMT. Daniel Dutton, a chaplain in both the South African and First World Wars, spoke in the debate opposing abolition, arguing: 'If military training was right it would not help the position one iota by making it voluntary'.[28] The motion in favour of abolition was carried by a vote of 150 to 47. The Assembly went on to affirm 'the duty of a Christian in relation to the State', unanimously declaring 'the inviolability of the rights of conscience'. They recognised that 'a Christian in the interpretation of his duty to Christ may feel obliged to refuse to render military service', claiming the right of exemption on religious grounds to military training under the 1912 amendment of the 1909 Defence Act.[29] These decisions were communicated to the government.

In April 1928 Richards reappeared in Court joined by two other Presbyterian divinity students,[30] Lex (Alexander) Miller and William Byrt, along with Leonard Usher, a teacher and Methodist lay-preacher; all of them claimed exemption from CMT. Dr Gibb travelled to Auckland and gave support when Richards' case was heard, and clergy provided *bona fides* supporting the men's religious convictions. The four cases were adjourned to give the appellants time to consider alternative service with the Boy Scouts.[31] The Scout Movement, however, could not assure the Court that it was willing to accept them if they were exempted because it did not know if they were suitable and if they had the requisite training. Also, under the statute, the Governor-in-Council, not the Court, had to make provision for alternative service. While the magistrate was ready to acknowledge the men's conscientious objection to military service he could not understand why they were not 'prepared to do some substitute service'. He refused their applications, ruling that they would be fined 'If they do not drill now'.[32]

The Public Questions Committee organised another deputation to F. J. Rolleston in his role as Minister of Defence. Gibb pointed to the large majority in the Presbyterian Assembly against CMT. He indicated that some magistrates outside Auckland had 'enabled conscientious views to be respected' and that a magistrate did not have the prerogative to suggest alternative service to an objector without the Governor-General having indicated what substitutes were approved. Rolleston expressed his concern that the Church 'should not take up a hostile attitude' or say that 'it was going to fight the matter out and decline to agree to any form of alternative service'. He looked for the Church and Richards to meet the Defence Department 'half way, as we have done, and agree to some alternative service'.[33] In response to Rolleston's appeal for compromise, the Auckland Presbytery answered that it still upheld 'the claim that the conscience clause of the Defence Act applies equally to all religious denominations'.[34]

Lee, when he spoke to the second reading of his second Repeal Bill in August 1928, indicated that although it was bound to be defeated, 'the number of converts grow and . . . the amount of hostility to compulsory military service grows'. Peter Fraser, who was imprisoned during the war for sedition for opposing conscription, with the Presbyterian objectors in mind, declared that 'you have either to respect their conscience, which is the only sensible thing to do, or else resort to all sorts of tyrannies to impose your will upon the persons who appear to be recalcitrant'. The vote, as Lee predicted, was ten in favour of repeal and fifty against.[35]

During the next eighteen months the columns of the Presbyterian Church magazine included frequent articles and letters both for and against CMT. There were appeals to the Church's role to support the State, with the view 'that the citizen in all civil matters owes obedience to constituted authority'.[36] Arguments were also advanced supporting the rights of conscience and opposition to war, with Duncan Hercus noting: 'Mr Richards objects fundamentally not to the possible causes for which war may be waged, but to the very institution and method of war.'[37] These debates were cast against the background of another argument that was taking place in the Presbyterian Church over the Peace Manifesto.

When the Assembly met in November 1928, Gibb reported that the Public Questions Committee had suggested to Mr Rolleston that the Governor-in-Council make provision for non-military alternative service for those given exemption. Nothing it seemed, however, had been done. In the meantime, the three Presbyterian students had not been prosecuted. They indicated they were willing to undertake approved non-military alternative service. The Assembly again reaffirmed its resolution on CMT, although with a smaller majority, ninety-nine votes to sixty, and approved the support given by the Committee to Richards, Byrt and Miller.[38] A Peace Manifesto originating from the national ecumenical Peace Committee set up in 1926, which included the 'outspoken and uncompromising declaration that the outlawry of war is the primary moral task of this generation', was also before the Assembly.[39] A modified resolution was agreed to, based on the 1926 Jerusalem International Missionary Conference's 'renunciation of war as an instrument of national policy' and 'the adoption of peaceful methods for the settlement of all international disputes'.[40]

Civil rights, alternative service and political pressure

The cases of Richards and Miller came before the Court again on 12 June 1929 when the magistrate ordered the withdrawal of their civil rights for ten years and a fine each of £5. Another student for the ministry, J. N. McDougall, was fined £1. Richards' and Miller's refusal to take up hospital duty in lieu of military service was contrasted with three Seventh-day Adventist youths who the same day had accepted this alternative. Miller wanted his exemption to be recognised as based on religious grounds and called for alternative service to be officially gazetted.[41]

Both Richards and Miller were the focus of public vitriol, the *New Zealand Herald* editorialising that it was 'their duty to obey the law'; they were doing 'shameful violence' to the word 'Conscience'; they were 'contumacious youths . . . flagrantly anti-social and utterly unworthy of the citizen privileges they have hitherto enjoyed'.[42] One correspondent, 'Son of the Manse', declared that 'these youths are not fit entrants for the Christian ministry'. In contrast, Ormond Burton, a decorated First World War veteran, at this stage an active Presbyterian layman who later became a Methodist minister and New Zealand's leading pacifist during the Second World War, responded that he was 'proud to identify myself with them', believing 'their stand to be the only one possible to any one who applies Christian ethics to the question of war and preparation for war'.[43]

After obtaining legal advice, the Presbyterian Public Questions Committee resolved that while the Church did not encourage refusal to participate in CMT it supported the rights of conscientious objection under the law. The Committee urged those offered alternative service to accept this if it was 'prescribed by the Governor-in-Council'; they regretted that Richards and Miller had not done this. At the same time, the Committee felt the sentence and fine given to them was 'unduly severe'. An opportunity to meet with the Minister of Justice was requested, with one of the points of discussion the determination as to whether magistrates could offer alternative service without the Governor-in-Council making provisions for it.[44]

A Presbyterian deputation met with T. M. Wilford, Minister of Justice. He responded to their submission by indicating that conscientious objection in future would be decided 'on the strength of individual cases' and not 'the basis of church or denominational connection'. The Governor-in-Council would go ahead and gazette prescribed alternative service. These concessions were welcomed. Wilford, however, refused to review Richards' and Miller's sentences, denying on the basis of their trials that they 'were bona fide conscientious objectors', classifying Richards instead as 'a political rather than a religious objector'. The deputation disagreed, viewing Richards' attitude as 'religious in essence'.[45] The same day, Labour politicians for a third time introduced into Parliament their Compulsory Military Service Repeal Bill.[46]

The seriousness with which the issues raised by the objections of Richards and Miller to CMT were being taken, and the public sensitivity around their cases, were seen in a deputation of ten Labour members of Parliament to the Prime Minister, Sir Joseph Ward, and T. M. Wilford on 12 July. The Leader of the Opposition, H. E. Holland, declared there was 'no question at all' about the students' *bona fides*. He deplored the withdrawal of their civil rights and the possibility they might be put in prison. Peter Fraser asserted 'that the interests of the country as a whole would be served far better by recognising the rights of these young men, who had an individual religious conscience'. Ward promised to take the matter to Cabinet, describing it as 'a peculiar case'. He was concerned though about a minister interfering with a court decision. When pressed, he agreed to bring before the Cabinet the possibility of the Governor-General withholding the execution of the arrest of the two students if they did not pay their fines.[47]

Alexander (Lex) Miller was a contemporary and fellow Presbyterian divinity student who joined Richards' protests against compulsory military training from 1928. He remained committed to social causes even as he pursued a notable academic career, which included appointment as the first Professor of Religion at Stanford University. Source: P-S15-6, Presbyterian Archives Research Centre, Dunedin.

Four days after the Labour delegation, Ward made a public statement and announced in the House of Representatives that he regretted 'it is not possible to reverse the decisions of the Magistrates' as this could only be done by a higher court. It was decided, however, to amend the law 'in the direction of exempting divinity students who apply for exemption from military training'.[48] Ward indicated that if Richards and Miller did not pay their fines they would go to gaol for two weeks and then could apply for exemption.[49] The unfairness of exempting only divinity students was raised immediately, with the Labour MP Edwin (Ted) Howard questioning Ward, 'What about Socialists?', while Alexander Harris, a Reform MP, exclaimed that 'The Government will wreck the whole defence system.'[50] The *Evening Star* editorialised that the limited exemption was 'the thin edge of the wedge'. The editor accused the Labour Party of eagerly seizing the conscientious objection agitation because their political objective was the 'abolition of the defence system'.[51]

When the Repeal Bill came up for its second reading at the end of July, the Labour MP W. J. Jordan, like Lee another war veteran, took the lead, stating that the measure was 'not one for the abolition of military training', but 'to abolish the compulsory sections in the Act' in favour of a voluntary system. His complaint was not with the defence forces, but with the expenditure involved when there were other pressing needs such as medical and dental services. For Jordan, 'to prepare for war, when there is no war expected, is absurd'. After a lengthy debate, with the Prime Minister indicating that only the government could initiate an alteration in the system of defence, the Bill was defeated forty-six to twenty-one.[52]

When they met to consider the Prime Minister's statement exempting divinity students, the Presbyterian Public Questions Committee urged that this 'should be extended to all persons whose conscientious objections to military training and service are certified by trustworthy witnesses', and that alternative service should be an obligation. They also asked that the heavy sentences imposed on Richards and Miller be reviewed. Strong views were expressed within the wider Church against the objectors. G. M. Thomson, Member of the New Zealand Legislative Council, for example, accused the objectors of 'posing as martyrs', 'with a perverted sense of duty' and dismissed them as 'cranks' whose actions savoured 'of vanity and obduracy'.[53] But they also had powerful supporters, including the Reverend J. H. MacKenzie, the clerk of the Presbyterian Assembly, who concluded that 'We should invite our young men to think peace, not to think war.'[54]

In mid-August, with the cases of Richards and Miller about to be heard again, Alun Richards' father wrote to the Prime Minister, concerned that Ward's statement that the law should take its course would result in prison sentences if the fines were not paid. He urged that the court hearing be deferred. Several days later he acknowledged Ward's telegram indicating that the magistrate had agreed to hold over his son's case for two months while Parliament made a decision as to how it was going to deal with exemptions.[55] This deferral also applied to eight others who had now applied for exemption on religious grounds.[56]

The issue of conscientious objectors was raised in the Legislative Council at the end of August 1929 by Sir James Allen, who was Minister of Defence during the war, and had overseen the strict administration of conscription. Referring to the recent 'agitation for exemption from military training and service on account of conscientious objection', and the current exclusive provision for 'religious beliefs', his motion called on the government to consider whether the law needed 'to include conscientious objectors' and to provide under alternative service, 'training for first-aid, ambulance, and stretcher-bearer work'. In his speech Allen reviewed the administration of exemption during the war and gave examples of objectors who appealed for exemption to avoid their responsibilities. His own preference was to leave things as they were, without any provision for conscientious objectors. Allen's distinction between religious and conscientious objectors reflected his narrow approach to exemption and the difficulty he believed objectors had in establishing their *bona fides*. Sir Thomas Mackenzie, New Zealand's High Commissioner in London during the war, supported Allen, arguing 'that every man fit to bear arms—whether parson, priest, or layman—ought to take his stand in defence of his country'.[57]

Increasingly the division among politicians and the public over CMT was, however, overtaken by international and national forces as the growing economic depression placed constraints on public expenditure. In November 1929, the newly elected Federal Labor government in Australia suspended CMT on financial grounds.[58] Meanwhile, further adjournments were given in October and November to the cases of Richards, Miller and others.[59] In December, the Defence Department told the Court that with arrangements underway for Richards, Miller and Byrt to do alternative service in Presbyterian orphanages, which they accepted, exemptions would not be opposed. The magistrate duly granted them exemption subject to the performance of alternative service. Two brothers, Neil and John McDougall, however, refused to do this and their exemption was declined.[60]

Church and community protest against CMT continued to grow in 1930. Baptist, Methodist, Congregational, and Presbyterian Churches, the Churches of Christ, the Society of Friends and the Women's Christian Temperance Union publicly continued to bring pressure on the government to abolish CMT.[61] In the view of Lionel Fletcher, a leading Congregational minister, compulsion was a 'violation of conscience'.[62] There were other groups, such as a newly formed Territorials Association, the New Zealand Manufacturers' Federation and the National Defence League, who defended the need for CMT.[63]

Sir Joseph Ward in April 1930 signalled a review of the defence system, and this was taken by many to include the suspension of CMT.[64] The Presbyterian General Assembly, which applied for the restoration of Richards' and Miller's civil rights, was notified in mid-May that 'the Governor-General has been pleased to cancel as from May 1 last the orders of deprivation'.[65] The Minister of Defence stated in the House on 15 July 1930 that compulsory military training, with the exception of school cadets, 'had been temporarily suspended'.[66] The reason given for this was to reduce military spending from £500,000 to £275,000.[67] Legislation validating the suspension was passed in August, with thirty-two in favour and seventeen against.[68]

Alun Richards' reflections on his role in opposing CMT

During the years when he became a lightning rod for the debates over CMT, Alun Richards successfully pursued his studies, completing a Master's degree with Honours in Education, and a Diploma in Journalism. Asked many years later who paid his fines, he said that he could not afford them and did not want to pay them; 'they were paid by well-wishers without my knowledge'. Initially, his action was a personal protest against CMT, a stand taken without his parents' knowledge. After his first court appearance, he recalled that David Herron, the minister at St David's, Khyber Pass in Auckland, gathered supporters around him, in Alun's words, 'to hedge their growing objection to the warlike indoctrination of young New Zealanders'. While Richards was criticised in the newspapers by some, he found that his public profile resulted in him being contacted by or introduced to 'a lot of interesting people', including: the novelist Rex Fairburn; Jack Bennett, C. S. Lewis' successor in Cambridge; the poet R. A. K. Mason; the bookseller and publisher Blackwood Paul; Colin Scrimgeour, 'Uncle Scrim'; and Labour Party people. He described these people as not necessarily pacifists or objectors, but 'part of the wave of disenchantment' following on from the First World War.[69]

At first, Richards did not welcome the publicity he gained, describing himself as 'a shrinking fellow'. But his objection was to 'the whole military system' and by 1928 his protest had 'moved from being an individual thing'. Given the withdrawal of his civil rights, which was regarded by people in his circle 'as something of a joke', the government decided to back off from making him into a martyr. He recalled that at one point he was about to accompany the Takapuna constable to Mount Eden gaol but was phoned 'half-an-hour beforehand' and told by the policeman that 'he'd been told not to come'. Richards believed this was a political decision to keep him out of gaol because the authorities 'felt that this would cause still more trouble'. He saw himself as 'just one of the bits in the uncoordinated movement' against CMT and 'was not really important in any way except as a catalyst'.[70]

Conclusion

Richards' implacable rejection, not only of CMT, but of the whole defence system because of his religious beliefs, provoked his confrontation with military authorities and the judgements of the Court against him. While he was only one among many who objected to CMT, he gained a much higher profile than others. In large measure that was due to his status both as a Presbyterian divinity student and son of a minister, and the groundswell of support he attracted from church leaders. There was general questioning in the churches of the continuing use of compulsion in military training and a strong desire following on from the First World War to promote peace. Presbyterian advocacy in particular, wider support in the community, and the growing number of other divinity students embracing Richards' opposition to CMT, helped moderate and change the government's attitude, leading them to grant exemption to divinity students. But this response only raised the issue of equity and the broader issue of exemption for non-religious objectors.

The decision to suspend CMT on pragmatic financial grounds saved the government from having to deal with an unresolved contentious issue but left unanswered the fundamental principle as to how to recognise conscientious or religious grounds for objection to military service. This problem reared its head again in the Second World War. In opposition the Labour Party had opposed conscription and CMT. When Labour was in government during the Second World War it reintroduced conscription in 1940. Ironically the Prime Minister was Peter Fraser, who was imprisoned in the First World War for opposing compulsory recruitment. The Labour government oversaw a system which rejected most appeals for exemption on conscientious and religious grounds, with some 800 imprisoned as defaulters; they were deprived of their civil rights for ten years.[71] In 1949, in the face of the Cold War and the perceived Communist threat, Fraser controversially, despite Labour's traditional hostility to compulsion, called for a referendum in support of CMT. Nearly four-fifths of the population supported the reintroduction of compulsory training.

For Alun Richards, his objection to CMT and war was more than a youthful protest. As a ministry student at the Presbyterian Theological Hall in Dunedin in 1931, his questioning of the social and political status quo in the context of the Depression made him something of an irritant, leading to him being asked to leave. He completed his theological study at New College in Edinburgh. Through a Student Christian Movement (SCM) European Conference he met and heard outstanding ecumenical leaders such as Lesslie Newbigin, William Temple and John Oldham. Newly married to Muriel Hunt, they travelled through Europe, including Nazi Germany and Communist Russia, visiting Java for an SCM conference on the way home to New Zealand.

Richards was ordained at Totara Flat on the West Coast in 1934, where he served for four years. He then took up a position with Victoria University College in extension education through the Workers' Education Association (WEA). In 1937, in the face of rearmament in Europe, he engaged in a debate over pacifism with Isaac Jolly, a long-time defender of the Presbyterian tradition of supporting the State, in the Presbyterian weekly the *Outlook*.[72] After the declaration of war in 1939, the editor of the *Outlook*, in response to a letter from Richards, pointed to the confusion in his thought 'which makes pacifism an essential part of Christian faith and doctrine'. The editor stated the Presbyterian position as one that respected conscience, recognising this would lead some to support and others to oppose war.[73]

Richards was controversially dismissed by the Victoria College professorial board after being unfairly accused of 'using the WEA for propaganda purposes' against the war.[74] He went on and worked for the Council of Organisations for Relief Services Overseas (CORSO), and served as editor of the *Outlook* (1948–55), in various parishes, and as first editor of the revived *New Zealand Methodist* (1966–67). When he died in 2000, an obituary described him as 'a thinker of considerable originality, and a man often ahead of his times' who 'never found it easy to work to instructions, or within structures'.[75]

Author's postscript

On 22 July 1983 when I interviewed Alun Richards, he had just returned from being out on Auckland Harbour as part of preparation for the forthcoming anti-nuclear protest against the visit of the USS *Texas* on 2 August. There was continuity between the reluctant student stirrer and the elderly protestor.

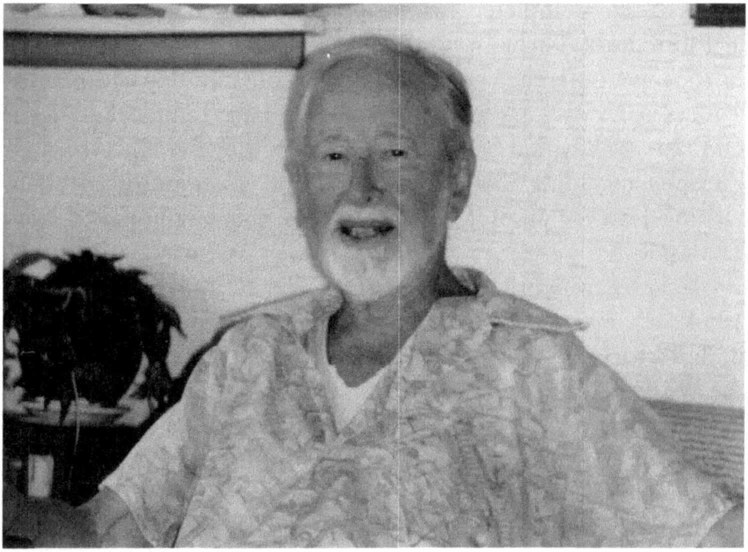

Alun Richards campaigned in support of peace and justice issues throughout his career; this included protests against nuclear weapons, and wider contributions to the peace movement in the 1970s and 80s. Source: Presbyterian Archives Research Centre, Dunedin.

9

Sects and War in New Zealand

Peter Lineham

The pacifists of New Zealand who belonged to the mainstream churches but held personal convictions against war have frequently told their story of being sentenced to the detention camps for refusing military service during the Second World War. Occasionally their accounts include shadowy references to another group of people who were also in the camps, described as 'fundamentalists' or 'Bible-bangers'.[1] Some accounts of the peace movement ignore these fundamentalist conscientious objectors.[2] These people never glamourised their experience and they have therefore been neglected.

All of the original soldiers in the First World War were volunteers, although there had already been a significant dispute over the requirement that young people be trained for military service, which provoked concern among religious and other opponents of war. In 1915 the National Registration Act required men to indicate their willingness to serve, and 8621 single men without dependants declared that they were unwilling. Furthermore, 819 single men classified themselves as having a religious objection to warfare and 260 a political objection.[3] Under the Military Service Act, which introduced conscription in November 1916, balloted men who were members of a religious group that had a documented objection to fighting prior to the beginning of the war were eligible for exemption. Some seventy-three men were exempted by the Military Service Boards on these grounds, drawn from the approved sects—initially the Quakers, but later the Christadelphians, and then the Seventh-day Adventists. Those who were exempted signed a declaration indicating their availability for civilian service if called upon. Sometimes even those who were not exempted were recommended for noncombatant military service in the Ambulance Corps.[4] At the end of the war some 273 men were held in prison for their refusal to serve, including 88 with religious objections. One schedule gives their religion, indicating that among those who objected on religious grounds there were 3 Catholics, 11 from the three largest Protestant churches, and 45 from sectarian groups (although 4 others had conscientious objections to fighting and altogether another 73 from the sects were also held for various reasons); 8 of the 88 are listed with no religion, and 21 with no stated religion. In December 1918, the Religious Objectors Advisory Board classified 113 prisoners as religious objectors, and these were released in September 1919. Others among the 273 may also have had religious grounds for their refusal to serve.[5]

In the Second World War the regulations were eased somewhat, with some recognition that there could be divergences within sects, and the choice of noncombatant duties in the Army was permitted by the Military Service Boards.[6] In October 1944 a count was taken of the religion of imprisoned objectors. Alongside the 157 members of main churches (68 Methodists, 32 Anglicans, 28 Presbyterians, 23 Catholics and 6 Baptists), and the 156 non-religious people, there were 248 sectarian Protestants. Of these, 107 were from the Christian Assemblies (Cooneyites), 78 Jehovah's Witnesses, 35 Brethren, 9 Seventh-day Adventists, 8 Christadelphians and 11 Pentecostals. Another 30 were unclassified.[7]

So sectarian Protestants were the largest group of those imprisoned.[8] The lack of public sympathy for these people was particularly evident. One columnist wrote in the *Observer*:

> The fanatic of any kind is a fanatic. . . . He loves to be a martyr when his idiotic vapourings get into print. No man seized by the military authorities should be allowed to bleat in print. . . . It doesn't matter a bit to the public whether a possible conscript is a Christadelphian, a Confucian or a humbug . . . the State isn't an advertising medium for religious cranks or people who want to give Germans a cup of tea for murdering their mothers.[9]

Main groups of conservative Christian objectors

This group of detainees probably expected hostility from the community towards their stand, for they should be classified as sectarian Protestants—members of small Protestant churches with high levels of commitment, tightly knit and eager to maintain their separateness from the broader religious and secular world. Scholars have long noted that there have been Christians who have dissented from the dominant church, whether Catholic or the state Protestant churches (Presbyterian, Lutheran and Anglican). Since the eighteenth century, denominations like Congregationalists, Baptists and Methodists have co-existed with the state church, and the term 'mainstream' churches has included all such churches. In contrast, the sects emphasised their distinctive theology or Bible interpretation, and consequently did not co-exist comfortably, although there were degrees of sectarianism.

Sects were a significant part of the New Zealand Christian landscape.[10] Disagreeing with the mainstream, they also vehemently disagreed with each other. Quakers, Plymouth Brethren, Latter-day Saints, Seventh-day Adventists, Christian Scientists, Christadelphians, and a range of smaller revivalist, millennial, new thought and reformist groups constituted a very diverse assortment. Together they accounted for about 15,142 people in the 1916 census, which was 1.3% of the population, and 44,437 in 1945, or about 2.6% of the population. These figures were not particularly high compared to the USA, but they attracted public attention because they were published.[11] Of these sects, some, including the Latter-day Saints, had no qualms about service in the military, but those sects that took the New Testament literally were bound to be challenged by the words of Jesus. While Quakers fit into this group, their theology and practice was far from fundamentalist or exclusive, and on account of the special exemptions from which they had long benefited, their members were more readily able to claim exemption from military service. The Salvation Army, also, was far more open than other small religious groups.

The tensions between the sects became very evident in wartime. Although they read the Gospel injunctions on peacemaking in the same way, in other respects their beliefs were very different. Their focus on scripture made them keen to debate with each other, but each group existed precisely because of deeply held convictions with which others disagreed. Two groups, the Plymouth Brethren and the so-called Cooneyites, contributed the bulk of the detainees and therefore detailed sections are devoted to them below. Yet a significant share of the detainees came from an assortment of other groups. The level of detainees is only one measure of the significance of the sect, so these other groups need to be identified and the distinctiveness of their response identified.

Seventh-day Adventists, a group that had arisen through the preaching of Mrs Ellen White and others in the USA after the debacle of William Miller's prediction of the end of the world in 1843, commenced New Zealand activity in 1885. They had 1534 adherents by 1916 and 5084 by 1945, including a significant group of Māori. They were best known for adherence to the Old Testament Sabbath and other laws, so their viewpoint on war was not widely known beyond the sect, but in fact they took the command not to kill literally. In May 1917 the American leadership provided evidence that members were not permitted to fight, and their objection to war was then upheld by the courts. This ruling remained despite widespread criticism in the media when a large group of Adventists was exempted at a Hamilton hearing.[12] In February 1917 the Adventist leaders estimated that about 160 members were at risk of being called up.[13] Adventists did not have to re-apply for exemption in the Second World War. Accepting military service in noncombatant roles, Adventists were dutifully loyal, and the denomination raised money for military ambulances.

Christadelphians were a British schism within the Restoration Movement (the Churches of Christ) which advocated the 'soul sleep' of those who died before the Day of Judgement. The movement arrived in New Zealand in the 1870s. In 1916 there were 1150 adherents, and in 1945, 1367, with particular concentrations in Wanganui and Otago. In 1911 and 1912 some Christadelphians objected to their sons joining the cadets, even when they were assigned non-military exercises.[14] Christadelphians were shown no sympathy by British military authorities, and this news must have troubled local adherents.[15] A Christadelphian territorial soldier, who had been called up prior to the introduction of conscription, was excused service when he expounded his view that this war was a fulfilment of prophecy.[16] When the Military Service Act was under consideration, the Christadelphian position was scrutinised in Parliament. One Legislative Councillor called them 'Castadelphians' and 'the religious Red Feds', but under the Act they qualified for exemption.[17]

It took some time for members and for the Military Service Boards which heard appeals against conscription to develop a consistent approach to Christadelphians. Christadelphian refusal to undertake military training had already troubled magistrates.[18] The first Christadelphians mistakenly accepted noncombatant duties in the Army but then appealed, producing written evidence of the beliefs of the ecclesia. The original text of the declaration signed by those whom the boards exempted from conscription was unacceptable to Christadelphians.[19] Early in 1917 the wording of the declaration was changed and consequently more were willing to sign it.[20] The boards were usually willing to exempt Christadelphians from wearing military uniforms while performing noncombatant duties. At first unbaptised adherents had their appeals dismissed, but in November 1917 they too were exempted.[21] National leaders of the Christadelphians kept a close watch on call-ups, and where necessary John M. Troup, the leading brother, would travel to the provinces to support adherents.[22] His daughter Alice served in the Prime Minister's Department and was able to put in a good word for fellow-members.[23] The Second World War regulations were prepared with the Christadelphians in mind, although it remained the responsibility of the individual member to seek help from his ecclesia.[24]

The Richmond Mission was a small Christchurch sect that was commenced by David and Florence Smith in 1911. Pacifism was integral to their gospel, along with a prophetic interpretation of the approaching end of the world. Seven of them declined to be called up and declined to sign the noncombatant declaration, and so were imprisoned. In July 1917 (inspired, no doubt, by the Adventists) they sought reconsideration of the status of five members in gaol. The Court declined to intervene, holding that the Mission had no status because the Smiths did not hold a marriage license.[25] Theodore Gibbs, grandfather of the National and ACT party leader, was also a member of this group who was called up.[26] In the Second World War, Mission leaders wrote to the Prime Minister, but lacking an official pacifist stance, the church could not help members before the court.[27]

There were a few Christian Israelites in the Dominion, most of them Wroeites, followers of one of the claimants to be heirs of Joanna Southcott, who had prophesied England's future during the Napoleonic wars.[28] They viewed Britain as inheriting all the Old Testament promises to Israel. In 1917 Arthur Hill, a member of the Society of the House of Israel, whose members dressed as Jews, appealed his call-up.[29] He was treated with derision. In the Second World War a clerk belonging to the House of David declared that 'We think this is Armageddon, an end of all things' and was sent into detention.[30] Among other groups in the First World War, five Spiritualists were held in prison, as were two each from the Unity Society of Practical Christianity and Christ's Peace Society, one from the Fellowship of Reconciliation, and others who failed to identify their sect to the court.[31]

In the Second World War, two significant new groups emerged. Pentecostalism is usually traced to the Azusa Street Revival in Los Angeles in 1906, although there were earlier examples of speaking in tongues. The first generation of Pentecostals appeared in New Zealand in the 1920s and they were very literal in their reading of the New Testament. By the time of the Second World War they had split into several groups. The largest group was the Assemblies of God, and Percy Robert Meek, a draftsman working for the government, was one member who refused to take up arms.[32] The Apostolic Church had a national structure and supported individual protestors but left the decision to the individual. The Vice President of the Church appeared in support of Graham Cecil Scadden of Wellington, while Albert Painter, an Auckland labourer, was supported by

APPEAL CASES

"NEUTRAL" ORGANISATION

JEHOVAH'S WITNESS

Three of the appeals which came before the No. 4 Armed Forces Appeal Board yesterday were based on conscientious objection. Two were dismissed outright, and in the third case, in which the appellant was Samuel Allan Powell, clerk and a member of the Exclusive Brethren, the board dismissed the appeal subject to the performance of non-combatant service in the Armed Forces, which the appellant had stated his willingness to undertake.

William Howard Boxall Bell, storeman, one of the conscientious objectors, said that he was a Jehovah's Witness. He admitted to the Crown representative (Mr. C. O. Bell) that in his two previous unsuccessful appeals against Territorial service he had stated that he was not prepared to undertake non-combatant service, and said that now he was willing to undertake any work that might be required of him in a civil capacity. His objection was to the taking of human life.

Supporting the appeal, Flurence J. White said that he was also a Jehovah's Witness.

Mr. Bell: Don't Jehovah's Witnesses as a rule want to be neutral?

Witness: Yes, they are neutral; they are not Christian Pacifists.

Therefore they would not be prepared to assist either side actively?—No, not either side.

And they consider both sides Satanic organisations?—That is so, because they are neutral.

If this man says he is prepared to assist in a non-combatant capacity in this war, he is acting contrary to Jehovah's teaching?—No, he would not be. That is quite all right, provided that he does not kill.

If he joins the Army, that is against Jehovah's teaching?—Oh yes, if he joins the Army.

The appeal was dismissed.

Smaller Christian sects such as the Brethren, Jehovah's Witnesses and the Christian Assemblies (Testimony of Jesus) were strongly represented among conscientious objectors to war service. These smaller groups were seldom met with understanding, or with sympathy, by either the public or the authorities. Source: *Evening Post*, 14 November 1941, 7.

the President of the Church. Despite this help, members who appealed were generally sent to the camps.[33] The Commonwealth Covenant Church believed that Britain was the inheritor of the promises to Israel (hence linked with the British Israelites who objected during the First World War). They produced several conscientious objectors to military service, some of them giving the courts colourful accounts of their faith.[34]

In the detention camps Pentecostals formed a small but rowdy group. David Grant describes Harry Gallus, a fire and brimstone preacher who held regular Sunday night services in Hautu Camp, undeterred by his lack of front teeth.[35] Some Pentecostals were disillusioned with denominational support, and Brian Aubone Snowden, when he appeared in court, insisted that he now only belonged to the Christian Pacifist Society.[36]

The most controversial group in the Second World War was the Jehovah's Witnesses, who were known in the 1940s as the Russellites, Millennial Dawn, the Watch Tower Society, or Rutherfordites. They were best known at that time for interpreting the biblical prophecies as indicating the return of Christ in the heavens in the twentieth century (although they revised the date several times). The census records them in New Zealand from 1911 and there were 177 in 1916. Pastor Charles Taze Russell, the founder, evidently visited Auckland in 1914, and one adherent was imprisoned during the First World War.[37] By 1945 there were 650 adherents in New Zealand, and this group had the worst experience of any religious minority in the Second World War, with 78 held in the camps. Believing that Armageddon was near at hand, they had no loyalty to any existing state and were only willing to defend fellow Witnesses.[38] Defying the state, they generally refused to take the oath of allegiance.[39] One conscript told the court that he would not soil his hands with any work for Satan's organisations.[40]

Nan Taylor and Harry (Peter H.) Ballis have documented how the group was banned from any public meetings at the outset of the war and then restricted in operations until 5 April 1945.[41] Most Witnesses who were called up were imprisoned and they were known as a very extreme group in the camps. At least one Witness left the movement after debates in the camp, but another 'Conchie' joined them while in detention.[42] Tom Harrison, a member interviewed in 1981, explained how the imprisoned Witnesses were shaped into a community through their imprisonment, developing experience in public speaking and in evangelism.[43]

Open and Exclusive Brethren

The second largest of the groups of conscientious objectors in the First World War was the Plymouth Brethren, a group of evangelicals with a particular interpretation of the end-time prophecies, founded in Great Britain in the 1820s and present in New Zealand from the 1840s. By 1916 they had 9758 adherents, and this number had doubled to 18,868 by 1945.[44] Sharply divided after the 1840s into Exclusive and Open Brethren, both groups objected to defilement from the world and sought to obey scripture literally, which led many members to object to conscription. During the First World War they were divided over military service. The editor of the Open Brethren magazine, *Treasury*, urged prayer for soldiers on both sides of the conflict.[45] Some more evangelistic Brethren were eager to support the Allied war efforts; some fifty-five Brethren volunteered prior to the introduction of the draft and thirty-five were drafted in the first twelve months of conscription.[46] But the introduction of conscription brought a flurry of Brethren objectors, who insistently claimed that believers must oppose the war. The Canterbury Military Service Board as a result sought clarification of the Brethren stance on the war, and consulted with other boards.[47] Some Brethren were very anxious to nullify the bad impressions created by the objectors. Since the Brethren rejected any formal organisation, they could only provide scriptural texts as evidence of their stance.[48] Brethren appeals were generally dismissed, often with a sarcastic reference to Brethren inconsistency.[49] In all, fourteen 'Brethren', two 'Gospel Hall' and seven 'Plymouth Brethren' (the latter probably signifying Exclusive Brethren) were imprisoned in the First World War.[50]

Some members sought to promote general Brethren opposition to the war. The central Open Brethren assembly in Dunedin in 1917 tried to rally support for the objectors, urging all assemblies to appeal to the Governor.[51] The letter had no effect. A number of Open Brethren leaders wrote a letter representing this position, but given the divergences it was impossible to maintain that noncombatancy was a fundamental tenet of Brethren beliefs.[52] The Open Brethren magazine acknowledged the tension among the Brethren over the issue.[53] Exclusive Brethren were split along the same lines.[54] John Olley, later a prominent Brethren missionary in Chad, and J. W. Clapham, later a Brethren missionary in Palestine, seem to have joined the Open Brethren while interned. Nevertheless, when Clapham wrote Olley's biography in 1961 he stated that they 'were thrown in contact . . . with a little company who seemed to be enjoying particularly happy and profitable times of Christian fellowship', omitting the fact that this was in a prison camp.[55] After the war the issue remained very divisive and people increasingly glossed over it. Those congregations that were more evangelistic and outward-looking saw the high price paid as unnecessary, especially when the noncombatant option became available.

In the Second World War, most Brethren accepted conscription, and then chose noncombatant service in the medical or transport divisions. A few were not prepared to serve in the military, and to support them a memorandum on Brethren views on war was presented to the Prime Minister.[56] Twelve Brethren cases were heard together in Wellington in February 1941. All were willing to undertake noncombatant work, so while their cases were dismissed, they were recommended for noncombatant duties.[57] Some forty Brethren were sent to the detention camps, compared to roughly one hundred who served in the Army.[58] Many future leaders were among the detainees.[59] The war widened divergences between more and less open Brethren. The eminent surgeon Gordon Anderson wrote to the *Evening Post* insisting that Brethren supported the war, and the members at Tory Street Hall issued a statement that 'they do not support objection to military service on religious grounds'.[60] In June 1941, most of the Open Brethren appeals were reheard and many people were released into noncombatant service. This was a substantial victory for the Open Brethren.[61]

Exclusive Brethren who accepted conscription during the Second World War consistently requested noncombatant duties, but some refused to obey the summons. The board was amused at one member who claimed exemption, for he worked in the munitions industry, but objected to firing guns.[62] But Brethren were capable of a very literal reading of Scripture which avoided broader conceptual principles.

The Testimony of Jesus or the Christian Assemblies

The largest group of conscientious objectors held in detention in both the First and Second World Wars came from the church with no name, called the 'Christian Assemblies' in the census, and identified in the courts as the Testimony of Jesus (although the former name was used in the Second World War, to the confusion of secular historians); outsiders called them the go-preachers, or the Cooneyites (after the name of one of their early leaders).[63] In the First World War they had 28 detainees, in the Second World War, 122, and only a tiny handful served in the military. The New Zealand branch of the sect has never before received any detailed academic attention.

The Cooneyites were a schism from the Faith Mission in Northern Ireland, which had become highly sectarian.[64] Eight workers were sent in pairs to Australia and New Zealand in 1905, preaching initially in inland Otago, rural Canterbury and Pukekohe.[65] By 1917 there were more than 730 members in New Zealand, so they were stronger in New Zealand than in Australia or England relative to the population.[66] By 1921 they claimed to have more than 1200 members.[67] The movement published no literature and members read no books except the Bible.[68] Weekly meetings took place in members' homes and the sect owned no property. There was no formal structure, there were no marriage celebrants and the only authoritative text was the New Testament (not the Old Testament). Somewhat paradoxically, the teaching of Jesus was read as a set of strict commandments.

Evangelists were the elite of the movement and they caused more problems for the authorities. There were between fourteen and twenty-four full-time evangelists during the First World

War; by 1942 there were fifty evangelists in New Zealand.[69] When members claimed to have received an inner call to be evangelists the annual convention had to confirm the call, and send them out in pairs for lifelong service. Evangelists gave away all their possessions to the poor, and looked to professed members for support.[70] They were not permitted to marry.[71] Unlike in the Brethren, women were called as evangelists.[72] In one case a fifteen-year-old seeking exemption from the cadets advised the Court that when he was twenty-one he intended to become an evangelist for the rest of his life.[73]

Three annual conventions were at the heart of the movement.[74] Evangelists' sermons at these events were quoted with some authority although another evangelist could contradict the teaching in a subsequent sermon. The first of the three conventions was at Avondale, and later held at Pukekohe; the second at Waikanae, then moving to Masterton and then to Ngaere in Taranaki; and the third at Winchester near Ashburton. These locations reflected the concentration of the movement.

Most early members came from small farming communities. There were groups of farm hands from Pukekohe, Waiuku and Riverhead around Auckland, and from Manawaru, Matamata, and other places in the Waikato. There was a significant cluster of supporters in southern Taranaki. The first military conscript brought before the military service board in the North Island was Frederick Peter Plews, aged twenty-five, an evangelist from Stratford.[75] In the Hawke's Bay, there was a gardener.[76] Cooneyites in the Wellington area included men employed in the public service. In the South Island there was a significant cluster of members in west and south Canterbury, and the first detainee in the south was Robert Clayton Patton of Mount Somers.[77] There were some twenty or more in Dunedin, others in Owaka, and a storekeeper and a farm labourer in Otokia.[78]

The courts took some time to identify the Testimony of Jesus, and the Defence Department never seems to have made any sense of them.[79] Members in 1917 insisted that they had been recognised as a pacifist religious body in England, but they never gained this status in New Zealand.[80] Nevertheless the sect was organised enough to employ a Wellington solicitor to send representations when members and especially evangelists were called up.[81] Cooneyites refused to serve in the Ambulance Corps or Army Service Corps, and refused to sign the declaration of noncombatancy.[82] Reason did not work with them. As usual, board members put test questions to them on their willingness to defend women and children, but objectors were unmoved.[83] One insisted that those who joined the Army did not deserve his help if they were wounded or dying.[84] Such views created great offence; a magistrate, J. W. Poynton, called the unwillingness to help a wounded soldier 'anti-social fanaticism'.[85] The same magistrate later claimed to have received a letter from the founder of the sect who had allegedly declared his willingness to shed his blood for the defence of Britain and expressed anger that his followers did not act in this manner.[86] Since Irvine, the founder of the sect, subsequently fell out with it, this letter may have come from him. Members were obdurate in the face of tongue lashing by magistrates. One appellant said 'they could shoot him if they liked'. By mid-1917 most courts had determined that membership of the Testimony of Jesus did not qualify anyone for exemption.[87] Some members qualified for exemption on other grounds, given their agricultural employment.[88] Two brothers who worked on a farm were asked to choose which one would remain behind, knowing that the one called up would refuse to serve and be imprisoned.[89]

Since the authorities had no idea how large the sect was, they were startled at the number of detainees. On 25 July 1917 the Third Wellington Military Service Board called in all detained members in order to consider whether the Testimony of Jesus should be recognised as having a formal objection to war. Sixteen cases were reviewed.[90] Sir John Findlay, who represented them, called as witnesses Wilson M'Clung, the overseer of the New Zealand movement, and J. E. Holtham, a leading member. Their testimony was rejected, because they supplied no written evidence other than the New Testament and reports of what had been said at the conventions after the commencement of the war.[91] Magistrates were perplexed by a religion that had no formal rules, creeds, ceremonies, buildings, marriage celebrants or name. The Boards were also troubled that different evangelists could take different positions on the matter of bearing arms, and was alarmed to hear that one member had volunteered yet remained a member of the sect.[92] So the Court ruled that the Testimony of Jesus did not meet the criteria prescribed in the Act.

Some members were persuaded at this time to sign the form requesting noncombatant service if their appeals were dismissed. The Board may have hoped that a change of heart was in the offing.[93] This did not occur. The next Cooneyite balloted, Arthur Webster, refused to sign the declaration, although a few weeks later Wilfred Davey did sign—but he worked at the Defence Department.[94]

Three months later when the issue of the exemption of ministers and priests from conscription became controversial, the government proposed to list qualifying denominations in a schedule to the Act. Provocatively, the MP for Wellington South and Labour leader, Alfred Hindmarsh, proposed adding the Testimony of Jesus to the list. Sir John Findlay, who had tried so hard to get them recognised as conscientious objectors, spoke in favour. Faced with this, Sir James Allen, the Minister of Defence, changed tack, leaving recognition of qualifying denominations to the courts. Parliament backed him.[95] When evangelist Frederick Plews sought exemption as a minister some months later, it was not granted.[96]

By 1917, twenty-two people had been called up, of whom sixteen had been placed in the camp for those refusing to serve. One of the notorious fourteen objectors taken to the Western Front was a member of the Testimony of Jesus, David Gray.[97] He was later said to have been sent to England in error, but the sheer number of Cooneyite detainees must have imperilled them.[98] All told, twenty-eight Cooneyites were held in detention during the First World War.[99] After the war ended, Cooneyites were among the early releases from Waikeria Prison.[100]

The Testimony of Jesus in the Second World War

Cooneyites were bitterly opposed to compulsory military training in the interwar years and were mostly exempted from it, although the Court refused exemption of one lad because the mother but not the father was a member of the Testimony.[101] In another case it insisted that the exemption needed to be reviewed every year.[102] In 1920 Wilson M'Clung corresponded with the Prime Minister about facilitating exemptions, but magistrates often ignored informal guidelines and sect members did not help their cause when they responded belligerently to compulsory military training.[103]

With the reintroduction of conscription in the Second World War the issue recurred. The sect this time issued a statement, but it was no help, for it said that participation in war was a matter of individual conscience. The Christian Assemblies continued to be penalised because they had no written tenets, and their emphasis on individual conscience meant that the sect could not be exempted.[104] Most members refused their call-up and were arraigned before the boards, and subsequently imprisoned, apart from a few exempted on medical grounds.[105] Members gave relatively consistent answers to such questions as whether they could love the commandant of the Belsen concentration camp.[106] One appellant described noncombatant service as similar to providing a first aid kit to a bank robber.[107] They boldly asserted their unwillingness to sign the oath of allegiance or to serve in the military ambulance, and their willingness to die before a firing squad rather than go against conscience.[108] The No. 2 Appeal Board became annoyed at the stereotyped answers members gave. William Hughes, who appeared before the Board in their support, insisted that each member had made their own conscientious decision, but the Board chair complained that some were not bright enough to do this.[109] Two Cooneyites did serve in the Army in noncombatant roles. They were two of four sons of the Richardson family from Palmerston North; their two other brothers went to the defaulters' camp.[110]

As early as December 1940 an evangelist asked the Wellington Manpower Committee to exempt him from service with the Territorials as a minister of religion. The claim was rejected.[111] Later the evangelists again sought exemption from military training on the grounds that they were ministers, noting that the United States military had recognised them as such. The New Zealand boards were generally reluctant, noting that one of them was licensed to conduct marriages. They also justifiably noted that the role of evangelist was self-appointed, and feared that all members might claim to be ministers.

Len J. Greenberg, who ran the camps, seemed to enjoy scriptural skirmishes with members of the sect.[112] He later claimed that he had proposed to the Cooneyites in detention that they offer to go to the Pacific under civilian control to assist the natives, but they had rejected the proposal.[113] In the camps they co-operated with the authorities and undertook the work they were assigned, for 'we didn't see anything in the detention camp setup that conflicted with our conscience. We were there by choice, not force.'[114]

In 1945 at the end of the war, Christian Assemblies members were among those given early parole by the Revision Authority. Evidence for their release given by William Hughes and Thomas Monteith indicated that 95% of the young men in the fellowship had refused to serve in the military.[115] Hughes told the Palmerston North sitting of the No. 2 Revision Board that even though 97% of members called up had refused to serve, one Board granted only 5.8% of appeals, whereas in another district 50.5% were allowed. He held that the Cooneyites were not unlike the Quakers in that individual conscience was the ultimate basis of their decision not to serve, but because the Quakers had written proof, their appeals were allowed.[116] He became more and more forceful as he made the same case before various Revision Boards around the country.[117]

In July 1946, Hughes, describing himself as senior minister (although not naming the church) forwarded to the Prime Minister a statement on the sect's attitude to military service agreed by the annual convention at Masterton in January 1946. The statement ended with a ringing declaration:

> we have the satisfaction of knowing that we have not made one wife a widow or one child fatherless in the countries who became enemies of the British empire during the recent world war. Our Missionaries were labouring in all those countries previous to the war, and we can go back to them with a good conscience, knowing that we did not go first with the Gospel, then with weapons of war, and then return again with the Gospel. We have felt that our attitude was the only

THE FOLLOWING STATEMENT WAS READ AT THE ANNUAL CHRISTIAN CONVENTION HELD AT TE ORE ORE, MASTERTON, ON 6th JANUARY, 1946, AND WAS AGREED TO WITHOUT A DISSENTIENT VOICE.

Most of us will remember a statement which I made from this platform four or five years ago to this effect that "our attitude towards war must be one of individual conscience, and if any person feels that they can go further than others in the matter they must not be penalised, and it must not make any difference to our fellowship". The years have now passed and the war is over. Although we declared in favour of this liberty of conscience, the result has been that 100 per cent of our men of military age have, because of freely exercised conscience on Christian grounds, found it impossible to take part in combatant warfare and 98 per cent found it impossible to take any part in warfare in any capacity.

122 members were committed to Defaulters' Detention. Of this number five ceased to attend the meetings of the fellowship in the Camps, but 117 remained faithful to the meetings and to their Christian profession.

Of this 117, 14 were released because of age or Medical grading, and all but one of the others applied for release on parole as genuine conscientious objectors. 86 were allowed and 14 refused. That is, of 116 men committed to Detention, 100 have been released and 16 are still held. Therefore it has been proved that through the freely exercised individual conscience, we are a people who are 100 per cent against war.

We may receive much blame for this but we have the satisfaction of knowing that we have not made one wife a widow or one child fatherless in the countries who became enemies to the British Empire during the recent world war. Our Missionaries were labouring in all those countries previous to the war, and we can go back to them with a good conscience, knowing that we did not go first with the Gospel, then with weapons of war and then return again with the Gospel. We have felt that our attitude was the only one which we could adopt consistent with our profession of loving Christ and His teaching and the souls of men of all nations whom He shed His blood to save.

(Signed) W. J. HUGHES.

The largest group of conscientious objectors held in detention in the First and Second World Wars came from a group that has never previously received scholarly attention in New Zealand. The Christian Assemblies (also known as the Testimony of Jesus, or Cooneyites) regarded their opposition to war as a matter of faithfulness to conscience and 'the Gospel'. Document supplied by author.

> one which we could adopt consistent with our profession of loving Christ and His teaching and the souls of men of all nations whom He shed his blood to save.[118]

The military camps had a profound effect on sect members. One member described his detention as one of the best experiences in his life, for 'There was nothing like being shut away to secure a complete picture of the pattern of life'.[119] Another compared his experience to that of Christ, who like him had no loyalty to any secular state.[120] Members generally forewent the few worldly pleasures the camp afforded, such as movies, dances and drinking.[121] Occasionally they got into trouble. One member who went AWOL to visit his wife was banned by the Assemblies from attending meetings in detention.[122] Another was found with an indecent picture in his back pocket, but denied that he had placed it there.[123] Another supported himself by catching and selling rabbits to internees.[124] Just one man left the sect in the camp; he remained a pacifist, although he now swore a bit.[125] Two others became full members while in detention.[126] In general the experience seems to have increased the dedication of members. Greenberg told the Court that members of the Christian Assemblies wanted their farms back. He suggested from his experience that members of the sect were not as self-denying as they portrayed themselves, although he may have been confusing evangelists with ordinary members.[127]

Conclusion

For all these sects the two world wars were traumatic. Courts often put appellants through their biblical paces. One member of the Second Military Court came to hearings with Cruden's Concordance at hand in order to discomfit appellants. He gleefully recorded how one man:

> quoted from the Bible about 'They that live by the sword shall die by the sword.' My Concordance came in handy, for I replied with the Master's order, 'Sell your clothing, and buy a sword.' I pointed out to the objector that we were not even asking him to buy one, as if he went to the front the Government was prepared to supply the arms.[128]

The courts got very frustrated with what seemed the absurd logic of sect members.[129] Their objections were partly to killing, partly eschatological, partly rejection of the defilement of the state. Because their sect was not recognised, they were required to defend their religious beliefs and show their conscientious refusal to kill. They were brave men with deep convictions.

Imprisonment was a grim experience and it was also intellectually demanding. The sectarian groups would try to convert the 'hoons' (the agnostics) and there was constant jostling and debate between the various groups.[130] The fundamentalists generally co-operated with the authorities, and so they incurred the annoyance of the 'absolutists' who opposed every aspect of the militarised state.[131] Nevertheless there were moments of community. At Rangipō in the Second World War there was a monthly church service in the camp held by the Taumarunui Brethren or the Taupō Presbyterians, and the Rangipō Methodist choir would participate.[132]

Overall the experience of the sectarian Protestants during both world wars initiated them into the coercive power of the modern state. Their sects had taken advantage of greater religious freedom, and New Zealand had placed few barriers to this type of religion. But the twentieth-century state logically embraced conscription as an aspect of democracy. The sects which paid the price for this had no particular hostility to the state, but they treated the commands of Jesus as higher than state laws. The state did not want to persecute religious groups, so it provided exemptions for sects while it rejected the claims of individual conscience. This distinction did not work well. The government's requirement that sects have formal rules barring fighting was naïve about the way that the sects operated, just as the sects were ignorant of the necessity that the state be obdurate. The state has become steadily more omnipresent over the last one hundred years, and religions have been forced to examine their consciences very deeply to decide how far their resistance to its tentacles should go. Every sect, no matter how opposed to war, had some members who chose to serve—including, in the First World War, 6 Christadelphians, 140 Plymouth Brethren, 7 Quakers, 9 Seventh-day Adventists and 12 Spiritualists.[133]

The law made provision for the exemption of those who had been members of exempted sects before the war. It was obviously concerned that large numbers of those reluctant to serve would join the Quakers or the Christadelphians, although the likelihood was surely low. It also subjected those who sought exemption to gruelling cross-examination, designed to prove not just their membership of the sect but also their convictions on war. This was a very tough requirement. If the conscience was not deemed sufficiently strong, then the appeal would be rejected. Frequently sects felt the indignity of their inability to stand alongside members as they were cross-questioned. Those sect members who were well prepared got much better outcomes. For the rest, people were in effect thrown to the dogs.

Few of the sects and their members were defiant in essence. This was evident by the bearing of the members in court and in the detention camps. They formed a distinctive group in the camps, rather more compliant with prison authorities than most other objectors, and they were therefore held in the more lightly guarded camps. The grimness of their experience of detention proved a rapid education for some. In the Brethren case there was a noticeable drop in conscientious objection in the Second World War and a preference for noncombatant service. Brethren and Adventists were eager to reach out for new members and their evangelists sought to reduce the obstacles to membership. The Testimony of Jesus and Jehovah's Witnesses were the least co-operative. Both seem to have taken some pride in persecution. The limited authority of local leadership in both groups prevented the voice of moderation being heard.

Sectarianism has flourished even more in recent years, while traditional religiosity has waned. New groups have appeared, and the Jehovah's Witnesses are now the tenth largest religious group in the country. The state chooses to hide its coercive powers towards religion at present, and contemporary warfare has little use for conscription, but the potential for another profound rift between sect members and the state remains.

10

Adventist Conscientious Co-operators and Jehovah's Witness Neutrals in New Zealand during the Second World War

Peter H. Ballis

Seventh-day Adventists and Jehovah's Witnesses have many features in common. The churches arose out of the same sociohistorical context, both being born in the wake of mid-nineteenth-century North American Christian millennialism. Prophetic exegesis and apocalypticism dominate the movements' outlooks. In their own peculiar ways, each is characterised by an attitude of exclusivism. In New Zealand, both have been minorities operating on the fringes of mainstream society. Seventh-day Adventists arrived in New Zealand in 1885, and by the turn of the century established a strong presence of some 1000 members spread across Auckland, Napier and Wellington.[1] Jehovah's Witnesses began their work in New Zealand in 1904. By the commencement of the Second World War, Adventist membership had grown to 3387; the Witnesses movement was still in its infancy with a membership estimated at less than 500.[2] Crucially, so far as this chapter is concerned, they also shared a longstanding history of pacifist objection to war. Surprisingly, however, during the war, the two churches responded to military conscription in New Zealand in strikingly different ways.

This chapter draws on previously unpublished correspondence, official documents and semi-structured interviews with Jehovah's Witnesses and Seventh-day Adventists who lived through the Second World War. It addresses three main issues: the social circumstances that dragged Seventh-day Adventists and Jehovah's Witnesses into conflict with the New Zealand government during the Second World War; their contrasting positions with respect to conscription; and how each was affected by their respective controversies.

Jehovah's Witness suppression

Writing in the late 1970s, sociologist Ken Jubber argued that 'persecution has been so persistent and of such an intensity that it would not be inaccurate to regard Jehovah's witnesses as the most persecuted religion of the twentieth century'.[3] From their arrival in New Zealand in 1903, Witnesses were a major target of denominational opposition. Christian churches denounced the movement as unchristian,[4] and condemned it as promoting 'the most debased of modern heresies'.[5] By 1940, criticism of its teaching had developed into outright hostility for the Jehovah's Witness movement generally. *Time* dubbed the movement 'the most irritating of US sects',[6] and *Smith's Weekly*, an Australian publication with considerable New Zealand circulation, labelled Witnesses a community of 'spies', 'communists', 'fifth columnists' and 'dangerous antiwar propagandists and pacifists who teach . . . converts to refuse to recognize the king of England and not to fight'.[7] Arguments in defense of the movement—for example, that their 'unusual' teachings did not in themselves make Witnesses 'open to a charge of active disloyalty'[8]—sounded fainthearted against a backdrop of public hysteria and religious bigotry.[9]

An unhappy incident on 13 October 1940 in Oamaru was the spark that transposed what until then had been primarily a religious protest into a political one.[10] The public meeting on that date, using the Watch Tower's United States president Judge Rutherford's recorded lecture 'Government and Peace', was to conclude more than four months of intense witnessing in the town. Two days before the lecture, Witnesses from Dunedin and Timaru distributed more than 2000 brochures and promoted the lecture in the community with loudspeakers and placards.[11] No one had anticipated the political furore their seemingly peaceful activities would precipitate. Part way through the evening's presentation, William Meehan, a returned soldier, intruded into the meeting with a rifle and bayonet concealed under his coat. In the scuffle that ensued when two Witnesses sought to disarm him, one man's hand was cut with the bayonet and a second was shot in the thigh.[12] With this incident the Jehovah's Witnesses minority immediately attracted media headlines across the country.

Fearing the incident would incite more stringent measures against the Society, Harold Gill, a leading spokesperson for the movement in New Zealand, telegraphed the Prime Minister assuring him that Jehovah's Witnesses were not responsible for the shooting, and as 'friends of the people' expressed willingness to co-operate with a government inquiry into the incident.[13] The Oamaru Returned Soldiers' Association (RSA)[14] sent a telegram to the NZRSA in Wellington, quoting *Smith's Weekly* allegations of Witness Nazi and pacifist activities, to urge the government to ban the sect before more trouble occurred.[15] The New Zealand government had already sought to curtail Witness activities for vilifying other religious organisations and for undermining 'national morale at a time when the nation was fighting for its life'. The Attorney-General now felt the situation necessitated 'a quicker method of putting an end to their activity'.[16] On 21 October 1940 the Attorney-General declared the Watch Tower Society a subversive organisation in accordance with Section 2A of the Public Safety Regulations 1940, thereby imposing a ban on all Jehovah's Witness activities in New Zealand.[17]

Robert Lazenby, who headed the movement's literature depot in Wellington, informed Jehovah's Witness leaders in Australia that the ban was sweeping and threated to end Witness activities in New Zealand:

> It covers the use of phonographs, witnessing from door to door, meetings, etc. For even two to meet together to discuss the furthering of the work is illegal. . . . Further, it is an offense to have in one's possession anything, or matter with a view to making or facilitating a subversive statement. The ban means that if we have in our possession books, magazines, gramophone records, we are liable to the penalties of the law. We may not call meetings or use any premises for the purpose of the organisation. We must not participate in the activities

> of, or aid, abet or encourage in any way the organisation, and must not express approval of it.[18]

Meehan's trial brought little comfort of justice for Witnesses. He was acquitted on the attempted murder charge, but was convicted on the minor charge of assault and sentenced to two months' hard labour.[19] 'Public opinion [was] with Barrabas', according to Harold Gill.[20] Police officers throughout the country were alerted to arrest and charge Witnesses who contravened the Regulations.[21] The Wellington RSA set up a 'Vigilance Committee' to assist the police in their work.[22] In smaller rural centres individual Witnesses experienced ostracism and physical harassment.[23]

The Regulations galvanised Jehovah's Witnesses into action. They interpreted the ban as God's call 'to fight for freedom and worship'.[24] At the Wellington headquarters, Reg Johnston partitioned off a section of the roof area to hide Watchtower literature and from there continued to distribute it around the country.[25] Johnston and his fellow Witnesses wrapped their Watchtower publications in plain covers to circumvent custom checks on wharves and in Post Offices.[26] At least 1000 copies of each issue of the Watchtower study guide were typed and distributed throughout New Zealand. Some members hid literature they kept in their homes 'under the carpet'.[27] The Keoghans hid their supply of *The Watchtower* in a forty-gallon drum which they buried in a friendly farmer's milking shed.[28] Most surprising of all is that door-to-door activities continued to feature as a central strategy for promoting their message. Alexander MacGillivray, the Society's secretary in Australia, called on Jehovah's Witnesses to remain defiant, advising them that 'the fight is on, and soon the battle of Armageddon will break'.[29]

Witnesses took every opportunity to test the government's commitment to the Regulations. Followers continued to meet in homes, sometimes with as many as forty-five persons gathered at a time.[30] On 30 November 1940, R. T. Reid, a retired school teacher and leader of the Auckland branch, received permission from Auckland's Superintendent of Police and from Auckland

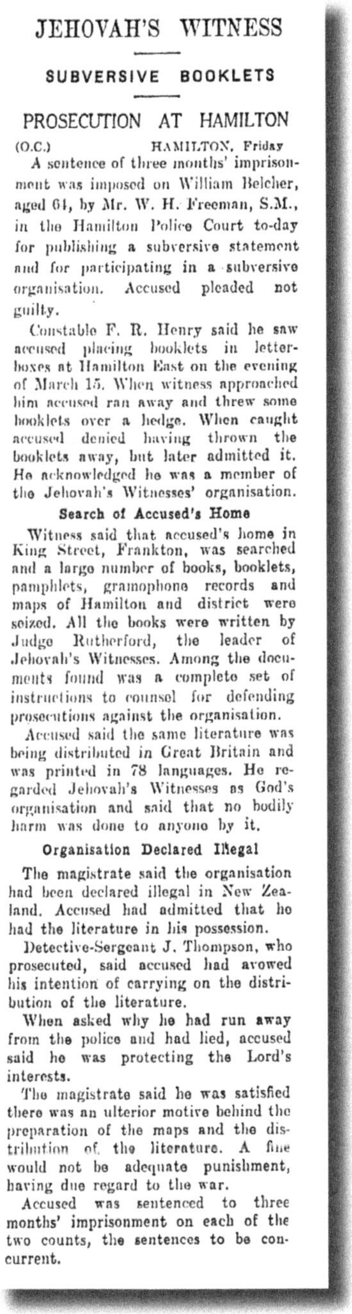

JEHOVAH'S WITNESS

SUBVERSIVE BOOKLETS

PROSECUTION AT HAMILTON

(O.C.) HAMILTON, Friday

A sentence of three months' imprisonment was imposed on William Belcher, aged 64, by Mr. W. H. Freeman, S.M., in the Hamilton Police Court to-day for publishing a subversive statement and for participating in a subversive organisation. Accused pleaded not guilty.

Constable F. R. Henry said he saw accused placing booklets in letter-boxes at Hamilton East on the evening of March 15. When witness approached him accused ran away and threw some booklets over a hedge. When caught accused denied having thrown the booklets away, but later admitted it. He acknowledged he was a member of the Jehovah's Witnesses' organisation.

Search of Accused's Home

Witness said that accused's home in King Street, Frankton, was searched and a large number of books, booklets, pamphlets, gramophone records and maps of Hamilton and district were seized. All the books were written by Judge Rutherford, the leader of Jehovah's Witnesses. Among the documents found was a complete set of instructions to counsel for defending prosecutions against the organisation.

Accused said the same literature was being distributed in Great Britain and was printed in 78 languages. He regarded Jehovah's Witnesses as God's organisation and said that no bodily harm was done to anyone by it.

Organisation Declared Illegal

The magistrate said the organisation had been declared illegal in New Zealand. Accused had admitted that he had the literature in his possession.

Detective-Sergeant J. Thompson, who prosecuted, said accused had avowed his intention of carrying on the distribution of the literature.

When asked why he had run away from the police and had lied, accused said he was protecting the Lord's interests.

The magistrate said he was satisfied there was an ulterior motive behind the preparation of the maps and the distribution of the literature. A fine would not be adequate punishment, having due regard to the war.

Accused was sentenced to three months' imprisonment on each of the two counts, the sentences to be concurrent.

After the Watch Tower Society was declared a subversive organisation in October 1940, its activities came under intense scrutiny. Despite pressure and considerable public opprobrium, some Jehovah's Witnesses maintained their ministries unmolested; others were less fortunate in evading the attention of the authorities. Source: *New Zealand Herald*, 29 March 1941, 8.

Mayor Ernest Davis to hold a public meeting in the Auckland Town Hall. Apparently more than 300 people attended this meeting.[31] The *New Zealand Truth* declared it an 'extraordinary ... meeting', and protested that 'Witnesses ... were permitted to stage a meeting in the Concert Chamber of the Auckland Town Hall while the law was still . . . being enforced by the courts ... elsewhere in New Zealand.'[32] These apparent inconsistencies added to public and official confusion as to what activities actually had been banned by the October Regulations.

Certainly, Witnesses interpreted the Regulations as a wholesale attack on religious freedom.[33] MacGillivray cabled the New Zealand Governor-General, Lord Galway, that the action of the New Zealand government 'savours Nazi Catholic Action'.[34] Telegrams to the Attorney-General protesting that the government's ban discriminated against Witnesses by denying them their 'right[s] as Christians to assemble and worship God with song, scripture and study' received vague and evasive replies. The Attorney-General stressed that the government felt compelled to act in response to the unfavorable climate Witness activity had generated in the community.[35]

At least twenty Jehovah's Witnesses were arrested during the first eight weeks of the Regulations.[36] Usually acting on information from private citizens, police arrested Witnesses suspected of subversive activities such as distributing Watchtower pamphlets and propagating their message through house visitation. The volume of arrests suggests the ban in fact had enticed the whole Jehovah's Witness community to the streets for a head-on confrontation with government. However, most cases of Witnesses charged with participating in the activities of a subversive organisation that were heard in courts did not result in convictions. The charges against W. A. Roberts, E. D. Ridling and J. Ridling were dismissed because the Crown prosecution had no proof that the 363 books and 27 gramophone records found in their possession were intended for public distribution.[37] Those against A. Belcher and W. McDonald were dismissed because the prosecution failed 'to connect the accused with the distribution of the pamphlets'.[38] The inability of the court to convict Witnesses highlighted the enthusiastic yet haphazard nature of police involvement. Harold Gill informed his colleagues in Australia that the unpredictability of the court rulings was in fact benefiting the Society by highlighting the injustice of their treatment. 'A few court cases before a police magistrate will do us no harm', Gill told MacGillivray.[39] Witnesses were determined to 'fight to death for freedom of thought, speech and assembly to worship Almighty God'.[40]

Jehovah's Witness leaders in Australia and New Zealand had sent telegrams to the King protesting against religious persecution.[41] The New Zealand Prime Minister Peter Fraser denied allegations of religious persecution, stating that the ban did not 'interfere with the right to worship', and that it was 'a prohibition on dissemination of literature and other propaganda directed against religious organisations'.[42] Nevertheless, the continuing demand for Witnesses to 'confine themselves to ordinary religious observances like the Churches and other religious bodies' was effectively a request that Jehovah's Witnesses stop being Witnesses.[43]

The government's heavy-handed action on a seemingly harmless and numerically insignificant sect soon compelled others in the community to voice their opposition. F. W. Doidge, the outspoken Member for Tauranga, condemned the 1940 Regulations as government action directed at pleasing voters in preference to 'an obscure sect with few votes in the community'.[44] The implications of the ban were also dawning on other church groups. On 6 May 1941, the Auckland Presbytery urged the Public Questions Committee to be vigilant against actions that would confine the Christian Church to worship and prevent the exercise of the right to proclaim religious truth, denounce error, and remedy social wrong.[45]

While government officials were adamant that 'there [had] been no attempt to stifle either freedom of conscience or freedom of religion',[46] the New Zealand Prime Minister informed the House that arrangements were on the way for 'Jehovah's Witnesses [to] carry out ordinary worship, like the people of other Churches'. On 8 May 1941, some seven months after the Public Safety Regulations were announced, a notice was published in the *New Zealand Gazette* announcing a partial lifting of the ban.[47] Despite this announcement, followers of the Jehovah's Witnesses were still being arrested and brought before district magistrates. Contradictory court rulings added to the complexity of the situation. The cases of Fred Holland and Irvine Keltie were dismissed because the magistrates did not consider that going door to door with a Bible was subversive.[48] Naida McLean successfully appealed to the High Court against her conviction; the Judge ruled that the counsel for the Crown had failed to prove that house-to-house witnessing 'was an activity [solely] of the [Witness] organization'.[49] While dismissing the case of seventeen-year-old Donald McGeachie, the Magistrate protested that 'there should be a straight out ban on this organisation or nothing at all, then we would know where we are'.[50] Others, however, such as Leslie Ward and Silas Martyn, were convicted merely because the magistrates felt duty bound to uphold the law.[51]

Adventist noncombatant co-operators

Adventists were acutely aware that they too had the potential to be banned under the National Service Emergency Regulations. Early in 1941, only months after the announcement restricting Jehovah's Witness activities, the New Zealand Conference President, H. G. Moulds, declared that 'a dark plot [had been] formulated by the agelong enemies of truth',[52] to frustrate an evangelistic campaign planned in Wellington. Advertising for a campaign lecture on 'The Little Horn of Daniel 7' attracted immediate protests from the local Catholic community. Responding to complaints, the Chief of Police issued an order to deport the Adventist evangelist. Both Adventists and the government immediately sought compromise. Not willing to be caught in yet another sectarian squabble, the Prime Minister and the Attorney-General accepted assurances from an Adventist lay delegation that the Adventist evangelist would restrict his opinions 'to biblical exposition and keep out of politics'.[53] More than 100 people converted to the Adventist faith as a result of N. C. Burn's outreach in Wellington.[54]

New Zealand Adventists had learnt some lessons on church–government relations from their experiences during the First

World War. A. W. Anderson, who headed the Religious Liberty Department of the Australian Union Conference, concluded:

> loyalty to the government means much more than a mere sentiment. Loyalty to the government means much more than to refrain from disloyal acts. A neutral is expected to refrain from such acts, but a citizen is not only expected to refrain from disloyal acts, but to actually render loyal service.[55]

Adventists were better prepared than possibly any other group in New Zealand to respond to the introduction of compulsory military service in 1940. The experiences of the Jehovah's Witness movement, and both government and public responses to it, reinforced in the consciousness of Adventist leaders that sensitivity and tolerance were crucial in time of national unrest. Adventist responses were, in many ways, a counterbalance to the perceived extremes of the Witnesses.[56] Driven by the conviction that, as upholders of the Ten Commandments, 'Seventh-day Adventists should be the best and most loyal citizens of the land',[57] the Adventist minority embarked on an all-out campaign to convince the community and the government of Adventist loyalty and co-operation in all matters—short of carrying arms and working on the Sabbath.

The establishment of its National Emergency Service was one such expression of Adventist loyalty to the State. Patterned after the Medical Cadet Corps, which was popular among Adventists in the United States,[58] and proclaimed as 'the greatest thing that has ever been attempted in [the Australasian] Division', the Service was calculated to disarm prejudice. The National Emergency Service was designed to attract 'the favourable attention of the public' by locating the Church at 'the head and not the tail' of welfare ministry during the war.[59] In New Zealand the National Emergency Service became an integral part of the Church's noncombatant stance and was promoted as the Adventist means of assisting the country with 'strong, acceptable and efficient noncombatant service'.[60] Watson called upon the Church members to convince New Zealanders that Seventh-day Adventists 'were not cowards'.[61]

A National Emergency Service branch was established in Christchurch in May 1939.[62] By the end of that year, in the South Island alone, the branch boasted a membership of 543 persons divided into 16 companies. The National Emergency Service program received immediate and unqualified support from New Zealand Adventists. By 1940, 160 Adventists had trained in First Aid, 30 had trained in Home Nursing, 38 had passed the hygiene examinations, and 37 had completed a course in air raid precautions.[63] In Wellington, fifty-two had enrolled with the St John Ambulance first aid classes, with that many again responding to the call of the National Blood Transfusion Service.[64]

Another more important intention of the National Emergency Service was to curry favour with the government. On 17 August 1939, a delegation consisting of the two New Zealand Conference Presidents and the Union Conference Religious Liberty Secretary outlined the program to the Minister of Defence to make it known that, at their own expense, Adventists had initiated to train and organise members into a skilled and disciplined army of noncombatant volunteers.[65] The Minister, duly impressed with the Adventist initiative, gave verbal assurance that Adventist 'religious convictions towards becoming members of the Armed Forces would be respected'.[66] These positive comments were sufficient to convince those 'who questioned the wisdom of undertaking this training',[67] and to give added incentive for continuing the scheme.

With the majority of Adventist members directly or indirectly involved in noncombatant training, the vote reaffirming Adventist commitment to noncombatancy as the official Seventh-day Adventist attitude to military service was all but decided. In January 1940 both the South New Zealand and North New Zealand Conference Sessions were unanimous in reaffirming their commitment to the traditional stance.[68]

The Adventist problems over conscription were not over, however. Introduction of the National Service Emergency Regulations in 1940 reawakened Adventist fears. Adventists were not sure where they stood with the government over these regulations.[69] The Conference President assured members that the position of Adventists was adequately covered under Regulation 21 of the Emergency Regulations, and that Adventist conscientious objectors could appeal to an Armed Forces Appeal Board.[70] The North New Zealand Conference President, Moulds, referred to the Minister of Defence's assurance that 'every consideration would be given to the position of [Adventists] relative to noncombatancy and the observance of the seventh-day sabbath'.[71]

In the meantime church leaders were occupied devising additional ways of making public Adventist loyalty to the State. In July 1940, the Union Conference donated a fully equipped ambulance to the New Zealand government.[72] Robert Semple, who was responsible for the national service portfolio, advised Moulds that the government accepted the gift as an expression of Adventist patriotism.[73] The Minister of Finance, Walter Nash, saw the ambulance as 'further evidence of the universal desire to assist the Dominion's war effort'.[74] Adventist generosity had breadth as well as depth. In Australia, the Union Conference placed at the disposal of the Commonwealth Government its entire stock of family tents, and although this entailed cancellation of the church's annual convention meetings even in New Zealand, Adventists felt this was a small price to pay in return for their civil liberties.[75] The Sanitarium Health Food Company offered to supply the forces with breakfast cereals at production cost.[76] In Christchurch, two Sanitarium vans were refurbished as auxiliary units for the St John Ambulance Brigade.[77] Even more extreme was the Union Conference recommendation 'that as a mark of respect and loyalty to our King and Country [churches] sing the National Anthem in the divine service'.[78] While some churches balked at the suggestion, others absorbed such patriotism as a matter of course.[79]

Church leaders justified these unprecedented expressions of loyalty on the grounds that they 'helped [Adventist] young men to prepare for noncombatant service'.[80] It is difficult to assess the effectiveness of these measures at persuading the government to accommodate Adventist Sabbatarian noncombatants. It is known, for example, that the government's communications with Seventh-day Adventists were used as a norm for addressing other religious minorities, such as the Open Brethren.[81]

What is clear is that, notwithstanding all they had done for the government, Adventist appellants were still receiving a mixed reception from Appeal Boards. L. C. Naden reported that 'some [Adventists] had their appeals allowed, others were recommended for alternative service, and still others had their appeals dismissed with a recommendation for noncombatant service only; and finally, there were a few whose appeals were dismissed with no recommendations whatsoever'.[82] The situation was less clear-cut than Adventists had anticipated.

One complicating factor was that Appeal Boards were not authorised to differentiate noncombatants from other conscientious objectors.[83] In effect, the Minister of Defence's assurances that Adventist religious beliefs would be respected were of little consequence.[84] Appeal Boards insisted that 'to succeed an [Adventist] appellant [had to] object to war on all sides, combatant and noncombatant'.[85] Defence authorities, though equipped to respond to the pacifist alternative, were unable to conceive of and thus provide for noncombatants. H. G. Moulds protested that the Minister of Defence had gone back on his word.[86]

On 7 February 1941, Moulds sent a telegram of protest to the Prime Minister, petitioning that the National Service Emergency Regulations 1940 'be amended to include the name of Seventh-day Adventists with that of the Society of Friends and Christadelphians' as conscientious objectors exempt from military service, so as to give statutory recognition to the Adventist position.[87] Mounting pressure from mainline churches, coupled with the Adventist protest, finally forced the government to accommodate noncombatants.

A second factor complicating the Adventist position was their socially awkward sabbatarianism. If there already was ambiguity over the definition of the terms 'noncombatant' or 'noncombatant service', the Seventh-day Adventist sabbatarianism added to the confusion. New Zealand Adventists felt they were doubly disadvantaged by the military service regulations: while noncombatancy may have satisfied the majority of objectors,

Adventists still had to negotiate to be exempted from 'non-essential' noncombatant duties between sunset Friday and sunset Saturday.[88] During Appeal Board hearings some Adventist appellants refused noncombatant duties for fear that their Sabbath convictions would not be respected. One protested that 'in the matter of Sabbath-keeping [Adventists] had in many cases met with a great deal of opposition from superior officers, who were invariably guided by their own attitude to the Sabbath-keeper'.[89]

Church leaders made every effort to familiarise government representatives with Adventist sabbatarianism. In May 1939, an Adventist delegation explained to Prime Minister Michael Savage that the Saturday Sabbath was a distinctive tenet of the Seventh-day Adventist faith and that the 24-hour period from sunset Friday to sunset Saturday was devoted to religious exercises.[90] Again, Moulds instructed the Minister of Defence that, in addition to being noncombatant, Adventists were also 'conscientious Sabbath keepers':

> we observe the Sabbath generally at considerable personal sacrifice and difficulty at times of peace, and sincerely find ourselves unable to do otherwise under the greater difficulty of the war.[91]

Adventists were willing to settle for a compromise regarding the military question; they were uncompromising over their Sabbath. In his 'Circular to Young Men of Military Age', Moulds reasoned that Adventist young men were being called to appear before the Armed Forces Appeal Boards, in order to testify for the Sabbath.[92] Meanwhile, the Union Conference voted 'wholehearted adherence to the Sabbath of the fourth commandment' and exhorted Adventist young men 'to observe faithfully the Sabbath under all circumstances'.[93] The Adjutant-General responded to letters of protest with a memorandum instructing that Adventists were to 'be struck off all duties from sunset Friday until sunset Saturday . . . [and] employed as fatigues on Sundays'.[94] The Sabbath also proved to be a 'thorn in the flesh' to Adventists posted with the forces. The problem arose with the Second New Zealand Expeditionary Force in the Middle

East because the government concession had been overlooked.[95] This situation, which ultimately was righted by the Minister of Defence,[96] underscores on the one hand the ongoing difficulties Adventists faced on account of their peculiar noncombatant stance, but, on the other, the willingness of Defence officials to accommodate them.

Witness defaulters and Adventist nonconformists

Jehovah's Witnesses neither sought, nor received, any concessions from the government. The police appear to have turned a blind eye to the Society's uninterrupted and persistent proselytising activities following the lifting of the ban, yet the steady flow of Jehovah's Witnesses into detention camps extended their gloom. Jehovah's Witnesses represented the second largest group in New Zealand detention camps: of 592 men reviewed in October 1944, 78 declared themselves members of the Watch Tower Society.[97] Paul Oestreicher's judgement that these men were 'impudent and abusive towards all authority'[98] fails to capture the Witness mindset.

There is an uneasy quiet about Witness objectors in the available Jehovah's Witness records dating from this period; no correspondence was entered into with Defence authorities by Society leaders on behalf of Witness followers. Appeals were characterised sometimes by loud outbursts of defiance and often by forthright affirmation of faith. One of only two Witnesses whose appeal was upheld expressed 'surprise' at the Appeal Board's decision.[99] There was a sense of inevitability to their protests,[100] and a monotonous predictability to handling of Witness appeals. Witnesses called up by ballot would fail to report for military service. They would refuse to take the oath of allegiance, appear for medical examination, consent to wear the uniform or obey orders of any sort.[101] When appearing before Appeal Boards, appellants would insist that they were neither pacifist nor antimilitarist, but simply 'neutral', rejecting noncombatancy as a compromise favouring militarism.[102] When questioned, they would declare their appeal to be based on the belief that 'all wars are man-made' and that 'fighting in this war will never stop more mass murder'.[103]

Witnesses viewed appearances before Appeal Boards as opportunities to articulate their faith. During his appeal, eighteen-year-old John Nelson launched into a lengthy tirade declaring that 'all nations at the present time were against God' and that Jehovah 'will destroy them at Armageddon'.[104] Even more daring, Sydney Tee declared that 'the Court also [was] on trial before the Supreme Court of Jehovah'.[105] Paton and Wilkins proclaimed they would not default to the laws of Jesus Christ.[106]

Appeal Boards faced with 'the difficult task of pronouncing on the sincerity of conscientious objectors' were less than sympathetic to the claimants.[107] Whangarei reservist Lance Harvey was labelled a 'slacker', other Witnesses were condemned as 'pure and unadulterated shirkers' and still others were dismissed for their considered 'desire to seek notoriety or to bask in the sunshine of martyrdom'.[108] R. T. Reid complained that genuine efforts to explain the Witness position were 'met with sarcasm, irony, veiled and open hostility and studied insults'.[109] In addition to having their appeals dismissed and being sent to detention camps for the duration of the war, the majority of Witnesses also had to serve from one to three months in prison for their noncompliance with the regulations.

Witnesses accepted detention as a corollary to their neutrality; circumscription was their price for conscience.[110] This mindset they transferred to the detention camps, displaying a sense of exclusivism and commitment to proselytising. In his autobiographical account of 'the microcosmic world of the concentration camps', Ian Hamilton states that the behaviour of 'Jay Dubs in the camps was the same as their behaviour elsewhere, not quite of this world'.[111] They transported their sectarian subdivisions to the camp setting, where they held their own study groups, conducted their own services, and even, in Whitanui Detention Camp, staged their own mini 'Theocratic Convention'.[112] Since they considered 'their main business . . . to make converts', their time in camp was largely occupied trying to win 'as many converts as they could within the precincts of the camps'.[113] At least five individuals are known to have converted to the Watch Tower Society while in detention.[114]

Conscientious objectors whose appeals against conscription were denied, and who continued to refuse service, were held indefinitely in detention camps; the last were released only as late as May 1946. These men at Hautu Detention Camp in 1943 included a number of Christian objectors. From left to right: Harold Hansen, Bernard Giles, Tom Smith, the Reverend Colin Clark and Jack Hamerton. Source: 1/2-037726-F, Alexander Turnbull Library, Wellington.

By comparison, only fifteen Seventh-day Adventists are known to have been detained as conscientious objectors.[115] Their presence suggests, however, that Adventists were less than united over the Church's noncombatant stance. The patriotism of Adventist administrators was received ambiguously by Church members. It made some so sensitive to public opinion that they voluntarily enlisted or did not appeal against militarism.[116] However, it strengthened a vocal minority to demand Adventist non-co-operation in all things pertaining to war.

The Adventists' exaggerated patriotism during the war years—illustrated by gifts to the State, sermons on 'Christian Patriotism' and prayers petitioning God 'to save the nation from the enemy'—was interpreted by some as compromise.[117] Adventist administrators attempted to clarify their position with adherents. According to C. B. Haynes:

> The belief of the Seventh-day Adventist does not require him to agitate against war, to oppose militarism, to be insubordinate, to oppose the military programme, or to stand apart from the military establishment and organisation.[118]

Others emphatically stated that:

> Noncombatancy is not pacifism. Noncombatancy is not antimilitarism. Noncombatancy is not conscientious objection to war. Noncombatancy is conscientious cooperation. . . . A Seventh-day Adventist noncombatant does not concern himself with what a government does or does not do. He concerns himself with his duty to his government in the light of his individuality to God. God's will to him comes first. He will cooperate with the government. . . . He will bear his country's flag. He will aid his country in its need.[119]

Statements such as these were a far cry from the First World War when Adventists chose prison rather than the uniform. These attitudes were interpreted as heralding wholesale abandonment of the sixth commandment, thereby adding to the number of voices accusing the Church of 'apostasy' and condemning it as having become 'luke-warm' through compromise.[120]

Feeling they had worked hard to facilitate the way for members to maintain their faith without persecution, Church administrators were less than sympathetic to nonconformist attitudes. Church officials even went to the extreme of attending uninvited the hearings of known Seventh-day Adventist conscientious objectors to ensure Appeal Boards knew that the stance of these individuals was not endorsed by the Church.[121] During the hearing of one such Adventist, L. C. Naden declared: 'Adventists greatly disliked being classed with conscientious objectors who refused to make any sacrifice or render any service to [the] country in time of war.'[122] During another hearing, E. J. Johanson pleaded with the Appeal Board in Christchurch not to be prejudiced against the movement as a whole by 'the few of our faith who do not subscribe to our position of noncombatancy'.[123] Not surprisingly, members embittered by the Church's apparent compromise over noncombatancy, and who refused to conform to the Church's ruling, made their protests by resigning their membership from the Adventist Church and declaring themselves members of the overtly pacifist Seventh-day Adventist Reform Movement.[124]

The numerous articles in Adventist publications during these years condemning 'the spirit of independence' and pleading for tolerance suggest that the divisions over conscription were extensive and that the activities of the Reform Movement were threatening.[125] By 1940 the Reform Movement had established a presence in Auckland, Hamilton, New Plymouth, Palmerston North, Masterton, Christchurch and Invercargill, and had become a major concern of Adventist administrators in both New Zealand conferences.[126] To combat the activities of the Reform Movement, in a most unusual move the North New Zealand Conference issued its own Statement of Fundamental Beliefs.[127] The Statement was intended to reinforce the official stance by welding the noncombatant position to the Church's belief system, and to marginalise the now vocal minority of its constituency advocating pacifism. Clauses 1–12 of the Statement outlined the distinctive Adventist doctrines. The next five points were an adaptation and expansion of the 'Religious Liberty' clause relating to noncombatancy, which was first introduced in the Constitution in 1923 and omitted from the 1942 revised Constitution.[128] This polemic was deemed appropriate and necessary by the situation.

Conclusion

The Seventh-day Adventists and the Jehovah's Witnesses took radically different stances to war, conscription and the state in New Zealand during the Second World War. At the conclusion of the Second World War nearly every individual Witness had a story to tell of police harassment, arrest and conviction, and time spent in prison, either for contravening the ban regulations or as defaulters. It seems ironic that, when the consequences of commitment were not as great, a circular addressed to 'The Jehovah's Witnesses Throughout New Zealand' called upon adherents to 'be tactful, friendly and kind to all. Avoid controversy and strife. Remember that the people we meet hold their beliefs sincerely and conscientiously. We must not hurt them.'[129] In 1945, Jehovah's Witnesses had arrived voluntarily at the very position the New Zealand government was hoping to force them to in 1940 using the strong arm of the law.

As early as mid-1941, Adventist Church leaders were celebrating the concessions they had won for Adventist noncombatants. A. W. Anderson proudly announced at the Union Conference Session that the Adventist 'noncombatant principles and . . . conscientious objection to engaging in military duties on the sabbath' were fully recognised and accommodated for by the government.[130] Some Adventist young men with the forces claimed they were 'treated like . . . kings'.[131] Church leaders saw this turn of events as evidence of God's leading, and as vindication for their expressions of patriotic zeal.[132] Statements of community approval for Adventist war support bolstered these convictions.[133]

The Adventist drive to present a united administrative front and maintain social cohesion required them to harness the evangelistic aspirations of members, exploit the political situation with a self-initiated patriotism and, finally, marginalise and expel deviating members. Whereas detention camp was the price Jehovah's Witnesses paid for their 'neutrality', their experiences during the war enhanced the solidarity of the Jehovah's Witness movement; in a real sense the Jehovah's Witness movement in New Zealand was born following the 1940 Regulations.[134]

By contrast, schism was the Adventist price for co-operation. The emergence of the Adventist Reform Movement—a group that combined the theological bias of Adventists with the social outlook of the Witness movement—was evidence of Adventism's shifting ideology. While the Adventist Church during the Second World War had remained true to its traditional position of noncombatancy, it had undergone a radical change of heart. New Zealand Adventists continued to be noncombatant in principle, but the movement had undertaken a metamorphosis by their adoption of an overt patriotism.

11

The Reverend Ormond Burton and his Antagonists during the Second World War

David Grant

Ormond Burton was New Zealand's most prominent pacifist during the Second World War. He was also New Zealand's best known Christian pacifist. The two points are not unrelated, for it was the strength of Burton's distinctively Christian convictions that drove him and a small group of Christian pacifist colleagues to pursue a highly visible and controversial anti-war campaign. This dissent continued, against immense pressure, even when all other expressions of public anti-war sentiment dissipated during the war.

This chapter provides an account of Burton's Christian pacifism, focusing on his actions during this war and the antipathy he experienced. Burton's antagonists were many. He encountered opposition from brethren within the Methodist Church and the New Zealand Christian Pacifist Society that he helped establish, but also and especially from the New Zealand State. This opposition was partly of Burton's own making. It also highlighted the changing fortunes of Christian pacifism in New Zealand during this period, and the particularly harsh attitude of the New Zealand State to wartime dissent when compared to the policies of its allies.

Burton before the Second World War

Ormond Burton was born in Mount Eden, Auckland, on 16 January 1893, the son of Beatrice and Robert Burton, a market gardener. The family shifted to Pukekohe in 1895, but returned to Auckland in 1902, where Burton excelled at Remuera Primary

School in literature, science, football and cricket. In Standard Five he won a scholarship to attend Auckland Grammar School, which he attended for four years, attaining matriculation.[1]

Although he was a successful scholar, it was nevertheless religious instruction, both at home from his pious mother, and at Sunday school and Bible Class, that would become the greatest influence on his character. He studied the New Testament assiduously, being attracted in particular to its tales of forgiveness and compassion. As a leading member of the Young Men's Bible Class Movement at St Luke's Presbyterian Church, Remuera, he led discussions among his peers, honing his talents as a public speaker and debater. At his first Easter Bible Camp in 1907 he publicly criticised a visiting evangelist who was intent on encouraging conversion through what Burton considered to be emotional and hypnotic propaganda. He later had intense personal religious experiences, which shaped him greatly. Yet Burton maintained the conviction, early formed, that a commitment to Christianity should be thoughtful and based solely on an unconditional love of Jesus Christ.

Burton was a boy of his time, however, and pacifism was a philosophy of the future. He recalls in his unpublished autobiography that he was profoundly stirred in 1900 by the 'outrageous impudence in the challenge of the uncivilised Boers to our Empire in South Africa'.[2] And after teachers' college training and a period sole-charge teaching—first at Waimana Primary School in the Bay of Plenty, then at Ahuroa in Northland—he volunteered to fight in the First World War, sailing to Egypt as a noncombatant with the No. 1 New Zealand Field Ambulance.

At Gallipoli he first tended wounded men on the hospital ship, the *Lutzow*, later transferring ashore as a stretcher-bearer. By May 1916 he was with the New Zealand Division in France. The following year, in the spring of 1917, he replaced a friend in the infantry who had been killed. In the field of battle Burton won a reputation for gallantry. Refusing home leave on all occasions he was wounded three times, and decorated by the British with the Military Medal and the French with la médaille d'honneur.

After the war he became a war historian. As early as 1917, Major General Sir Andrew Russell had asked him to write a short history of the New Zealand Division; on publication it was distributed to every soldier who had served in France in the Division. This was followed, in 1922, by a history of the Auckland Regiment—a work that had formed the basis of his Master's thesis at Auckland.[3] In the early 1930s he wrote another war book, a memoir of his experiences and those of his fellows, called *The Silent Division: New Zealanders at the Front 1914–1919*. It was highly praised for its stark realism and eulogies of the self-sacrifice of the common soldier.[4]

Yet by now Burton was a deeply committed pacifist. He had fought in the war because he believed the destruction of Prussian militarism would usher in a new age of peace and freedom for all time through forgiveness and reconciliation under God. But he was horrified and angry at the vengeful provisions of the Treaty of Versailles. Coupled with the carnage he had observed on the battlefield, often for no good purpose, this led to an epiphany; he became a propagandist for absolute Christian pacifism—first expressed publicly at the Student Christian Movement's 1922 Conference at Solway College in Masterton. One contemporary called his conversion 'akin to that of St Paul'.[5]

By this time, he had been barred from teaching because he refused to take the oath of allegiance to the Crown, arguing that it conflicted with his duty to God. Surprisingly, in 1924, the State rescinded this decision after adding a conscience clause that Burton could sign. He taught in primary schools until 1930, when he began teaching at Wesley College, a Methodist Boys' School near Tuakau. There he persuaded the school to ban the cadet corps, the first boys' high school in New Zealand to do so, and cajoled all but the headmaster to stop using corporal punishment.

In 1933, he decided to train as a clergyman—not in his own Presbyterian faith, as that Church refused to employ him as a probationer unless he went to theological college—nor as a Home Missionary, because the Church only wanted trained men. Instead he trained as a Methodist when their 1934 Conference accepted his application as a married probationer.[6] The following year he was appointed as the third minister in the Wellington Central Circuit in charge of the Webb Street Methodist Church. The area was a slum—a 'surrounding mass of paganism'—as he referred to it.[7] The church was run-down. Burton and his wife Nell worked hard and built up numbers in the congregation and Bible Class. Nell singlehandedly revitalised the Sunday school. Burton was a charismatic speaker. On Sunday afternoons he held open forums in the nearby Basin Reserve where he would argue the faith with hundreds of atheists, agnostics, communists, rationalists and the otherwise curious. Increasingly, as the war approached, the debate centred on Christian pacifism. Some argued, a few heckled, but many stood in silence, captivated often, although rarely swayed by the power of Burton's oratory.

In March 1936, he founded the Christian Pacifist Society of New Zealand (CPS) with his circuit steward A. C. (Archie) Barrington. It was a restricted organisation in that only communicant members of churches were allowed to belong, as Burton believed that only Christians had the strength of purpose to be genuinely anti-war.[8] On Friday nights from January 1938, a small number of members held poster parades through the city, walking with sandwich boards with anti-war slogans draped around their necks from the Webb Street church to Allen Street in the central city. There, Burton would speak, mostly by this time about New Zealand not becoming involved in the forthcoming conflict. By the middle of 1939, some 428 Christians, mostly Methodists, belonged to the Society, though only a small number of these adherents were active on the streets.[9]

Peter Fraser and anti-war protests

Burton's anti-war beliefs were fundamental, irrespective of worldly circumstances. The day after the Second World War was declared, in September 1939, Burton and two other pacifists—fellow Christian Neil Traill and Michael Young of the Peace Pledge Union (PPU)—mounted a rostrum outside Parliament; to a curious crowd, they condemned the war, demanding that the New Zealand government not become involved. Under Emergency Regulations only hours old, expressing such views in public was unlawful and all three were arrested for obstructing a constable. They were taken to the Central Police Station and thereafter to Mount Crawford Prison.[10] Some hours later a bemused Burton was brought back to the police station to be confronted by no less a person than the Deputy Prime Minister, Peter Fraser.

The relationship between these two men is intriguing. In 1922, Burton had joined the Labour Party as he had found common ground with many of its early leaders. Fraser, Walter Nash, William Jordan, James McCombs, Harry Holland and Robert Semple were all either practising Christians, or had come from church backgrounds, and espoused a social gospel of love, brotherhood and altruism towards the country's poor. By 1924, Burton had won enough respect within the movement to be elected to the executive of the Auckland Labour Representation Committee. The following year he became its senior vice-president. Rules concerning collective responsibility were passed soon afterwards, however; these were an affront to the individualistic Burton and he left the Party. Yet he remained friends with most of these leaders through into the 1930s. He even hosted Fraser at his home when Fraser came to Whangarata to campaign in the Raglan electorate during the 1928 election, though Burton himself stood as an independent Christian Socialist in the Eden electorate.[11]

In 1939, Fraser had both respect and affection for Burton, whom he regarded as the country's only genuine pacifist. Who could be more genuine, he believed, than a returned soldier from a war? Yet Fraser was also concerned, naïvely, that Burton, as a returned serviceman and charismatic speaker, might become the nucleus of a large and embarrassing anti-war pressure group. He pleaded with Burton to desist from further anti-war ministrations and, patronisingly, tried to persuade him to go back to his good work among the alcoholics in Webb Street.[12] Fraser went further, providing the surety that Burton and his two friends could be released on bail. Burton politely but firmly resisted Fraser's entreaties. He and his two friends were released after two nights in jail. Within two days he returned to his rostrum in Allen Street, and later in Swan Lane, a no-exit way off Cuba Street not used by traffic. He was arrested again and fined £10.[13]

Burton soon became a public figure, the press highlighting his speeches and speedy arrests. The police warned him that they had heard that angry members of the Returned Services' Association were threatening to disrupt CPS meetings by throwing speakers off their podiums, and that they were powerless to do anything about it. It was a scare tactic, which Burton and his fellows ignored. Yet within days the Wellington City Council banned public meetings in streets, public places and reserves under its jurisdiction. On 12 October 1939, it refused to sanction any more CPS Friday night poster parades in the city. Despite the noose tightening, more and more crowds were coming to the anti-war rallies—out of curiosity and Friday night 'entertainment', it has to be said, rather than sympathy. As a consequence, the CPS shifted its regular meetings to the Manners Street Reserve, or 'Pigeon Park' as Wellingtonians colloquially referred to it. It was a convenient site. A large triangle of lawn bounded by two prominent thoroughfares, Dixon and Manners Streets, allowed for convenient public access; the drinking fountain, built to commemorate the site of the first Christian sermon in Wellington, made an ideal speaking platform. Burton was again arrested in December and fined £20 for 'disturbing the peace'.[14]

Later, in January 1940, he was sharing a speaking platform in Quay Street, Auckland, with a communist activist in front of about 500 people—including soldiers and sailors, some of whom were drunk and who constantly interrupted him. One melee, close in, saw Burton pushed off the rostrum, but he remounted it and continued to talk against the police sergeant in charge, who soon arrested him for disturbing the peace. In court, Burton argued that the meeting was orderly until the servicemen arrived—a point with which the magistrate concurred—but he was found guilty anyway and fined.[15]

This was the prelude to the most dramatic anti-war meeting, which occurred in Pigeon Park on 9 February. The initial curiosity centred on Wellington's outspoken mayor, T. C. A. (Tommy) Hislop, who during a recruiting rally three days earlier had castigated all war dissenters as 'shirkers', stating that he would do everything in his power to prevent them meeting publicly in Wellington. 'If they want a fight they can have it', he told the press. They featured his remarks and accordingly a huge crowd of onlookers, estimated at close to 6000, crowded Pigeon Park the following Friday.[16] Burton feared a cataclysm. He recalled the trepidation he felt as he arrived to speak:

> The mayor clearly meant to force the hand of the government. . . . I was very much afraid that I might be put under some sort of preventive detention so it would be made to appear that I had failed to be present through fear. Consequently, I kept well out of the way until a few minutes before 8pm. . . . The whole area was packed. Near the fountain there were many soldiers in uniform and patriotic songs were being sung. More police were scattered about than I had ever seen before and for everyone in uniform there would be another in plain clothes.[17]

As he moved forward to speak to a crowd swathed in silence, a police inspector forbade him to proceed, putting an arm out to stop him. Burton evaded him, quickly mounted the rostrum, just managing to blurt out 'Ladies and gentlemen!' before being hauled down, arrested and taken to the Central Police Station. William O'Reilly, a young communist, and A. C. Barrington, who followed, received the same treatment. Yet the crowd's reaction was interesting. When the police hauled Barrington off, the crowd chanted 'give him a chance'. When Hislop moved forward to speak, a significant number cried 'Heil Hislop'.[18] While few agreed with the pacifist message, they were incensed with the abrogation of civil rights; they wanted people who did not agree with the State's actions to be allowed to express their views in public.

The State's reaction was entirely the opposite. After J. L. Stout SM sentenced Burton to a month's hard labour for 'obstructing a constable in the execution of his duty' the government, soon afterwards, imposed the third and toughest round of emergency legislation to date. It widened police powers to prohibit all meetings or processions 'likely to be injurious to public safety' and granted them the authority to search without warrants premises suspected of being used for subversive activities. The

Ormond Burton was the most prominent face of the Christian Pacifist Society, itself the most visible base of anti-war protest during the Second World War. The headline of this *Observer* billboard from 1940 says it all. Image supplied by author.

term 'subversive' was widened, too, to include any comment that was likely to cause 'disaffection' to his Majesty, disrupt the morale of the civilian population or cause undue harm to public safety. That, of course, could include just about anything. It was deeply ironic that these measures were almost identical to those the Massey Government passed during the First World War, which saw Fraser and three of his cabinet colleagues (Semple, Tim Armstrong and Paddy Webb) jailed for sedition for publicly opposing military conscription early in 1917.[19]

The government's emergency rules addressed all anti-war dissent. Since the war began, however, other groups, such as the PPU and the barely existing Peace Council, had kept their witness behind closed doors. Because it was the only remaining outspoken organisation, the new rules primarily affected the CPS. On release from prison, Burton went straight back to Pigeon Park in defiance of the government's new measures, only to be rearrested after speaking just three words: 'Now Jesus Christ. . .' Magistrate Stout was irascible. 'The time has come', he said, 'to treat offenders like you without kid gloves . . . the people are getting restless because of the anti-recruiting campaign carried on by your society under the guise of Christian pacifism.' This time Stout sentenced Burton to three months' hard labour.[20]

The Christian Pacifist Society splits

Not all CPS members agreed with Burton's aggressive anti-war stance. In October 1940, the organisation underwent a crisis. In light of the government's deepening intransigence and increasing intolerance of wartime dissent, delegates to the CPS's conference split into two opposing groups. On one side were those who wished to retreat into a quietist 'peacemaking' organisation. This group, led by the Reverend Alun Richards and Thurlow Thompson, worried that the CPS might be banned altogether as a 'subversive' organisation. It was an understandable concern. They called on the CPS to stop confronting the government over its policies.[21] As Richards argued:

> Democracy is gone. Our task now comes not to be that of a Christian Pacifist Society but of a Christian Society.

> We must lead but do it in a way that will not destroy our organisation and therefore avoid head-on clashes with authority. The primary function of our Society is to make its witness effective as an educational body—the executive needs to be more discreet.[22]

Moreover, CPS branches in Hamilton, Palmerston North, Christchurch and Dunedin had already retreated from public activity.

On the other side, the 'war-opposers', led by Burton and Barrington, were adamant that they had to continue their vigorous and public Christian pursuit against war, knowing full well that such activity meant a direct route to prison. Burton argued that there had to be room for individual choice; restricting such freedom would contravene one of their fundamental convictions. Probably as a consequence of Burton's eloquence and mana (prestige, authority, influence), Richards' motion that the CPS henceforth work as a collective conscience failed by just

Delegates to the pivotal 1940 annual conference of the Christian Pacifist Society. Ormond Burton is seated third from left in the second row, flanked on either side by Archibald Barrington and his wife, Nell, who appears rather tired and strained. Alun Richards is seated at the extreme right; the flag behind him was carried in parades and displayed at other public events. Image supplied by author.

two votes. Richards was disappointed and argued that if the Society as a whole had a chance to vote, his cautionary measure would have won. The 'aggressive' tactics of the few, he said, had whipped up an unwelcome hysteria against the organisation.[23]

Even if the vote had gone against Burton and his allies, it would have made no difference. In January 1941, Burton issued a circular urging branches to more 'dynamic' action. This circular followed a second unsuccessful meeting in November between Burton and other pacifists with Fraser, now Prime Minister, and senior government officials, where Burton requested that the CPS be allowed to continue its open witness against war. Arguably, it was only owing to Burton's prominence and erstwhile friendship with Fraser that these meetings were even held.[24]

Burton's arguments in this meeting were bewildering to those he was trying to persuade. 'Our own sufferings are irrelevant', he said. 'If the Japanese invaded we would try to be as friendly as possible . . . the greatest service we could render would be the conversion of the malignant mind of those who were the Dominion's enemy.'[25] The other-worldly nature of this message made it easy for Fraser to reject. Fraser claimed that it was preferable for the CPS to suffer a temporary handicap than to continue publicly and face possible extinction. He was adamant that he could not permit anything that was 'subversive' of the war effort.[26] In light of this, it is notable that the CPS was never in fact banned as a subversive organisation, despite its continued open campaigning under Burton—a rare liberal outcome during this period.

After this meeting, the activists that remained organised a speaking roster in Pigeon Park every Friday evening between 14 March and 6 June of 1941. As soon as they mounted the rostrum to speak they were removed, often roughly, by police, arrested, and later imprisoned for three to twelve months' hard labour. The latter sentence was imposed on Burton (whose turn had been on 18 April), Barrington and Arthur Carman, because they were the ringleaders. There was no pretense of impartiality. Chief Justice Michael Myers instructed the juries in the latter cases to find the men guilty.[27] In effect these men were tried twice—in the Magistrates' Court for 'obstructing a constable', and then in the Supreme Court for 'holding or attempting to hold a prohibited meeting'. Apart from a small number of Christian pacifists speaking in Auckland ('following Ormie's direction', as one of them said), that signalled the end of Christian pacifist open-air witness.[28]

Expulsion from the Methodist Church

Burton adjusted to prison life with little anxiety. A much greater hurt occurred when he was expelled from his beloved Methodist Church in June 1942. In his autobiography he described it as the 'worst of all things to happen'.[29] Personally painful, the action also reflected the Church's turning against thoroughgoing principled pacifism—a rejection of the CPS's position as well as its anti-war activism.

Despite the strong pacifist sentiment redolent among some of its clergy, in May 1940 the Methodist Annual Conference overwhelmingly endorsed a 'Manifesto on Peace and War', which stipulated that pulpits were to be used neither for recruiting agencies nor as propaganda platforms to encourage young men to refuse service. In view of the majority opinion assenting to the war, albeit reluctantly in most cases, it was a reasonable compromise. Burton, however, regarded the ruling as a slap in the face and refused to acknowledge it. For him, Christianity and pacifism were interdependent. In rebuttal, he wrote *A Testament of Peace*, his own manifesto on which he would base his further ministrations.[30] Burton restated his belief that it was his duty to preach peace as a living testament to the life of Jesus Christ: the tougher worldly circumstances made it for one to accept or even understand the pacifist position, the harder one must try to proselytise it.[31]

Burton barely survived in the Webb Street parish as it was. The Wellington Synod, led by the Reverend Jonathan Haslam, a former CPS member who had now turned against its agenda and become one of Burton's chief antagonists in the Church, refused to invite him back for a sixth year on the central circuit. But the May 1940 Conference accepted a proposal from Burton's long-time friend, the Reverend Percy Paris, that Webb Street be made a separate circuit, and Burton was reappointed.

Matters came to a head at the next Annual Conference in 1942. Burton was charged by the 'war party', as he uncharitably called them, which included senior clergy and the Conference president, Reverend William Walker, with refusing to accept the discipline of the Church. They moved to expel him. A clash on the floor ensued. Walker urged Burton to resign his post. Burton refused, claiming that the Church had no right to sanction him save for heresy or 'grave immorality'. Most delegates agreed with the Manifesto, but others argued that expelling Burton would split the Church. In the absence of a clear process the debate dragged on. Finally, Walker, losing patience, instructed the delegates to choose 'him or me'. The vote to expel Burton was carried by seventy-five to forty-five. Significantly, over 100 abstained. This vote was remarkable. That forty-five supported Burton and many more abstained spoke volumes for the stature he held among his fellows in the Church, despite his contrary views, firmly held.[32]

Burton was devastated. Barrington recalled: 'I left the church with Ormond and saw a strong man weeping'.[33] In the dark days of 1942, non-conformists within the Church were embarrassing, and a tense atmosphere pervaded the assembly at the point at which Burton was expelled. As E. W. Hames, the Methodist Church historian, noted: 'Mr Walker was technically right and acted properly but Mr Burton made his point. He left an irritant in our conscience.'[34] Now expelled, Burton secured a labouring job in a cool store, while the family left the Webb Street manse and rented a house in nearby Aro Street. Burton remained estranged from Methodism until 1955. He worshipped until then, with his family, at St Peter's Anglican Church, Wellington.

The Blair trial and State antipathy

After his release from his twelve-month sentence following the infamous 'Hislop' meeting, Burton became editor of the Christian Pacifist Society's newsletter, the *Bulletin*. The newsletter, at that time banned from being distributed openly, was a collection of cyclostyled sheets sent through the post to members. In his first issue he wrote, naturally enough, a report on his good friend

Barrington, who had recently been acquitted, upon appeal, of sedition charges that had been brought against him as the *Bulletin*'s editor. This first issue also included a mild anti-war poem by a Waikato pacifist, Clarice Templar, and an article by Basil Dowling critiquing the First World War poetry of Wilfred Owen. Yet the issue was intercepted by Chief Censor J. T. Paul who determined that it was 'subversive' under the Emergency Regulations. Burton was then arrested and indicted on three counts: editing a subversive document, publishing a subversive document and attempting to publish a subversive document.

On 23 October 1942, he was back in the dock, this time facing Judge Archibald Blair. The Supreme Court was packed. At first things seemed to go well. Blair and Burton exchanged good-natured pleasantries. Barrington recorded that the proceedings were courteous with 'flashes of wit between judge and prisoner'.[35] Burton himself recalled:

> He very generously offered to have my case deferred to the next session if he thought that I had not had enough time for preparation. I was anxious however, for the case to go through because Rob [Burton's son] was due to start at Wellington College at the beginning of 1943. Things would be bad for him in any case but to start high school at the very moment I was being jailed would be shocking.[36]

Defending himself, Burton's summing up to the jury was succinct:

> When parliament has abrogated its function the Jury becomes a last line of defence of the people's freedom. . . . Here am I charged with doing neither more nor less than I have done these last 20 years—and incidentally doing it privately amongst people who share my views—not doing it publicly or among soldiers. . . . I ask you to acquit me—not that I may be saved from imprisonment—but that something more important than myself shall live—the real freedom to think and to speak as conscience dictates.[37]

These comments appeared to antagonise Blair, who henceforth pushed aside any pretense of impartiality. Glaring at Burton, he told him that if Burton and his colleagues were allowed to go on doing this work then everybody would feel like laying down their arms and letting the Nazis or the Japanese take over the country. 'The British people', Blair continued, 'put up with a . . . lot of cranks and until we find them doing mischief we do not interfere—while they kept quiet about it it was all right, but there always comes a time when their mouths have to be shut.'[38] He then instructed the jury to find Burton guilty.

Thus charged they did; they had no choice. But when the jury returned they added a strong recommendation for mercy. The maximum sentence under the Emergency Regulations for printing 'subversive material' was twelve months' imprisonment, a punishing sentence in itself. In a very dubious legal manipulation, Blair ignored that. Instead, he claimed jurisdiction under a rarely used 1910 amendment to the Crimes Act, which allowed for a maximum eleven years' imprisonment—one year for sedition in wartime, and up to ten further years for reformative detention if a judge was satisfied that a 'criminal' would benefit from such a sentence.[39] Blair explained he would not impose the maximum sentence, but give credence to the jury's recommendation of leniency by only giving him two and a half years. The final humiliation was when Blair offered to release him immediately if Burton would promise not to speak or write in support of pacifism for the rest of the war, knowing that he would refuse—which he did.

Blair's sentence remains one of the most reprehensible judicial judgements in New Zealand's legal history. He simply wanted, with the State's implicit connivance, to see Burton confined for as long as possible, hopefully until the war was over. It is noteworthy that there were no more prosecutions of Christian Pacifist Society *Bulletin* editors after that, nor was there any other police attention on Christian pacifists—those still in the community were living and worshipping very quietly. Yet the malevolence did not end there. After a month in Mount Crawford, Burton was packed off to Napier Prison, a long distance from his wife and two children, as well as friends in Wellington. Already, on the instructions of B. L. Dallard, the Director of Prisons, Barrington was banned from seeing him in Mount Crawford on the basis that an ex-prisoner could not visit an inmate.[40]

The outcome of Burton's trial caused international outrage. Lord Ponsonby, a former leader of the Labour Party in the British House of Lords, gathered written support from sixteen other parliamentarians in both houses of parliament urging Minister of Justice Rex Mason to release him. H. Runham Brown, president of War Resisters' International in Great Britain, began an international telegram campaign calling for Burton's deliverance. Mason ignored both sets of entreaties. In the United States, sixteen bishops wrote to the Ministry of Internal Affairs calling for clemency for Burton.[41] Other theologians, Christian pacifists, civil libertarians, and politicians in Australia, Canada and the United States also protested in vain. These individuals included Reinhold Niebuhr, the prominent, stridently non-pacifist theoretician and Professor of Applied Christianity at Union Theological Seminary in New York, whose Barthian theology and attitudes to war Burton rejected.[42] Conversely, as if to salve a collective guilty conscience, the chairman of the Prisons Board twice urged Burton to accept early release, on condition that he promise not to engage in further pacifist activity. In April 1944, Dallard went further, threatening to confine Burton indefinitely if he continued to refuse this offer. It was an idle threat and Burton ignored all appeals.[43]

Burton did not despair. He expected to be imprisoned and this foreknowledge, along with his deep Christian faith, allowed him to make the adjustment effortlessly. He spent his time reading, gardening, and writing two books: one, called *Bart*, was about his dog; the second, an account of his prison experiences simply titled *In Prison*, was published in 1945.[44] In the meantime, his ever dutiful and hard-working wife Nell took a leading role in keeping the CPS alive in Wellington, as well as bringing up two children.

Burton had not set out to be a martyr. He had not wanted to go to jail. 'I have a wife, children and a job I am very keen on and I am not interested in being separated from them for any period', he told a journalist in 1940.[45] With the end of street speaking in 1941, he simply wanted to continue his Christian witness against war. His beliefs did not waver and his antagonists continued to fear that because he was well known and widely respected, harm could be done—indeed the country's morale could be affected—if he remained in the community, free to talk or write. That was a fantasy. In reality, Burton's fundamental message appealed to very few. It was uncompromising State and judicial reaction that caused the most distress among humanitarians, pacifist or otherwise.

Burton and the context of State antagonism

The approach of the New Zealand State to dissent during the Second World War continued its earlier tough stand against pacifist objectors—a position that was uncompromising even compared with other Allied states. In many ways, Burton's experience was a product of this general climate. During the First World War, New Zealand had treated its few pacifists and conscientious objectors harshly; most objectors failed the Appeal Board system and were sent to jail or compulsory work camps. The governments of Great Britain and Australia both imposed similarly tough sanctions at that time; Britain, like New Zealand, sent imprisoned objectors to the front line in France to try to make them fight.[46]

At the outbreak of the Second World War the Labour Government's commitment to assist Britain was sincere and uncompromising, as its citizenry was expected to be. Even before war began, the government passed a group of ten Emergency Regulations in order to curb 'contrary' behaviour. Thirty more were added by the end of December 1939.[47] These measures gave the State an immense power, which intensified during the 'phony war' period (September 1939 to May 1940) as various liberal and Christian New Zealanders questioned not only the war itself, believing that the conservative Great Britain was more concerned about Bolshevik Russia than Nazi Germany, but also the possible introduction of military conscription—then already talked about, but anathema to traditional labourites.[48]

This early crackdown affected the CPS directly. On 8 October 1939, the organisation's mail, detailing arrangements for its forthcoming national conference over Labour weekend, was seized by the newly appointed censor, J. T. Paul. A protest from CPS secretary Barrington to Fraser was ignored and a second approach from CPS member Edward Dowsett to Paul brought a curt response that CPS material was no longer 'suitable' for transmission by post.[49] There followed over the next six months up to the end of May 1940 a succession of measures that aimed to stifle any criticism of the war and New Zealand's participation in it.

The Fraser government's intensifying intransigence towards malcontents stands in striking contrast to the British response. After the First World War there had been widespread criticism within Britain among folk of standing—writers, actors, scholars, academics, trade union leaders, and various politicians and gentry—that pacifists and conscientious objectors had been punished far too harshly. Thousands had languished in jail for long periods, many suffered mental breakdowns and some had died. This, critics claimed, had abrogated the traditional British right to dissent, which since the Reformation had become an inalienable and integral part of the British way of life, frequently lauded and defended with great passion. Such criticism continued into the late 1930s, despite increasing fascist aggression in Europe and Asia. In May 1939, British Prime Minister Neville Chamberlain indicated to the House of Commons that there would be no persecution of people who had deep-seated scruples against militarism; in the same debate, the Archbishop of Canterbury implored the House of Lords—and the country—to respect the pacifist conscience. Later, in March 1941, during the deepest days of the Blitz, Chamberlain's successor Winston Churchill rejected a call that war critics should not have access to the British Broadcasting Corporation, declaring that anything in the nature of persecuting or victimising this community was 'odious to the British people'.[50]

Unlike in New Zealand, there was only one law passed concerning anti-war activity. The October 1939 British Emergency Powers (Defence) Act recognised that such activity was the concern of a relative few and therefore unlikely to threaten national security. Defence Regulation 18B of this Act, under which those suspected of sympathising with the enemy could be confined indefinitely, was used not against pacifists but rather the bleating of Oswald Mosley's British Union of Fascists and a few recalcitrant communists. Unlike in New Zealand, pacifists kept speaking in open forums. Lex Miller, a founding member of the NZCPS and, since 1938, minister of St John's Presbyterian Church, Stepney, informed Barrington in March 1941 that even during the Blitz, pacifists' meetings continued in Hyde Park and on Tower Hill in London, the police attending only because the speakers might be physically attacked by opponents.[51]

Indeed, the care of the British government to protect the rights of the pacifist voice during this war was remarkable. George Lansbury MP, the respected grand old man of British socialism and prominent PPU activist, summed it up in 1940 when he commented that Britons possessed rights and privileges that no other country allowed in wartime.[52] One Christian pacifist wrote that he found the liberal climate frustrating: 'The State has been more ingenious than we imagined it could be. British totalitarianism has found a way of assimilating pacifists. . . . There is a feeling somehow that we have been diddled!'[53] As a strategy for containing a dissident minority, British policy was effective. Open-air pacifist meetings faded away as absolute rejection of war became increasingly difficult to justify with the war so close at hand.

In Australia, too, there was similar concern that the anti-militarist voice not be stifled. Late in 1939, conservative Prime Minister Robert Menzies told his parliament that 'the greatest tragedy that could overcome our country would be for it to fight a successful war in defence of liberty and lose its own in the process'.[54] He was as true as his word. Under his government's October 1939 National Security Act, no pacifist, or pacifist organisation, was ever banned or prosecuted in Australia.[55]

Peter Fraser's role in the New Zealand response was significant. In contrast to Chamberlain, Churchill and Menzies, he felt no discomfort introducing Emergency Regulations designed to stifle opposition to the war. Unbending and self-assured, Fraser was less concerned with scruple than an overwhelming desire that everyone agree with him. Within his own party, rigid controls were imposed so that those with traditional left-wing labourite opinions who possessed anti-war or anti-conscription sympathies were silenced. One notable example was Cabinet minister Tim Armstrong (jailed along with Fraser in 1917), who told Burton as late as October 1939 that he would be a 'very disappointed man' if Labour ever lent itself to military conscription.[56] When Cabinet approved Fraser's demand for its introduction in July 1940, there were no dissenting voices.

Thereafter, led by city councils, which slowly banned the use of public places where pacifists like Burton could address crowds, and members of the judiciary like Stout and Blair, who falsely denigrated Burton and his colleagues as 'anti-conscription agents', a raft of pressure groups demanded consent—the powerful Returned Services' Association, a Defence League (formed in 1937), a newly formed right-wing People's Movement, farmers and business groups, as well as the political opposition and the metropolitan press. Fraser obliged. The great majority of New Zealanders agreed with him. Unlike Great Britain's heterogeneous and tolerant society, New Zealand's was comparatively insular and suspicious. New Zealanders reacted to pacifists emotionally, with feelings ranging from scepticism to outright hostility from those who wished to see them punished as shirkers and traitors. Particularly when the 'phony war' came to an abrupt end, there was no middle ground. Support for maintaining civil liberties faded under the demands of the 'war situation' and the great majority of pacifists retreated when the last batch of war regulations, passed in May 1940, forbade their public presence.

Peter Fraser misread his erstwhile friend Ormond Burton's charismatic abilities in believing that he could become the focus of a large and 'damaging' anti-war pressure group. In reality the pacifist message was the preserve of very few. Fraser met Burton three times, formally and informally, prior to the big meeting of October 1940. He was not surprised by Burton's continuing 'aggression' in pursuing a strident opposition to the war on fundamentalist Christian grounds. When ever-increasing fines had no impact on Burton and his friends continuing their open-air proselytising, prison seemed the only choice in this conformist society. Fraser and Burton shared similar personality traits: pugnacity, intransigence and a tendency towards authoritarianism. Despite their former friendship and continuing mutual regard, Burton's incarceration became inevitable.

After the War

Burton's post-war story is remarkable. After his expulsion from the Methodist Church, he laboured briefly before finding work as a night-shift cleaner at Wellington Technical College. A post-war teacher shortage led to an invitation in 1946 from the school board, which knew of his teaching qualifications, to teach English to night classes. He moved into the day school the following year and in 1950 became head of the department. In 1953, he was appointed the school's principal. Finally, in 1955, the Methodist Conference allowed him back into the fold. Posted to Ōtaki, he revitalised the local church.

Though Burton retained his pacifist faith, it included an increasing intolerance towards non-Christian pacifism, which he regarded as an armchair philosophy 'lacking in passion—not of the nature of tears and sweat. As with political liberation it is only able to provide amenities rather than provide a new structure.'[57] This retrospective judgement was patently untrue. Michael Young, Lincoln Efford, Lucy Gibson and Biddie Oldfield were humanist pacifists who remained resolute in their commitment throughout the war and suffered because of it. Young, in particular, spent most of the war as a protesting military defaulter incarcerated in prison, often in solitary confinement.[58] Burton also criticised the PPU's pledge for lacking depth of conviction, and claimed that the British PPU had little significance from the beginning of the war.[59] Again, his judgement was narrow-minded and erroneous. Led by the ebullient Anglican cleric, Canon Dick Sheppard, the PPU had by far the largest membership of any British pacifist organisation during the war, peaking at 136,000 in April 1940. Of its original thirty-seven sponsors from December 1934, twenty-six remained, while others like Dame Sybil Thorndike had joined. Its publication, *The Peace News*, long since banned in New Zealand as a 'subversive' publication, still commanded a healthy distribution of 20,000 late in 1944.[60]

Burton's belief that only the church had the faith, commitment and depth to end war precluded him from participating in an attempt by a diverse group of peace activists—including Christian pacifists—to establish a multi-faceted Peace Council in 1946. He also refused to work with 'loose' federations such as the Campaign for Nuclear Disarmament in the 1950s and 1960s. When in 1966 the CPS's international counterpart, the International Fellowship of Reconciliation, opened its doors to non-Christian members to survive, Burton was horrified. After campaigning, unsuccessfully, for the CPS to disaffiliate in protest, he sadly resigned from the movement he had co-founded thirty years earlier.[61]

Burton also refused to compromise his conservative theological dogma. In 1968 he regarded Lloyd Geering's radical challenge to the orthodox view of the resurrection as heresy. In rebuttal, he wrote *To Whom Shall We Go?*, an exposition of traditional orthodoxy that helped generate considerable public debate on religion and the Church.[62] He was often pessimistic in his later years, recoiling from attacks by liberals and the failure of the wider Church to embrace pacifism as orthodox. But he remained outwardly cheerful and caring as a parish clergyman, visiting every parishioner in his flock as often as he could. His proclivity for hard work never dimmed. After retiring in January 1960, he wrote a short biography of early missionary Octavius Hadfield,[63] and a massive autobiography, 'A Rich Old Man', which remained unpublished because he refused publishers' demands to reduce it. Interested in Christian history, he guided visitors around the historic Rangiātea Church and later travelled to Wellington to preach and march against the Vietnam War. He died on 7 January 1974, survived by his wife Nell and his two children Robert and Mary.

Conclusion

Ormond Burton was the most high-profile victim of State and judicial intolerance against dissenters during the Second World War. His experience was partly a product of hostile attitudes within New Zealand society towards non-conformity in general and pacifism in particular. It also followed from the stubbornly punitive stance that the New Zealand State adopted. Burton's pacifism was thoroughgoing, principled and based upon a rigorously applied Christian conviction. Perhaps surprisingly, this conviction set him at odds with his own Methodist Church, which, of the larger churches in New Zealand, had been the most fully imbued with a pacifist ethic prior to the war. In this conflict, Burton's own intransigence undoubtedly played a part, as it did in his confrontation with the State. The Church's insistence that its ministers not use pulpits for either recruiting or extolling pacifism had been fair and reasonable. Burton's outright rejection of that position, and production of an alternative 'peace' document, was egocentric and prejudicial. Burton was not a 'consensus' man. The biggest surprise, in hindsight, was that so few ultimately voted to banish him. This reflected his charisma, the longstanding esteem for him within the Methodist family and the respect that his ministry in the deprived Webb Street parish had kindled. For Burton had many antagonists, but also many admirers—often the very same people.

Burton's experiences must be viewed within the context of wartime intolerance of the New Zealand State towards dissenters. Nevertheless, there were occasional flashes of liberality. If Burton had been tried in the Supreme Court in 1942 not by Archibald Blair but by a different judge, the outcome might have been different. In an earlier trial, A. C. Barrington's guilty verdict for supposedly 'seditious' material he had printed while editor of the *Bulletin* was challenged in the three-man Court of Appeal. There, Judge David Smith contended that juries in sedition cases needed to become guardians of *bona fide* speech and expression: 'Criticism delivered in good faith may be necessary for the safety of the State and they (the jury) should allow for the heat of the moment and not subject the passages to any narrow or jealous review . . . when a judge sees fit I see no reason why that practice should not be adopted in a trial for an offence under these regulations.'[64]

The Court ruled two to one in Barrington's favour. He was set free.

Notes

1. Christianity, Peace and Opposition to War – Geoffrey Troughton

1 For a window into many of these events and projects, and historians' contributions, see ww100.govt.nz.

2 For example, Steven Loveridge, ed., *New Zealand Society at War, 1914–1918* (Wellington: Victoria University Press, 2016); Steven Loveridge, *Calls to Arms: New Zealand Society and Commitment to the Great War* (Wellington: Victoria University Press, 2014); Kate Hunter and Kirstie Ross, *Holding on to Home: New Zealand Stories and Objects of the First World War* (Wellington: Te Papa Press, 2014).

3 See Scott Worthy, 'A Debt of Honour: New Zealanders' First Anzac Days', *New Zealand Journal of History* (NZJH) 36, no. 2 (2002): 185–200; Graeme Ferguson, 'Chunuk Bair and the Search for Identity', in *Mapping the Landscape: Essays in Australian and New Zealand Christianity—Festschrift in Honour of Professor Ian Breward*, edited by Susan Emilsen and William W. Emilsen (New York: Peter Lang, 2000), 222–37; Maureen Sharp, 'Anzac Day in New Zealand, 1916–39', NZJH 15, no. 2 (1981): 97–114.

4 See, for example, the 'Voices Against War' project, led by Margaret Lovell-Smith at www.voicesagainstwar.nz.

5 *Field Punishment No. 1*, directed by Peter Burger (Lippy Pictures, 2014); David Grant with paintings by Bob Kerr, *Field Punishment No. 1: Archibald Baxter, Mark Briggs and New Zealand's Anti-militarist Tradition* (Wellington: Steele Roberts, 2008); Archibald Baxter, *We Will Not Cease* (Auckland: Cape Catley, 2003).

6 Matt. 5:9, 5:43–48, 22:34–40. The literature on forms of early Christian pacifism is extensive. There are useful accounts in Lisa Sowle Cahill, *Love Your Enemies: Discipleship, Pacifism, and Just War Theory* (Minneapolis: Fortress Press, 1994), esp. 15–54; and Roland H. Bainton's classic study, *Christian Attitudes Toward War and Peace: A Historical Survey and Critical Re-evaluation* (New York: Abingdon Press, 1960), esp. 53–84.

7 William T. Cavanaugh, *The Myth of Religious Violence: Secular Ideology and the Roots of Modern Conflict* (New York: Oxford University Press, 2009); Christopher Hitchens, *God is Not Great: How Religion Poisons Everything* (New York: Twelve, 2007).

8 Nicholas Thompson, 'The Escaped Nun: Taking the Sectarian Temperature of Nineteenth Century New Zealand', in *Sacred Histories in Secular New Zealand*, edited by Geoffrey Troughton and Stuart Lange (Wellington: Victoria University Press, 2016), 72–86; Rory Sweetman, '"How to behave among Protestants": Varieties of Irish Catholic Leadership in Colonial New Zealand', in *The Irish in New Zealand: Historical Contexts and Perspectives*, edited by Brad Patterson (Wellington: Stout Research Centre for New Zealand Studies, 2002), 89–90.

9 Notably, for example, Michael King, *The Penguin History of New Zealand* (Auckland: Penguin, 2003).

10 'God Defend New Zealand' was first published and set to music in 1876; this became the national song in 1940, and a national anthem in 1977. On the history of this anthem, see Max Cryer, *Hear Our Voices, We Entreat: The Extraordinary Story of New Zealand's National Anthems* (Auckland: Exisle Publishing, 2004); Ashley Heenan, *God Defend New Zealand: A History of the National Anthem* (Christchurch: School of Music, University of Canterbury, 2004).

11 As earlier noted in Megan Hutching, '"Mothers of the World": Women, Peace and Arbitration in Early Twentieth-Century New Zealand', NZJH 27, no. 2 (2005): 173–85.

12 For example, Ernest Crane, *I Can Do No Other: A Biography of the Reverend Ormond Burton* (Auckland: Hodder and Stoughton, 1986); David Grant, *A Question of Faith: A History of the New Zealand Christian Pacifist Society* (Wellington: Philip Garside Publishing, 2004); Zane Mather, '"To Leaven the Lump": A Critical History of the Anglican Pacifist Fellowship in New Zealand' (MA thesis, Victoria University of Wellington, 2011).

13 For example, Elsie Locke, *Peace People: A History of Peace Activities in New Zealand* (Christchurch: Hazard Press, 1992); Maire Leadbeater, *Peace, Power and Politics: How New Zealand Became Nuclear Free* (Dunedin: Otago University Press, 2013); Kevin P. Clements, *Back from the Brink: The Creation of a Nuclear-free New Zealand* (Wellington: Allen & Unwin, 1988); Trevor Richards, *Dancing on Our Bones: New Zealand, South Africa, Rugby and Racism* (Wellington: Bridget Williams Books, 1999); Geoff Chapple, *1981: The Tour* (Wellington: Reed, 1984). For contrast, Laurie Guy, *Shaping Godzone: Public Issues and Church Voices in New Zealand 1840–2000* (Wellington: Victoria University Press, 2011), esp. 235–355; Allan K. Davidson, *Christianity in Aotearoa: A History of*

Church and Society in New Zealand (3rd ed., Wellington: Education for Ministry, 2004); Christopher Nichol and James Veitch, 'Rucking for Justice: Apartheid, the Churches and the 1981 Springbok Tour', in *Religion in New Zealand*, edited by Christopher Nichol and James Veitch (2nd ed., Wellington: Tertiary Christian Studies Programme, 1983), 287–312.

14 Geoffrey Troughton and Philip Fountain, eds., *Pursuing Peace in Godzone: Christianity and the Peace Tradition in New Zealand* (Wellington: Victoria University Press, forthcoming).

15 Malcolm McKinnon, 'Opposition to the War in New Zealand', in *One Flag, One Queen, One Tongue: New Zealand, the British Empire and the South African War 1899–1902*, edited by John Crawford and Ian McGibbon (Auckland: Auckland University Press, 2003), 28–45; Megan Hutching, '"Turn Back This Tide of Barbarism": New Zealand Women Who Were Opposed to War, 1896–1919' (MA thesis, University of Auckland, 1990); Hutching, 'Mothers of the World', 173–85.

16 H. E. Holland, *Armageddon or Calvary: The Conscientious Objectors of New Zealand and 'The Process of Their Conversion'* (Wellington: Maoriland Worker, 1919), 5–6.

17 Angela Ballara, *Taua: 'Musket Wars', 'Land Wars' or Tikanga? Warfare in Māori Society in the Early Nineteenth Century* (Auckland: Penguin, 2003), 153–62; A. P. Vayda, *Maori Warfare* (Wellington: Polynesian Society, 1960), 119–24.

18 On this see Geoffrey Troughton, 'Missionaries, Historians and the Peace Tradition in New Zealand', in *Te Rongopai 1814 Takoto te pai! Bicentenary Reflections on Christian Beginnings and Developments in Aotearoa New Zealand*, edited by Allan Davidson, Stuart Lange, Peter Lineham and Adrienne Puckey (Auckland: General Synod Office of the Anglican Church in Aotearoa New Zealand and Polynesia, 2014), 243–44. See also, for example, Phyllis L. Garlick, *Peacemaker of the Tribes: Henry Williams of New Zealand* (London: Highway Press, 1939); A. H. Reed, *Marsden of Maoriland: Pioneer and Peacemaker* (Dunedin: A. H. & A. W. Reed, 1938).

19 Malcolm Falloon, 'The Tārore Story: Sorting Fact from Fiction', in Troughton and Lange, 40–53.

20 For example, Mary-Anne Woodfield, 'Sowing the Gospel of Peace: Missionary James Watkin at Karitāne and Wellington, 1840–1855' (MA thesis, Victoria University of Wellington, 2016).

21 See Lachy Paterson, *Colonial Discourses: Niupepa Māori, 1855–1863* (Dunedin: Otago University Press, 2006); Lyndsay Head, 'The Pursuit of Modernity in Maori Society: The Conceptual Bases of Citizenship in the Early Colonial Period', in *Histories, Power and Loss: Uses of the Past—A New Zealand Commentary*, edited by

Andrew Sharp and Paul McHugh (Wellington: Bridget Williams Books, 2001), 97–121.

22 For example, Lyndsay Head, 'Wiremu Tamihana and the *Mana* of Christianity', in *Christianity, Modernity and Culture: New Perspectives on New Zealand History*, edited by John Stenhouse and G. A. Wood (Adelaide: ATF Press, 2005), 58–86; Evelyn Stokes, *Wiremu Tamihana: Rangatira* (Wellington: Huia, 2002).

23 On Te Whiti as a prophet, see Bronwyn Elsmore, *Mana from Heaven: A Century of Maori Prophets in New Zealand* (Tauranga: Moana Press, 1989); *Like Them That Dream: The Maori and the Old Testament* (Tauranga: Moana Press, 1985). See also Paul Morris, 'The Provocation of Parihaka: Reflections on Spiritual Resistance in Aotearoa', in *Parihaka: The Art of Passive Resistance*, edited by Te Miringa Hohaia, Gregory O'Brien and Lara Strongman (Wellington: Victoria University Press, 2001), 105–16.

24 Danny Keenan, *Te Whiti O Rongomai and the Resistance of Parihaka* (Wellington: Huia, 2015). See also Hazel Riseborough, *Days of Darkness: The Government and Parihaka, Taranaki, 1878–1884* (revised edition, Auckland: Penguin, 2002); Dick Scott, *Ask That Mountain: The Story of Parihaka* (Auckland: Heinemann, 1975).

25 Peter Oettli, *God's Messenger: J. F. Riemenschneider and Racial Conflict in 19th Century New Zealand* (Wellington: Huia, 2008), 222.

26 Octavius Hadfield, *One of England's Little Wars* (London and Edinburgh: Williams and Norgate, 1860); *The Second Year of One of England's Little Wars* (London and Edinburgh: Williams and Norgate, 1861); *A Sequel to "One of England's Little Wars"* (London and Edinburgh: Williams and Norgate, 1861).

27 Steven Oliver, 'Te Rauparaha, Tamihana', www.teara.govt.nz/en/biographies/1t75/te-rauparaha-tamihana; W. H. Oliver, 'Te Whiwhi, Henare Matene', www.teara.govt.nz/en/biographies/1t89/te-whiwhi-henare-matene; Mason Durie, 'Te Rangiotu, Hoani Meihana', www.teara.govt.nz/en/biographies/1t67/te-rangiotu-hoani-meihana; Tina White, 'Who Was the Daughter of Peace?', *Manawatu Standard*, 9 April 2016, www.stuff.co.nz/manawatu-standard/lifestyle/78642162/Who-was-the-Daughter-of-Peace.

28 Religious Objectors Advisory Board to Minister of Defence, 20 March 1919, www.nzhistory.net.nz/war/nzers-who-resisted-ww1.

29 Allan K. Davidson and Peter J. Lineham, *Transplanted Christianity: Documents Illustrating Aspects of New Zealand Church History* (5th ed., Auckland: Kereru, 2015), 4.1 and 6.3.

30 For example, Hutching, 'Mothers of the World', 180. On the 1916 Act and issues relating to exemption, see Paul Baker, *King and Country Call: New Zealanders, Conscription and the Great War* (Auckland:

Auckland University Press, 1988); David Littlewood, '"Willing and Eager to Go in Their Turn"? Appeals for Exemption from Military Service in New Zealand and Great Britain, 1916–1918', *War in History* 21, no. 3 (2014): 338–54.

31 Thomas Kennedy, 'Why Did Friends Resist? The War, the Peace Testimony, and the All-Friends Conference of 1920', *Peace and Change* 14, no. 4 (1989): 355–56. See also Peter Brock, *Varieties of Pacifism: A Survey from Antiquity to the Outset of the Twentieth Century* (Syracuse: Syracuse University Press, 1998); Hugh Barbour, 'The "Lamb's War" and the Origins of the Quaker Peace Testimony', in *The Pacifist Impulse in Historical Perspective*, edited by Harvey L. Dyck (Toronto: University of Toronto Press, 1996), 145–58; Peter Brock, *Pioneers of a Peaceable Kingdom: The Quaker Peace Testimony from the Colonial Era to the First World War* (Princeton: Princeton University Press, 1971).

32 Elizabeth Plumridge, 'Quaker Conscience in War: The Goldsbury Family, New Zealand, 1914–1918', unpublished paper presented at 'Peace, not war, shall be our boast': Historical, Theological and Contemporary Perspectives on Peace and Christianity in New Zealand, Victoria University of Wellington conference, 18–20 November 2015; Margaret Lovell-Smith, 'The Case of Noel Goldsbury', www.voicesagainstwar.nz/exhibits/show/conscription--and-those-who-ob/the-case-of-noel-goldsbury--a-.

33 K. R. Adams, 'The Growth and Development of the Society of Friends in New Zealand, 1840–1920' (MA thesis, University of Canterbury, 1986), 29–40, 85–86, 104–106.

34 See R. L. Weitzel, 'Pacifists and Anti-militarists in New Zealand, 1909–1914', NZJH 7, no. 2 (1973): 143, 146.

35 Locke, 35–36; Jim McAloon, 'Radical Christchurch', in *Southern Capital: Christchurch: Towards a City Biography, 1850–2000*, edited by John Cookson and Graeme Dunstall (Christchurch: Canterbury University Press, 2000), 177.

36 Laurie Guy, 'Baptist Pacifists in New Zealand: Creating Division in the Fight for Peace', *Baptist Quarterly* 40 (2004): 488–99.

37 J. Ayson Clifford, *A Handful of Grain: The Centenary History of the Baptist Union of N.Z., Volume 2—1882–1914* (Wellington: NZ Baptist Historical Society, 1982), 114–15; John Tucker, 'The Ancient Word in the Modern World: The Preaching of J. J. North', in Troughton and Lange, 147–48.

38 See Martin Sutherland, *Conflict and Connection: Baptist Identity in New Zealand* (Auckland: Archer Press, 2011).

39 Allan K. Davidson, 'Peace and Pacifism: New Zealand Presbyterians 1901–45', in *Reforming the Reformation: Essays in Honour of Principal Peter Matheson*, edited by Ian Breward (Melbourne: Australian Scholarly Publishing, 2004), 181–96.

40 For example, Allan K. Davidson, *New Zealand Methodist Chaplains and Ministers at War*, Wesley Historical Society (NZ), Proceedings no. 101 (Auckland: Wesley Historical Society (NZ), 2016); Dickon John Milnes, 'The Church Militant: Dunedin Churches and Society During World War One' (PhD thesis, University of Otago, 2015); Ross M. Anderson, 'New Zealand Methodism and World War I: Crisis in a Liberal Church' (MA thesis, University of Canterbury, 1983).

41 Peter Lineham, 'The Rising Price of Rendering to Caesar: The Churches in World War One', in Loveridge, ed., *New Zealand Society at War*, 190–205; Allan Davidson, 'New Zealand Churches and Death in the First World War', in *New Zealand's Great War: New Zealand, the Allies and the First World War*, edited by John Crawford and Ian McGibbon (Auckland: Exisle Publishing, 2007), 447–66; Peter Lineham, 'First World War Religion', in Crawford and McGibbon, 467–92; Hugh Laracy, 'Priests, People and Patriotism: New Zealand Catholics and War, 1914–1918', *Australasian Catholic Record* 70, no. 1 (1993): 14–26.

42 Lawrence H. Barber, *The Very Rev. James Gibb: Patriot into Pacifist* (Dunedin: Presbyterian Historical Society of New Zealand, 1973).

43 J. E. Cookson, 'Pacifism and Conscientious Objection in New Zealand', in *Challenge to Mars: Essays on Pacifism from 1918 to 1945*, edited by Peter Brock and Thomas P. Socknat (Toronto: University of Toronto Press, 1999), 293.

44 Cookson, 'Pacifism and Conscientious Objection in New Zealand', 294.

45 J. E. Cookson, 'Illiberal New Zealand: The Formation of Government Policy on Conscientious Objection, 1940–1', NZJH 17, no. 2 (1983): 120–43; Cookson, 'Pacifism and Conscientious Objection in New Zealand', 306.

2. Samuel Marsden and the Origins of a New Zealand Christian Peace Tradition – Geoffrey Troughton

1 This perspective, highlighted in A. T. Yarwood, 'The Missionary Marsden: An Australian View', *New Zealand Journal of History* 4, no. 1 (1970): 20–33, has persisted. For criticism of the 'flogging parson' moniker that has often been applied to him, and signs of rehabilitation of Marsden's image in Australia, see Andrew Sharp, 'Samuel Marsden's Civility: The Transposition of Anglican Civil Authority to Australasia', in *Law and Politics in British Colonial Thought: Transpositions of Empire*, edited by Shaunnagh Dorsett and Ian Hunter (New York: Palgrave Macmillan, 2010), 133–136; Michael Gladwin, 'Flogging Parsons? Australian Anglican Clergymen, the Magistracy, and Convicts, 1788–1850', *Journal*

of Religious History 36, no. 3 (2012): 386–403, esp. 398. See also Michael Gladwin, *Anglican Clergy in Australia, 1788–1850: Building a British World* (Woodbridge: Royal Historical Society/ Boydell Press, 2015).

2 See J. B. Marsden, ed., *Memoirs of the Life and Labours of the Rev. Samuel Marsden* (London: Religious Tract Society, 1858); A. H. Reed, *Marsden of Maoriland: Pioneer and Peacemaker* (Dunedin: A. H. & A. W. Reed, 1938); and for a notably harsh assessment, see Richard Quinn, *Samuel Marsden: Altar Ego* (Wellington: Dunmore, 2008).

3 Josiah Pratt to Thomas Kendall, 18 March 1814, MS_0054_031, Hocken Library, Dunedin (HL).

4 Yarwood, 'The Missionary Marsden', 31. A. T. Yarwood, *Samuel Marsden: The Great Survivor* (Wellington: A. H. & A. W. Reed, 1977) was the standard, virtually unrivalled biography from its publication through to the recent appearance of Andrew Sharp's remarkable study, *The World, The Flesh and the Devil: The Life and Opinions of Samuel Marsden in England and the Antipodes, 1765–1838* (Auckland: Auckland University Press, 2016).

5 See Geoffrey Troughton, 'Missionaries, Historians and the Peace Tradition in New Zealand', in *Te Rongopai 1814, 'Takoto te pai!': Bicentenary Reflections on Christian Beginnings and Developments in Aotearoa New Zealand*, edited by Allan K. Davidson, Stuart Lange, Peter Lineham and Adrienne Puckey (Auckland: General Synod of the Anglican Church in Aotearoa New Zealand and Polynesia, 2014), 228–45.

6 Peter J. Lineham, 'Missions and missionaries—Māori converts', www.teara.govt.nz/en/missions-and-missionaries/5.

7 Keith Newman, 'Peacemaking in the Musket Wars—The Impact of the Gospel', presentation at the War, Remembrance and Reconciliation Study Day, Anglican Pacifist Fellowship, Auckland, 7 November 2015, www.converge.org.nz/pma/apf/apf15-kn.pdf.

8 William Yate, *An Account of New Zealand and of the Formation and Progress of the Church Missionary Society's Mission in the Northern Island* (London: Seeley and Burnside, 1835), 175.

9 Important recent additions to the literature on the CMS and early missions in New Zealand include: Tony Ballantyne, *Entanglements of Empire: Missionaries, Māori, and the Question of the Body* (Auckland: Auckland University Press, 2015); Angela Middleton, *Pēwhairangi: Bay of Islands Missions and Māori 1814 to 1845* (Dunedin: Otago University Press, 2014); Timothy Yates, *The Conversion of the Māori: Years of Religious Change, 1814–1842* (Grand Rapids: Eerdmans, 2013).

10 Michael Gladwin, 'Marsden's Generals: The Metropolitan Roots of Marsden's Mission', in *Launching Marsden's Mission: The*

Beginnings of the Church Missionary Society in New Zealand, Viewed from New South Wales, edited by Peter G. Bolt and David B. Pettett (Oxford: Latimer Trust, 2014), 13–29; Sharp, *The World, The Flesh and the Devil*, 23–30.

11 From around that time the Missionary Society was known as the London Missionary Society (LMS), and in 1818 this name was formalised.

12 Samuel Marsden to Avison Terry, 7 October 1814, in Marsden, *Memoirs*, 94.

13 Atholl Anderson, Judith Binney and Aroha Harris, *Tangata Whenua: A History* (Wellington: Bridget Williams Books, 2015), 168. Anne Salmond's reference to an 18-month stay apparently conflates the total time spent at Parramatta; see Anne Salmond, *Between Worlds: Early Exchanges Between Maori and Europeans, 1773–1815* (Auckland: Viking, 1997), 417.

14 Samuel Marsden to Josiah Pratt, 19 November 1811, MS_0498_240, HL.

15 *Proceedings of the Church Missionary Society*, 1810, 104–106.

16 Ballantyne, *Entanglements of Empire*, 126–34; Vincent O'Malley, *The Meeting Place: Māori and Pākehā Encounters, 1642–1840* (Auckland: Auckland University Press, 2012), 168–69. The word Rātapu (Sunday) brings together the terms rā (day) and tapu; the latter is often translated as holy or sacred, but is more fully and effectively rendered as something prohibited, restricted and under the protection of atua (supernatural beings, ancestors).

17 Henry Williams Journal, 1 July 1827, in *The Early Journals of Henry Williams, 1826–1840, Senior Missionary in New Zealand of the Church Missionary Society*, edited by L. M. Rogers (Christchurch: Pegasus Press, 1961), 60.

18 Malcolm Falloon, '"Openings of Providence": The Shaping of Marsden's Missionary Vision for New Zealand', in Bolt and Pettett, 136. See also Meredith Lake, 'Samuel Marsden, Work and the Limits of Evangelical Humanitarianism', *History Australia* 7, no. 3 (2010): 57.1–57.23.

19 Sermon 28, in David Pettett, 'Transcription of Samuel Marsden's Sermons' (2014), https://myrrh.library.moore.edu.au:443/handle/10248/5508.

20 These were sometimes formed from improvised materials such as sheets. See Henry Williams Journal, 23 March 1828 and 30 October 1831, *Early Journals*, 115, 199.

21 See John Rawson Elder, ed., *The Letters and Journals of Samuel Marsden, 1765–1838: Senior Chaplain in the Colony of New South Wales and Superintendent of the Mission of the Church Missionary Society in New Zealand* (Dunedin: Coulls, Somerville Wilkie, Ltd. and A. H. Reed for the University Council, 1932), 86–90;

John Liddiard Nicholas, *Narrative of a Voyage to New Zealand*, vol. 1 (London, 1817), 123–25. Marsden's account emphasises his initiative in brokering the reconciliation. Nicholas suggests that Ruatara made the initial approach.

22 Marsden considered that Te Pahi had been confused with Te Puhi, a chief of the Ngāti Uru hapū (sub-tribe) of Whangaroa, who had instigated the attack with his brother Te Ara (George) and Ngāti Pou people from the Whangaroa heads. See Angela Ballara, 'Te Pahi', www.teara.govt.nz/en/biographies/1t53/te-pahi; Peter G. Bolt, 'The *Boyd* Set-back to Marsden's Mission: The View from New South Wales', in Bolt and Pettett, 61–78.

23 Samuel Marsden to Ruatara, 9 March 1814, in Alison Jones and Kuni Jenkins, *Words Between Us—He Kōrero: First Māori-Pākehā Conversations on Paper* (Wellington: Huia, 2011), 57.

24 Elder, 89.

25 Hugh Carleton, *The Life of Henry Williams*, vol. 1 (Auckland: Wilsons and Horton, 1874), 26; A. H. Reed, *Heroes of Peace and War in Early New Zealand* (Wellington: A. H. & A. W. Reed, 1959), 66–67, which is otherwise largely obsessed with his heroic tramping.

26 Marsden, *Memoirs*, 96–97, citing Isaiah 52:7.

27 Thomas Kendall Journal, 31 March 1815, in *Missionary Register*, August 1817, 345.

28 Elder, 118–19.

29 Elder, 146, 260–61, 268–69, 274–77.

30 Anderson, Binney and Harris, 170.

31 Marsden, *Memoirs*, 141.

32 Elder, 146.

33 Jones and Jenkins, 131–42; Malcolm Prentis, 'A Thirst for Useful Knowledge: Samuel Marsden's Māori Seminary at Parramatta, 1815–1827', in Davidson, Lange, Lineham and Puckey, 139–52.

34 Samuel Marsden to Josiah Pratt, 7 February 1820, MS_0057_012, HL.

35 *Missionary Register*, November 1834, 511–12.

36 Martin Ceadel, *Semi-Detached Idealists: The British Peace Movement and International Relations, 1854–1945* (Oxford: Oxford University Press, 2000), 12–32; Peter Brock, *Pacifism in Europe to 1914* (Princeton: Princeton University Press, 1972), 367–406; Paul Laity, *The British Peace Movement 1870–1914* (Oxford: Oxford University Press, 2001), 13–36.

37 Gareth Atkins, 'Christian Heroes, Providence and Patriotism in Wartime Britain, 1793–1815', *The Historical Journal* 58, no. 2 (2015), 393–414.

38 Carleton, 12–13.

39 Henry Williams, 7 October 1819, in Carleton, 18.

40 Clive Barrett, *Subversive Peacemakers—War Resistance 1914–1918: An Anglican Perspective* (Cambridge: Lutterworth Press, 2014), 7–8.

41 For example, Rom. 5:1.

42 See Sermons 15, 45, in Pettett, 'Transcription of Samuel Marsden's Sermons'.

43 Sermons 34, 38, in Pettett, 'Transcription of Samuel Marsden's Sermons'.

44 Henry Williams, 14 March 1830, in Carleton, 83.

45 Cited in William Ellis, *History of the London Missionary Society*, vol. 1 (London: John Snow, 1844), 25–26.

46 *Proceedings of the Church Missionary Society*, 1810, 107.

47 Josiah Pratt to John King, Dinah Hall and William Hall, 29 August 1811, MS_0498_239, HL; Josiah Pratt to Thomas Kendall, 18 March 1814, MS_0054_031, HL, citing Romans 12:18.

48 William Hall Journal, 29 May 1816, 3–8 June 1816, William Hall Papers, 1816–1855, MS-1411, Auckland War Memorial Museum.

49 *Proceedings of the Church Missionary Society*, 1810, 107.

50 Elder, 123.

51 *Missionary Register*, July 1820, 307.

52 Sharp, *The World, The Flesh and the Devil*, 217.

53 Marsden to LMS Directors, 30 January 1801, CWM/LMS/03/02, Australia Incoming Correspondence, Box 1A 1798–1811, School of Oriental and Asian Studies (SOAS), University of London; cf. Journal of William Shelley and Rowland Hassell, Parramatta, New South Wales, 1800 (22–30 April 1800), CWM/LMS/03/05 Australia/Journals/Box 1, 1800–1842, SOAS.

54 John Butler accused him of some duplicity in this respect, claiming that Marsden delivered gunpowder to local chiefs as part of land purchases, and also traded in lethal weaponry such as bayonets: John Butler Journal, 23 August 1821, in *Earliest New Zealand: The Journals and Correspondence of the Rev. John Butler*, compiled by R. J. Barton (Masterton: Palamontain and Petherick, 1927), 165–66.

55 Judith Binney, *The Legacy of Guilt: A Life of Thomas Kendall* (Auckland: Oxford University Press, 1968), 56–57, and esp. 68, 86.

56 Elder, 259.

57 Sarah Dingle, 'Gospel Power for Civilization: The CMS Missionary Perspective on Maori Culture, 1830–1860' (PhD thesis, University of Adelaide, 2009), 131–32.

58 Elder, 162.

59 Elder, 89.

60 Elder, 260.

61 Elder, 347.

62 Elder, 387.

63 Elder, 295.

64 Elder, 113–14.
65 Elder, 386–88.
66 Anderson, Binney and Harris, 182.
67 Anderson, Binney and Harris, 182.
68 This began with advertising of the New South Wales government orders of 1813 and 1814 that threatened penalties for ships and crew who insulted or injured Pacific natives.
69 Marsden to Governor Ralph Darling, 2 August 1830, CO/209/1, New Zealand 1830–1835, National Archives, UK (Kew).
70 For an insightful recent exploration of the dynamics of missionary ideas and activity and imperial expansion in New Zealand, see Tony Ballantyne, 'Humanitarian Narratives: Knowledge and the Politics of Mission and Empire', *Social Sciences and Missions* 24 (2011): 233–64.
71 Elder, 58.
72 Isa 2:4 (King James Version): 'and they shall beat their swords into plowshares, and their spears into pruninghooks: nation shall not lift up sword against nation, neither shall they learn war any more'. Also Mic. 4:3.

3. Te Waharoa's War and Missionary Visions of Peace – Peter Lineham

1 Henry Williams Journal, 10 March 1833, in *The Early Journals of Henry Williams, 1826–1840, Senior Missionary in New Zealand of the Church Missionary Society*, edited by L. M. Rogers (Christchurch: Pegasus Press, 1961), 292.
2 Henry Williams Journal, 7 March 1833, 291.
3 Alfred Nesbit Brown Journal, 4 August 1835, in Journals, 1835–1850 (typescript), vol. 1, 1835–1838, 20, Alfred Nesbit Brown—Papers, Auckland War Memorial Museum Library.
4 Henry Williams Journal, 27 August 1831, 17 October–18 November 1831, 190, 194–204.
5 Henry Williams Journal, 23 March 1832, 237; the journey was from 26 March–11 May 1832.
6 Henry Williams Journal, 9 January 1833 and 7 February 1833, 273, 278.
7 Henry Williams Journal, 7 February 1833, 279–80.
8 Henry Williams Journal, 1 March 1833, 287–88; quote, 3 March 1833, 289.
9 Henry Williams Journal, 18 March 1833, 297.
10 Henry Williams Journal, 21 March 1833, 299.
11 Henry Williams Journal, 11 November 1833, 344–45.
12 Henry Pilley, *The New Zealand Missionary* (Cheltenham: William Wight, 1838), 34.

13 Henry Williams Journal, 17 November 1833, 349.

14 William Williams Journal, 26 December 1833 (Tauranga), 2 January 1834 (Waikato), in CMS microfilm papers C/N096 AJCP, Reel 234; John Wilson Journal, 28 December 1834, in John Alexander Wilson, *Missionary Life and Work in New Zealand* (London: SPCK, 1889), 6.

15 L. W. Melvin, 'Te Waharoa of the Ngatihaua', *Journal of the Polynesian Society* 71, no. 4 (1962): 361–78, especially 363.

16 Evelyn Stokes, 'Te Waharoa, Wiremu Tamihana Tarapipipi', www.teara.govt.nz/en/biographies/1t82/te-waharoa-wiremu-tamihana-tarapipipi.

17 Henry Williams Journal, 14–17 November 1833, 346–48.

18 John Alexander Wilson, *The Story of Te Waharoa: A Chapter in Early New Zealand History* (Auckland: Daily Southern Cross, 1866), vi; Evelyn Stokes, *Wiremu Tamihana: Rangatira* (Wellington: Huia, 2002), 15–16.

19 William Williams Journal, 2 September 1834, CMS microfilm C/N094 AJCP, Reel 234.

20 Brown Journal, 3 September 1834, in *Missionary Register*, November 1835, 526. See also William Williams Journal, 14 and 20 September 1834, in *Missionary Register*, November 1835, 525.

21 See *Missionary Register*, July 1835, 309.

22 Wilson Journal, 23 September 1834, 18.

23 Brown Journal, 29 January 1835, in *Missionary Register*, December 1835, 556.

24 Brown Māori Letters, cited and translated in Stokes, 29.

25 William Fairburn Journal, 14–20 September 1835, Fairburn Letters and Journals, 1828–1849 (typescript), 79–80, KIN108/.00/1, 11546, John Kinder Theological Library, Auckland; Brown Journal, 19 September 1835 and 12 October 1835, 29, 32.

26 Stokes, 30–31.

27 Melvin, 371.

28 For discussion see D. M. Stafford, *Te Arawa: A History of the Arawa People* (2nd ed., Auckland: Reed, 1982), 226–27.

29 *Missionary Register*, June 1838, 291–92.

30 Brown Journal, 13 and 22 January 1836, 43, 44.

31 Stokes, 33.

32 Brown Journal, 21, 29, 31 March 1836, 51–53.

33 Brown Journal, passim April–August 1836.

34 Samuel Knight Journal, in *Missionary Register*, June 1838, 295–96.

35 Knight Journal, 296.

36 Knight Journal, 296.

37 *Missionary Register*, June 1838, 296.

38 Wilson Journal, 25 August 1836, 48–49.

39 Brown Journal, 25 August 1836, 80.
40 Brown Journal, 19 October 1836, 89–90. See Malcolm Falloon, 'The Tārore Story: Sorting Fact from Fiction', in *Sacred Histories in Secular New Zealand*, edited by Geoffrey Troughton and Stuart Lange (Wellington: Victoria University Press, 2016), 40–53.
41 *Missionary Register*, June 1838, 297, citing Morgan and Knight.
42 Melvin, 375.
43 Knight and Pilley, 14 September 1836, in *Missionary Register*, June 1838, 297.
44 Morgan to CMS, 14 September 1836, in Jan Pilditch, ed., *The Letters and Journals of the Reverend John Morgan, Missionary at Otawhao*, vol. 1 (Glasgow: Grimsay Press, 2010), 37–39.
45 Stokes, 41.
46 Morgan, 47, 52.
47 Brown Journal, 22 September 1836, 85–86.
48 Stokes, 42.
49 Wilson Journal, 18 June 1836 and 18 August 1836, 38, 47.
50 Helen Garrett, *Te Manihera: The Life and Times of the Pioneer Missionary Robert Maunsell* (Auckland: Reed, 1991), 54.
51 Wilson Journal, 2, 10 April 1836, 31–32.
52 Brown Journal, 9 April 1836, 55–56.
53 Wilson Journal, 3 May 1836, 33.
54 Brown Journal, 3 January, 28 February, 6 April, 8 April, and 24 July 1836, 41, 49, 54–55, 76.
55 Brown Journal, 6 April 1836, 54–55.
56 Brown Journal, 7 January 1836, 41.
57 Brown Journal, 1 May 1836, 60.
58 Wilson (at Mokoia) to Anne Marie Wilson (Pūriri), 14 September 1836, *Missionary Life and Work*, 54.
59 Wilson Journal, 26 August 1836, 52.
60 Wilson Journal, 27 March 1836, 29.
61 Brown Journal, 15 June 1836, 70.
62 Wilson Journal, 26–27 March 1835, 28–29.
63 Brown Journal, 21 March 1836, 51.
64 Brown Journal, 25 May 1836, 65–66.
65 Brown Journal, 19 July 1836, 75.
66 Brown Journal, 15 August 1836, 78.
67 Melvin, 368.
68 Brown Journal, 17–22 September 1838, 152.
69 Fairburn Journal, 23 August 1835, 76.
70 Fairburn Journal, 17 September 1835, 79.
71 Brown Journal, 28 May 1836, 66.
72 Brown Journal, 6 September 1838, 150.
73 Brown Journal, 20 January 1837, 101.
74 *Missionary Register*, April 1839, 198.

75 Morgan to CMS, 9 January 1836, *Letters and Journals*, vol. 1, 34.
76 Brown Journal, 2 January 1837, 97.
77 Brown Journal, 30 May 1836, 67.
78 Brown Journal, 6 June and 30 July 1835, 10, 14.
79 Brown Journal, 6 December 1835, 38.
80 Brown Journal, 9 and 21 October 1838, 153, 157.
81 Brown Journal, 18–20 January 1837, 99–102.
82 Brown Journal, 17–22 September 1838, 152.
83 Brown Journal, 20 October 1836, 90.
84 Brown Journal, 3 September 1838, 150.
85 Brown Journal, 6 September 1838, in *Missionary Register*, January 1840, 57.
86 Brown Journal, 16 August 1839, in Journals (typescript), vol. 2, 1839–1843, 16. Brown Journal, 24–29 July 1843, in *Missionary Register*, November 1844, 489; Brown Journal, 17 January 1849, in *Missionary Register*, July 1851, 322.
87 Brown Journal, 11 August 1836, 77; Morgan, *Letters and Journals*, vol. 1, 43.
88 William Williams, 24 March 1839, cited in *Missionary Register*, August 1840, 382–83.
89 See Lyndsay Head, 'Wiremu Tamihana and the *Mana* of Christianity', in *Christianity, Modernity and Culture: New Perspectives on New Zealand History*, edited by John Stenhouse and G. A. Wood (Adelaide, ATF Press: 2005), 58–86.

4. Te Mānihera, Kereopa and Christian Peacemaking among Māori – Stuart Lange

1 Richard Taylor Journal, 1833–1873, qMS, WTU, Vol. 3–7, Auckland War Memorial Library; also Richard Taylor, *Te Ika a Maui, or New Zealand and its Inhabitants* (London: Wertheim and Macintosh, 1855).
2 John Houston, *Maori Life in Old Taranaki* (Wellington: Reed, 1965); Tony Sole, *Ngāti Ruanui: A History* (Wellington: Huia, 2005); John Te H. Grace, *Tuwharetoa: A History of the Maori People of the Taupo District* (Wellington: A. H. and A. W. Reed, 1959).
3 Sole, 145.
4 Sole, 145.
5 Taylor, *Te Ika*, 359; Grace, 365.
6 Houston, 83; Sole, 147.
7 Sole, 150.
8 Taylor Journal, 8 January 1845.
9 Taylor Journal, 18–24 January 1845.
10 Grace, 373, 384.
11 Taylor Journal, 16 June, 28 June, 7 July, 8 July 1846.

12 Wiremu Te Tauri was a rangatira of Ngāti Te Rangiita, Ngāti Tūwharetoa and Te Āti Haunui-a-Pāpārangi. He had become a Christian in Taupō, but settled in Whanganui after marrying. See 'Wiremu Eruera Te Tauri', www.nzhistory.govt.nz/politics/treaty/signatory/8-121.
13 Taylor Journal, 14 February 1847, 8–9 March 1847.
14 Taylor Journal, 28–29 June 1846.
15 Grace, 375.
16 Taylor Journal, 5–6 July 1846. Taylor gave the teacher at Rotoaira 'a lecture on his idleness'.
17 Alfred Nesbit Brown Journal, 27 November 1847.
18 Taylor, *Te Ika,* 361, 366; Grace, 377.
19 Taylor Journal, 24 December 1846.
20 Taylor Journal, 25 December 1846.
21 Taylor Journal, 24–25 December 1846, 6 January 1847; Taylor, *Te Ika*, 357.
22 Taylor, *Te Ika*, 358. Taylor usually recorded what people said in indirect rather than direct speech. He did not usually use 'Te' before the names of chiefs.
23 Luke 6:27.
24 Ian Church, 'Poutama, Te Manihera', www.teara.govt.nz/en/biographies/1p27/poutama-te-manihera.
25 Taylor, *Te Ika,* 357–8; Taylor Journal, 22 March 1847.
26 Taylor Journal, 28 December 1846.
27 Taylor, *Te Ika*, 358. Here tapu means to be set apart, under sacred restriction and protection.
28 Taylor, *Te Ika*, 358. Grace, 376, followed by Sole, 175, confused Porou-ta-whao in the Manawatū with Poro-ō-tarao in the King Country.
29 Taylor, *Te Ika*, 358.
30 Taylor Journal, 20 March 1849.
31 Taylor, *Te Ika*, 359.
32 Taylor, *Te Ika*, 366.
33 Taylor, *Te Ika*, 360.
34 Taylor, *Te Ika*, 360. For this part of the narrative, *Te Ika* contains more accurate information than the first reports noted in Taylor's Journal (e.g., 22 March 1847) which were entered before he arrived and was able to check the facts with local people.
35 Taylor, *Te Ika*, 360.
36 Taylor Journal, 23 March 1847; Grace, 377; one of Taylor's teachers later dubbed her 'Herodias, who asked for Manihera's life' (Taylor Journal, 6 March 1849).
37 Taylor, *Te Ika*, 360–61; Williams, 324.
38 Houston, 90, as recited by a kaumātua in 1955; Sole, 175–77; Grace, 379.
39 Taylor, *Te Ika*, 361.

40 Taylor, *Te Ika*, 361.
41 Taylor Journal, 23 March 1847.
42 Taylor, *Te Ika*, 361.
43 Taylor Journal, 1 April 1847; Taylor, *Te Ika*, 362; Sole, 177.
44 Taylor, *Te Ika*, 362, 476 (Appendix I).
45 Taylor, *Te Ika*, 362–63.
46 For example, Taylor Journal, 20 April 1847.
47 Taylor, *Te Ika*, 363.
48 Taylor Journal, 21 April 1847.
49 Taylor, *Te Ika*, 364–65.
50 Taylor Journal, 22 April 1847; Taylor, *Te Ika*, 364–65.
51 Taylor, *Te Ika*, 365.
52 Grace, 366.
53 Grace, 380.
54 Taylor, *Te Ika*, 366.
55 Taylor, *Te Ika*, 366.
56 Taylor, *Te Ika*, 366–67.
57 Taylor Journal, 24 April 1847.
58 Taylor Journal, 30 April 1847.
59 Taylor, *Te Ika*, 368.
60 Taylor Journal, 24 February 1849; Sole, 177.
61 Taylor, *Te Ika*, 368.
62 Sole, 177; Taylor Journal, 28 February 1849.
63 Taylor Journal, 12 March 1849.
64 Taylor Journal, 12 March 1849.
65 Taylor, *Te Ika*, 369.
66 Taylor Journal, 12 March 1849.
67 Taylor, *Te Ika*, 369.
68 Taylor Journal, 12 March 1849.
69 Taylor Journal, 13 March 1849.
70 Taylor Journal, 12, 13 March 1849.
71 Taylor Journal, 13 March 1849.
72 Taylor, *Te Ika*, 369–70.
73 Taylor Journal, 11 March 1849.
74 Taylor, *Te Ika*, 368–69.
75 Brown Journal, 13 November 1849.
76 S. J. Brittan, G. F., C. W. and A. V. Grace, eds., *A Pioneer Missionary among the Maoris: Being Letters and Journals of Thomas Samuel Grace* (Palmerston North: G. H. Bennett & Co.: n.d.), 56, 59.
77 John Richardson, *The First Christian Martyr of the New Zealand Church* (Exeter: W. Roberts, 1854), 51.
78 Archdeacon Macmurray, 'New Zealand Martyrs', *New Zealand Herald*, 18 March 1916.
79 Watson Rosevear, *Waiapu: The Story of a Diocese* (Hamilton: Paul's Book Arcade, 1960), 33.

80 Ken Booth, ed., 'March 13 Kereopa and Te Manihera of Taranaki: Martyrs at Turangi', *For All the Saints: A Resource for the Commemorations of the Calendar* ([Hastings]: The Anglican Church in Aotearoa New Zealand and Polynesia, [1996]), 85–90.

81 The remains of the two men were reinterred there in 1967, when the tailrace of the Tokaanu power station was routed through the location of Te Waiariki including its pā and urupā (cemetery). See New Zealand Waitangi Tribunal, *Turangi Township Report 1995 (Wai 84)* (Wellington: Brooker's, 1995), 149–52.

82 H. W. Monaghan, *From Age to Age: The Story of Church of England in the Diocese of Wellington, 1858–1958* (Wellington: Diocese of Wellington, 1957), 21.

83 James Cowan, 'Manihera's Farewell', in *Hero Stories of New Zealand* (Wellington: Harry H. Tombs, 1935).

84 A. S. Thomson, *The Story of New Zealand Past and Present: Savage and Civilized* (London: Murray, 1859), 319, 322.

85 William Williams, *Christianity among the New Zealanders* (London: Seeley, Jackson, and Halliday, 1867), 322–28; S. Tucker, *Southern Cross and Southern Crown* (London: James Nisbet, 1859), 261–62.

86 Houston; Grace; Sole; Keith Newman, *Bible and Treaty: Missionaries among the Māori—A New Perspective* (Auckland: Penguin, 2010), 213–16, though some details are not quite correct (215).

87 Allan K. Davidson, *Christianity in Aotearoa: A History of Church and Society in New Zealand* (3rd ed., Wellington: Education for Ministry, 2004), 18; note also the segment in the DVD documentary, Stuart Lange, *Te Rongopai. 200 years of the Gospel in Aotearoa, 1814–2014* (Auckland: Glass Eye Productions, 2014).

88 See Geoffrey Troughton, 'Missionaries, Historians and the Peace Tradition in New Zealand', in *Te Rongopai 1814 Takoto te pai! Bicentenary Reflections on Christian Beginnings and Developments in Aotearoa New Zealand*, edited by Allan Davidson, Stuart Lange, Peter Lineham and Adrienne Puckey (Auckland: General Synod Office of the Anglican Church in Aotearoa New Zealand and Polynesia, 2014).

89 Taylor Journal, 6 March 1849.

5. A Peaceable Puritan? Rutherford Waddell and God's Own Country – John Stenhouse

1 *New Zealand Truth*, 2 June 1927.

2 Historian Michael Snape criticises histories that rely too uncritically on anti-war literature in 'Church of England Army Chaplains in the First World War: Goodbye to "Goodbye to All That"', *Journal of Ecclesiastical History* 62, no. 2 (2011): 318–45.

3 Paul Baker, *King and Country Call: New Zealanders, Conscription and the Great War* (Auckland: Auckland University Press, 1988); Allan Davidson, 'New Zealand Churches and Death in the First World War', in *New Zealand's Great War: New Zealand, the Allies and the First World War*, edited by John Crawford and Ian McGibbon (Auckland: Exisle Publishing, 2007), 447–66; Peter Lineham, 'First World War Religion', in Crawford and McGibbon, *New Zealand's Great War*, 467–92.

4 Ian Breward, 'Rutherford Waddell', www.teara.govt.nz/en/biographies/2w1/waddell-rutherford.

5 The following biographical sketch draws on John Collie, *Rutherford Waddell: Memoir and Addresses* (Dunedin: A. H. Reed, 1932) and Rutherford Waddell, *My Pathway to Christ: A Confession of Faith* (Dunedin: New Zealand Bible, Tract and Book Society, 1920).

6 On Kathleen, and Waddell's relationships with women, see John Stenhouse, 'The Passionate Pastor: The Cultural Performances of the Reverend Rutherford Waddell', *Journal of New Zealand Studies* NS 15 (2013): 23–35.

7 On Waddell's role in anti-sweating see Stenhouse, 'The Passionate Pastor', 25–28.

8 Waddell's anti-sweating committee included Rachel Reynolds and Winifred Bathgate from his own St Andrew's congregation and William Downie Stewart of Knox Church.

9 Leading figures in this group included Stewart, Reynolds, George Fenwick, John Jago, and Henry Shacklock.

10 *Christian Outlook* (Outlook), 10 July 1897, 277.

11 *Otago Daily Times* (ODT), 8 November 1888.

12 *New Zealand Tablet* (Tablet), 23 January 1880, 17.

13 Tablet, 9 November 1888, 1.

14 Outlook, 27 October 1894, 438.

15 Outlook, 24 February 1894, 13.

16 Stenhouse, 'The Passionate Pastor', 28–29.

17 Outlook, 25 September 1897, 409.

18 Outlook, 24 November 1894, 492.

19 Sean Brosnahan, 'Rutherford Waddell: An Ulster Radical in Otago's Scottish Kirk', in *Ulster-New Zealand Migration and Cultural Transfers*, edited by Brad Patterson (Dublin: Four Courts Press, 2006), 131–44.

20 For Waddell's views on prohibition and suffrage, see ODT, 1 February 1889; 11 July 1891.

21 Supporters included William Hutchison, John Jago, Robert Stout, Harriet Morison, Rachel Reynolds, Winifred Bathgate and Helen Nichol. The Dunedin Women's Christian Temperance Union supported prohibition, suffrage, Sabbath observance and Bible-in-Schools.

22 Tablet, 8 September 1893, 17, 27–28; 15 September 1893, 17.
23 Kenneth W. Turner, 'Henry Smith Fish and the Opposition to the Female Franchise in Dunedin, 1890–93' (BA Hons long essay, University of Otago, 1985).
24 *Otago Workman*, 6 July 1892.
25 The following account, and quotations, draw from the report in ODT, 6 July 1892.
26 Outlook, 14 August 1897, 337.
27 Outlook, 11 February 1899, 3–4.
28 John Crawford and Ian McGibbon, eds., *One Flag, One Queen, One Tongue: New Zealand, the British Empire and the South African War 1899–1902* (Auckland: Auckland University Press, 2003).
29 *New Zealand Parliamentary Debates*, 28 September 1899, 110, 76.
30 See further, Ian McGibbon, 'The Origins of New Zealand's South African War Contribution', in Crawford and McGibbon, *One Flag*, 1–11.
31 *Evening Star* (ES), 23 October 1899.
32 ES, 23 October 1899.
33 ODT, 24 October 1899.
34 Outlook, 21 October 1899, 3–4.
35 Outlook, 28 October 1899, 3–4.
36 See further, John Coffey, *Politics, Religion and the British Revolutions: The Mind of Samuel Rutherford* (Cambridge: Cambridge University Press, 1997).
37 Outlook, 28 October 1899, 4.
38 Outlook, 28 October 1899, 4.
39 This account, and all quotations in this paragraph, draw from the report in ES, 4 November 1899.
40 John Stenhouse, 'The Rev. Dr James Copland and the Mind of New Zealand "Fundamentalism"', *Journal of Religious History* 17, no. 4 (1993): 475–97.
41 Outlook, 4 November 1899, 4–5.
42 For Gibb's talk on Christian socialism to the Fabian Society, see *Otago Witness*, 19 October 1899.
43 Outlook, 28 December 1901, 4.
44 Outlook, 11 January 1902, 3–5.
45 Outlook, 25 January 1902, 33.
46 ES, 15 January 1902.
47 Outlook, 25 January 1902, 2.
48 ES, 20 April 1914.
49 ES, 5 December 1914.
50 Lineham, 'First World War Religion', 471–2.
51 ODT, 1 June 1916.
52 ODT, 17 June 1916.
53 *Minutes of Methodist Annual Conference*, 1917, 117.

54 ODT, 19 June 1916.
55 ODT, 20 June 1916.
56 ODT, 21 June 1916.
57 ODT, 21 June 1916.
58 ES, 22 June 1916.
59 Davidson, 'New Zealand Churches and Death'; Lineham, 'First World War Religion'.
60 See further, H. Larry Ingle, *First Among Friends: George Fox and the Creation of Quakerism* (New York: Oxford University Press, 1994).
61 ODT, 15 February 1889. See further, Stenhouse, 'The Passionate Pastor', 22–35.
62 ODT, 27 June 1916; for a letter from 'Hoani' criticising Ramsay as a tiresome controversialist see ODT, 30 December 1892.
63 ODT, 27 June 1916.
64 ES, 4 April 1918.
65 Rutherford Waddell, *Killed in Action* (Dunedin: New Zealand Bible, Tract and Book Society, 1919), foreword.
66 Waddell, *Killed in Action*, 8–10.
67 Waddell, *Killed in Action*, 14–16.
68 Lineham, 'First World War Religion'.
69 Collie, *Rutherford Waddell*, 7.
70 Tony Ballantyne, *Webs of Empire: Locating New Zealand's Colonial Past* (Wellington: Bridget Williams Books, 2012), 290.

6. Comrades in Arms: Germany, the *War Cry* and the Salvation Army during the Great War – Harold Hill

1 A short earlier version of this research was published in *War Cry*, 18 April 2015, 5–7.
2 *War Cry*, 16 January 1915, 3.
3 See Andrew Francis, *To Be Truly British, We Must Be Anti-German: New Zealand, Enemy Aliens and the Great War Experience 1914–1919* (Bern: Peter Lang, 2012); also Steven Loveridge, 'A German is *Always* a German?: Representations of Enemies, Germans and Race in New Zealand c.1890–1918', *New Zealand Journal of History* 48, no. 1 (2014): 51–77.
4 Val Burr, '*German*-ating the Seeds of Anger: The Great War's impact on Germans in Manawatu and Rangitikei, New Zealand' (BA Hons research exercise, Massey University, 1996).
5 *Dominion*, 22 September 1915.
6 *War Cry*, 28 November 1914, 7.
7 *War Cry*, 12 December 1914, 5.
8 *War Cry*, 2 January 1915, 8.
9 *War Cry*, 6 February 1915, 7.

10 *War Cry*, 28 August 1915, 2.
11 *War Cry*, 7 November 1914, 2.
12 *War Cry*, 26 December 1914, 5.
13 *Otago Daily Times*, 22 May 1915.
14 *War Cry*, 20 February 1915, 7.
15 *War Cry*, 3 June 1916, 3.
16 *Evening Post* (EP), 16 May 1930.
17 *War Cry*, 2 January 1915, 3.
18 *Wanganui Chronicle*, 11 January 1915; *Dominion*, 15 January 1915; *New Zealand Truth*, 3 July 1915.
19 *War Cry*, 2 December 1916, 1.
20 *War Cry*, 6 April 1918, 7.
21 Albert Shaw Clifton, 'The Salvation Army's Attitudes and Actions in War Time, 1889–1945' (PhD thesis, King's College London, 1989), 258–61; also Shaw Clifton, *Crown of Glory, Crown of Thorns: The Salvation Army in Wartime* (London: Salvation Army, 2015).
22 Rebecca Carter-Chand cites these from Bundesarchiv, Berlin-Lichterfelde, R5101 Reichministerium für die kirchlichen Angelegen/Verschiedene einzelne Religionsgemeinschaften, in 'The Politics of Being Apolitical: The Salvation Army and the Nazi Revolution', *Word and Deed* 18, no. 2 (May 2016): 3–30.
23 Frederick Coutts, *The Better Fight: The History of The Salvation Army, Vol. VI, 1914–1946* (London: Hodder and Stoughton, 1973), 22.
24 Rebecca Carter-Chand, 'Doing Good in Bad Times: The Salvation Army in Germany 1886–1946' (PhD thesis, University of Toronto, 2016), 7.
25 *The Salvation Soldier's Song Book* (New York: Salvation Army 1880), #248, cited in Philip Davisson, 'Sweeping Through the Land: Postmillennialism and the Early Salvation Army', *Word and Deed* 5, no.2 (May 2003): 42.
26 Harold Begbie, *Life of William Booth, Founder of the Salvation Army*, vol. 2 (London: Macmillan, 1920), 237–38.
27 *Officer*, January 1893, 4.
28 Reprinted in *War Cry*, 19 September 1914, 4.
29 *War Cry*, 5 August 1916, 4.
30 *War Cry*, 26 September 1914, 5.
31 *War Cry*, 7 November 1914, 2.
32 Richard Collier, *The General Next to God* (London: Collins, 1965), 250; Catherine Bramwell Booth, *Bramwell Booth* (London: Rich & Cowan, 1933), 353.
33 *War Cry* (UK), 24 October 1914, 6, quoted in Clifton, 'The Salvation Army', 124.
34 *Maoriland Worker*, 9 January 1918, 5.

35 *War Cry*, 1 August 1915, 5.

36 Military personnel file: Hill, William Charles Frederick—WW1 79921—Army, R18048109, Archives New Zealand (ANZ).

37 Sheward's farewell is recorded in the St Albans Corps History Book, held at the Salvation Army Heritage Centre and Archives—Te Rua Mahara o Te Ope Whakaora, Trentham. He is also mentioned in *War Cry*, 24 June 1916, 8; 16 September 1916, 7; 2 November 1918, 3.

38 Military personnel file: Sheward, William—WW1 7/2149—Army, R7816716, ANZ.

39 *NZ Tablet*, 20 September 1917, 26, cited in Laurie Guy, *Shaping Godzone: Public Issues and Church Voices in New Zealand, 1840–2000* (Wellington: Victoria University Press, 2011), 253.

40 *Marlborough Express*, 18 October 1916.

41 EP, 13 September 1917.

42 *Poverty Bay Herald*, 15 September 1917; *Thames Star*, 25 September 1917.

43 Peter Clayworth, 'Brass and Pipe Bands—Military Bands, 1900 Onwards', www.teara.govt.nz/en/brass-and-pipe-bands/page-2.

44 *War Cry*, 4 March 1915, 3; *Press*, 27 October 1916; EP, 2 March 1917; Cyril Bradwell, *Fight the Good Fight: The Story of the Salvation Army in New Zealand 1883–1983* (Wellington: Reed, 1982), 103.

45 Clifton, 'The Salvation Army', 254–76. The varying extent of support noted conceivably reflected cultural values and the degree of independence from the British centre which the different territories felt able to assert.

46 *Press*, 4 August 1915.

47 *Maoriland Worker*, 19 May 1915, 4.

48 Published in sheet music format as Henry C. Goffin, *The Sailor* (Wellington: H. Warren Kelly, 1916); *Feilding Star*, 29 March 1916; *Free Lance*, 24 March 1916.

49 Quoted in Clifton, 'The Salvation Army', 274.

50 *War Cry*, 6 September 1919, 3.

51 The New Zealand Salvation Army Archive holds only two soldiers' war-time journals; neither reflects on this question.

52 In protest at Bramwell Booth's refusal to allow his brother Herbert to sit on the platform at a meeting when their visits to Auckland happened to coincide in 1920, Salvationist organisers reserved a vacant chair where Herbert might have been seated. Ford C. Ottman, *Herbert Booth: A Biography* (New York: Doubleday, Doran & Co., 1928), 366.

53 Ottman, 340.

54 Herbert Booth, *The Saint and the Sword* (New York: Doran & Co., 1923).

55 Allan K. Davidson, *Christianity in Aotearoa: A History of Church and Society in New Zealand* (3rd ed., Auckland: Education for Ministry, 1990), 100, citing *The Outlook*, 2 May 1927, 7.
56 EP, 6 June 1927. The Manifesto is reprinted in Allan K. Davidson and Peter J. Lineham, *Transplanted Christianity: Documents Illustrating Aspects of New Zealand Church History* (5th ed., Auckland: Kereru, 2015), section 5.45.
57 EP, 26 April 1932.
58 EP, 26 April 1932.
59 David Grant, *Out in the Cold: Pacifists and Conscientious Objectors in New Zealand during World War II* (Auckland: Reed Methuen Ltd, 1986), 88.

7. Under the Surface: Archibald Baxter's Christian Faith – David Tombs

1 For a concise biography see David Grant, 'Baxter, Archibald McColl Learmond', www.teara.govt.nz/en/biographies/3b19/baxter-archibald-mccoll-learmond.
2 Archibald Baxter, *We Will Not Cease* (Auckland: Cape Catley, 2012), 19. Unless indicated otherwise, all page references hereafter are to the 2012 edition, which includes a Foreword by Michael King, first published in 2003.
3 See David Grant with paintings by Bob Kerr, *Field Punishment No. 1: Archibald Baxter, Mark Briggs and New Zealand's Anti-militarist Tradition* (Wellington: Steele Roberts, 2008), especially 41–64.
4 *Field Punishment No. 1*, directed by Peter Burger (Lippy Pictures, 2014).
5 Grant, 'Baxter', 40; Grant, *Field Punishment*, 38.
6 'Imprisoned Conscientious Objectors, 1916–1920', www.nzhistory.net.nz/war/the-military-objectors-list.
7 Michael King, *Interview with Millicent Baxter*, transcribed by Christine Catley (October 1978), MS-3099/014, Hocken Library, Dunedin, 15, 31.
8 Frank McKay, *The Life of James K. Baxter* (Auckland: Oxford University Press, 1990), 7.
9 McKay, 11.
10 Penny Griffith, *Out of the Shadows: The Life of Millicent Baxter* (Wellington: PenPublishing, 2015), 81.
11 Cited in Griffith, 81.
12 James K. Baxter, *James K. Baxter: Complete Prose, Vol. 2, Return to Dunedin, 1966–1968*, edited by John Weir (Wellington: Victoria University Press, 2015), 148; the entire four-volume corpus is available online as *The James K. Baxter Complete Prose Collection*, www.nzetc.victoria.ac.nz/tm/scholarly/tei-corpus-baxter.html.

13 McKay, 1–6.
14 Griffith, 78.
15 Baxter, 19. Baxter does not name the speaker, but Michael King suggests that it was probably A. R. Barclay; see Michael King, 'Foreword', in Baxter, 7; also Griffith, 79.
16 Millicent Baxter also notes her husband's 'pacifism and socialism'; Millicent Baxter, *The Memoirs of Millicent Baxter* (Whatamongo Bay: Cape Catley, 1981), 53.
17 Paul Baker, *King and Country Call: New Zealanders, Conscription and the Great War* (Auckland: Auckland University Press, 1988), 59.
18 Baxter, 22–23; H. E. Holland, *Armageddon or Calvary: The Conscientious Objectors of New Zealand and 'The Process of Their Conversion'* (Wellington: Maoriland Worker, 1919), 76.
19 Baxter, 33.
20 Baxter, 76–91.
21 Holland, 79; Baxter, 115.
22 Baxter, 215. Baxter refers to Mitchell as 'Colonel Simpson' in *We Will Not Cease*, owing to the publisher's legal concerns about naming the important individuals in his story other than the fourteen objectors. See Grant, *Field Punishment*, 62.
23 Baxter, 119–21. The place Baxter referred to as Oudredoum is now known as Ouderdom.
24 Baxter, 131–33.
25 Baxter, 150.
26 On the fates of the others, see 'Afterword', in Baxter, 214–15.
27 The book was subsequently republished in Christchurch by Caxton Press, in 1968, and then in Auckland by Cape Catley, in 1980, 1983, 2003 and 2012. It was also published by Penguin New Zealand in 1987.
28 Griffith, 182.
29 King, *Interview*, 31.
30 Other writings by Baxter include a 100-line poem, 'The Vision', influenced by the work of Robert Burns, and an unpublished novel on a Scottish farming family in Otago during the Gold Rush: MS 0975/195 and MS 1136/24, Hocken Library, Dunedin. Neither work deals directly with Baxter's war experiences. See also Liam McIlvanney, 'The Visionary Voyages of Robert Burns', in *Jacobitism, Enlightenment and Empire, 1680–1820*, edited by Allan I. Macinnes and Douglas J. Hamilton (London: Pickering & Chatto, 2014), 173–92.
31 Archibald Baxter Letter to Parents, 5 March 1918, J. T. Paul Papers, MS-0982/752, reprinted in Gavin McLean and Ian McGibbon, eds., *The Penguin Book of New Zealanders at War* (Auckland: Penguin Books, 2009), 90–91.
32 Millicent Baxter, 51, 57.

33 McLean and McGibbon, 91.
34 McLean and McGibbon, 91.
35 McLean and McGibbon, 91.
36 Baxter, 134–35.
37 Holland, 75.
38 Holland, 75–76.
39 Holland, 76.
40 Holland, 76.
41 Holland, 76.
42 Holland, 76.
43 Holland, 87.
44 'New Zealand Expeditionary Force: Attestation for General Service', Baxter, Archibald McColl Larmond—WW1 47814—Army, R22273524, Image 37, Archives New Zealand (ANZ).
45 On the book as a work of literature, see Rod Edmond, '"It's your submission we want, Baxter!" Archibald Baxter's *We Will Not Cease: The Autobiography of a Conscientious Objector*', *Journal of New Zealand Literature* 33, no. 2 (2015): 142–59.
46 King, 'Foreword', 8.
47 'Thou shalt not kill' (Matt. 5:21); 'Turn the other cheek' (Matt. 5:39); 'Do good to them that hate you' (Matt. 5:44; Luke 6:28).
48 Baxter, 21–22.
49 Baxter, 21.
50 Baxter, 19.
51 David S. Keen, 'Feeding the Lambs: The Influence of Sunday Schools in the Socialization of Children in Otago and Southland, 1848–1901' (PhD thesis, University of Otago, 1999).
52 See especially Geoffrey Troughton, 'Jesus and the Ideal of the Manly Man in New Zealand after World War One', *Journal of Religious History* 30, no. 1 (2006): 45–60; John Stenhouse, 'God, the Devil, and Gender', in *Sites of Gender: Change and Continuity in Southern Dunedin, 1890–1939*, edited by Barbara Brookes, Annabel Cooper and Robin Law (Auckland: Auckland University Press, 1999), 313–47.
53 Baxter, 19.
54 See Isa. 40:3; Matt. 3:3; Mark 1:3; Luke 3:4; John 1:23.
55 Baxter, 31.
56 Baxter, 21.
57 Baxter, 19.
58 In a similar way, his elder son, Terence, was named after the Irish playwright, politician and nationalist, Terence MacSwiney, who died on hunger strike in Brixton prison in 1920.
59 Baxter, 102–3.
60 Baxter, 104.
61 Baxter, 119.

62 Baxter, 103.
63 Field punishment took the form of a prolonged stress position that grew increasingly painful and damaging as the hours passed. On Field Punishment as a form of torture, see David Tombs, 'The Politics of Torture: The Findings of the US Senate Intelligence Committee Report on Torture', Archibald Baxter Memorial Trust, Annual Peace Lecture, 2015, University of Otago, 21 September 2015, www.archibaldbaxtertrust.com/2015-prof-david-tombs/.
64 Baxter, 123.
65 Dickon John Milnes, 'The Church Militant: Dunedin Churches and Society During World War One' (PhD thesis, University of Otago, 2015), 110–18.
66 Troughton, 50.
67 Baxter, 123.
68 *Illustrated Sunday Herald*, 29 October 1916. See Clive Emsley, 'Why Crucify Tommy?' *History Today* 62, no. 11 (November 2012): 27–33.
69 See Baxter, 135.
70 Holland, 86.
71 Holland, 86.
72 King, *Interview*, 15 (original ellipses). Later in the interview, Millicent adds: '. . . he was extremely . . . he was devoutly religious—he really was', although she might be speaking here of Archibald's later years; see *Interview*, 30.
73 King, *Interview*, 16.
74 Baxter, 44.
75 Baxter, 44–45.
76 King, *Interview*, 15.
77 King, *Interview*, 16.
78 King, *Interview*, 16.
79 King, *Interview*, 16.
80 King, *Interview*, 31.
81 Griffith, 180.
82 'History Sheet', Archibald Baxter files, Image 1, ANZ.
83 McKay, 5–6.
84 McKay, 5–6.
85 H. H. Rowdon, 'The Early Brethren and Baptism', *Vox Evangelica* 11 (1979): 55–64.
86 'Men on whose behalf the Board is unable to make any recommendation: Schedule No. 5', 1, in 'The Report of the Religious Advisory Board', 1919, AD1 734 10/407/15, ANZ; see: www.nzhistory.net.nz/files/documents/cos/religious-advisory-board.pdf.
87 'Men whose cases were investigated by the Religious Objectors Advisory Board', 9, 14, in 'The Report of the Religious Advisory Board'. On 22 May 1918, Hugh was discharged from prison on

remission; his case came before the Board in Dunedin on 18 February 1919. Donald was sentenced to an additional two years, and released on 21 November 1919; his case came before the Advisory Board on 5 March 1919 whilst he was still in Waikeria Prison.

88 Archibald Baxter files, Image 33, ANZ.

89 Grace Davie, *Religion in Britain Since 1945: Believing Without Belonging* (Oxford: Blackwell, 1994).

90 Baxter, 'The Vision'; James K. Baxter, *Complete Prose*, 192. See also James K. Baxter's poem, 'To My Father' (1954), in which the poet honours his father by composing in what John Dennison identifies as '"Burn's Metre", the Standard Habbie stanza'. John Dennison, '"Old Masters and Violent Moderns": Baxter, Burns, and T. S. Eliot', *Journal of New Zealand Literature* 30 (2012): 101–2; James K. Baxter, 'To My Father', in *Selected Poems of James K Baxter*, edited by Paul Millar (Manchester: Carcanet, 2010), 54–56.

91 Baker, 58.

92 Holland, 80.

93 Baxter, 77; also James K. Baxter, *Complete Prose*, 192, on Burns as an ancestral Scots figure.

8. Compulsion or Conscience: Alun Richards and Opposition to Compulsory Military Training, 1927–1930 – Allan K. Davidson

1 'My Conscience', *Auckland Star* (AS), 16 June 1927.

2 For Presbyterian attitudes towards war see Allan K. Davidson, 'Peace and Pacifism: New Zealand Presbyterians 1901–1945', in *Reforming the Reformation: Essays in Honour of Principal Peter Matheson*, edited by Ian Breward (Melbourne: Australian Scholarly Publishing, 2004), 181–96.

3 Defence Act 1909, Part VI. In 1912 the age of eligibility was raised to fourteen.

4 Defence Act 1909, Part IV.

5 Defence Amendment Act 1912, s.65.2, 3.

6 R. L. Weitzel, 'Pacifists and Anti-militarists in New Zealand, 1909–1914', *New Zealand Journal of History* 7, no. 2 (1973): 128–47.

7 Military Service Act 1916, s.18.1.e.

8 *New Zealand Methodist Times*, 17 March 1917, 6; *New Zealand Baptist*, January 1917, 2.

9 *Church Gazette*, Supplement, December 1916, VI.

10 *Proceedings of the General Assembly of the Presbyterian Church of New Zealand* (PGA), 1917, 48.

11 *Evening Post* (EP), 18 December 1916; *Grey River Argus*, 22 February 1917; *Press*, 28 February 1917.

12 *Taranaki Daily News*, 16 January 1918.

13 David Grant, 'Conscientious Objectors', in *The Oxford Companion to New Zealand Military History*, edited by Ian McGibbon (Auckland: Oxford University Press, 2000), 116.
14 Joint Defence Committee on a Proposed Scheme of Organization and Training of the New Zealand Military Forces, *Appendices to the Journals of the House of Representatives*, 1920, I.12A, 2–3.
15 PGA, 1922, report 184–86, resolution 33.
16 PGA, 1926, 34; 1924, 43.
17 PGA, 1926, 93.
18 PGA, 1926, 24.
19 *Press*, 15 June 1927.
20 *New Zealand Parliamentary Debates* (NZPD), 3 August 1927, vol. 207, 211, 216, (for the full debate, 209–42).
21 'Deputation from the Labour Members of Parliament to the Prime Minister (Rt. Hon. Sir Joseph Ward) and Minister of Defence (Hon. T. M. Wilford) at Wellington, 12th July, 1929', and statement by A. M. Richards. Army Department, Registration—Exemption religious objectors—General File, Series 8638, Record 227/9/1, Archives New Zealand (ANZ). The statement is annotated: 'Copy forwarded by Mr. Hunt, S. M. on 27/8/27. Original was filed about May or June of 1927.'
22 *Otago Daily Times* (ODT), 29 September 1927.
23 *New Zealand Herald* (NZH), 15 September 1927.
24 AS, 17 September 1927.
25 *Outlook*, 9 August 1926, 18.
26 AS, 19 October 1927.
27 AS, 20 October 1927.
28 *Outlook*, 28 November 1927, 14.
29 PGA, 1927, 25–26, 50, 200–203.
30 The Presbyterian Church distinguished 'divinity students', those in pre-training at university, from 'ministry students', those who were undergoing theological training and preparation for ministry.
31 NZH, 5 April 1928.
32 NZH, 19 April 1928.
33 NZH, 10 May 1928.
34 NZH, 16 May 1928.
35 NZPD, 2 August 1928, vol. 271, 1036 (for the full debate, 1018–56).
36 R. J. Cuming, 'The Presbyterian Church and Compulsory Military Training', *Outlook*, 21 May 1928, 9.
37 D. M. Hercus, 'The Richards Case', *Outlook*, 18 June 1928, 28.
38 PGA, 1928, 38, 213–15.
39 PGA, 1928, 215.
40 PGA, 1928, 42.
41 NZH, 13 July 1929.

42 NZH, 13 June 1929.
43 NZH, 17 June 1929; 18 June 1929. On Burton, see further the chapter by David Grant below.
44 ODT, 3 July 1929.
45 *Outlook*, 22 July 1929, 8.
46 NZPD, 10 July 1929, vol. 221, 260.
47 'Deputation from the Labour Members of Parliament'.
48 NZPD, 16 July 1929, vol. 221, 374.
49 AS, 16 July 1929, 9.
50 NZPD, 16 July 1929, vol. 221, 374.
51 EP, 17 July 1929.
52 NZPD, 31 July 1929, vol. 221, 782, 786, 801–802.
53 *Outlook*, 22 July 1929, 33.
54 *Outlook*, 29 July 1929, 25.
55 Morgan Richards to Prime Minister, Takapuna, 12, 13, 17 August 1929. Army Department, Registration—Exemption religious objectors—General File, Series 8638, Record 227/9/1, ANZ.
56 AS, 14 August 1929, 5.
57 NZPD, 30 August 1929, vol. 222, 715.
58 AS, 1 November 1929; NZH, 19 November 1929.
59 NZH, 10 October 1929; 14 November 1929.
60 NZH, 19 December 1929.
61 NZH, 7 March 1930; *Press*, 12 March 1930; EP, 21 April 1930; 21 May 1930; NZH, 24 May 1930.
62 NZH, 7 March 1930.
63 *Press*, 21 June 1930; NZH, 10 July 1930; 15 July 1930; EP, 11 July 1930.
64 AS, 17 May 1930.
65 NZH, 29 May 1930. Alun Richards, in oral interviews with the author and his son, maintained that his civil rights were not restored. Allan Davidson interview with the Reverend Alun Richards, 22 July 1983 (tapes in author's possession). Telephone conversation with Rhys Richards, 17 May 2016.
66 NZPD, 15 July 1930, vol. 224, 309.
67 NZH, 17 July 1930.
68 NZPD, 15 August 1930, vol. 225, 303–34.
69 Interview with the Reverend Alun Richards.
70 Interview with the Reverend Alun Richards.
71 Grant, 'Conscientious Objectors', 117; J. E. Cookson, 'Appeal Boards and Conscientious Objectors', in *Kia Kaha: New Zealand in the Second World War*, edited by John Crawford (Auckland: Oxford University Press, 2000), 173–98.
72 A. M. Richards, 'Why do Christians Differ about Pacifism', *Outlook*, 26 April 1937, 16; 3 May 1937, 29–30; 10 May 1937, 21–22; Isaac Jolly, 'Why do Christians Differ about Pacifism: The

Non-Pacifist Position', *Outlook*, 28 June 1937, 15–17; 4 July 1937, 30–31; 12 July 1937, 18–20.

73 'The Things That Are Not Caesar's', *Outlook*, 1 November 1939, 3.

74 Alun Richards, 'An exact as possible recital of the events of my dismissal', WEA Papers, 386-2/04, Alexander Turnbull Library, Wellington.

75 'Richards, Rev. A. Morgan', in Register of New Zealand Presbyterian Church Ministers, Deaconesses & Missionaries from 1840, Rennie to Robertson, www.archives.presbyterian.org.nz/Page194.htm.

9. Sects and War in New Zealand – Peter Lineham

1 David Grant, *Out in the Cold: Pacifists and Conscientious Objectors in New Zealand during World War II* (Auckland: Reed Methuen, 1986) 157; Paul Baker, *King and Country Call: New Zealanders, Conscription and the Great War* (Auckland: Auckland University Press, 1988), 170–78.

2 Elsie Locke, *Peace People: A History of Peace Activities in New Zealand* (Christchurch: Hazard Press, 1992).

3 *Appendices to the Journal of the House of Representatives* (AJHR), H-35, 1916; this does not contain the references to religious dissenters cited in Baker, 171.

4 David Littlewood, 'Striking a Balance: The Military Service Boards', in *New Zealand Society at War, 1914–1918*, edited by Steven Loveridge (Wellington: Victoria University Press, 2016), 112–26.

5 AJHR, H-19, 1917, 1918 and 1919; Baker, 243.

6 Nancy M. Taylor, *The Home Front: The New Zealand People at War*, vol. 1 (Wellington: Government Printer, 1986), 248–51; also J. E. Cookson, 'Illiberal New Zealand: The Formation of Government Policy on Conscientious Objection, 1940–1', *New Zealand Journal of History* 17, no. 2 (1983): 120–43.

7 Taylor, 275, citing L. J. Greenberg, 'The Men Who Would Not Serve—Being the Record of Defaulters' Detention in New Zealand 1941–46', War History Narrative, R12677443 (ADQZ 18912 W914 57/b, 106), Archives New Zealand (ANZ), Wellington. This is a slightly different list from the 1943 National Service Department, cited in Allan Handyside, *Indeterminate Sentence* (Wellington: Philip Garside Publishing, 2005), 99.

8 Taylor, 279, citing Paul Oestreicher, 'They Would Not Fight: Being a Survey of the Position of Conscientious Objectors and Military Defaulters in New Zealand during World War II' (MA thesis, Victoria University College, 1955).

9 *Observer*, 3 March 1917.

10 See Ernst Troeltsch, *The Social Teaching of the Christian Churches* (English translation, London: George Allen and Unwin, 1931 (German edition 1912)), in which the sectarian aspect of some Protestants is emphasised; also Michael Hill, 'The Social Context of New Zealand Religion: "Straight" or "Narrow"?' in *Religion and New Zealand's Future: Proceedings of the Seventh Auckland Religious Studies Colloquium, May 2–3, 1981*, edited by Kevin J. Sharpe (Palmerston North: Dunmore Press, 1982), 23–46.

11 The visiting French sociologist André Siegfried commented on these groups in *Democracy in New Zealand*, edited by David Hamer (Wellington: Victoria University Press, 1982), 310, 311, 313–14.

12 See, for example, *Feilding Star*, 2 May 1918; *Auckland Star* (AS), 2 May 1918; *Manawatu Times*, 7 May 1918. See Peter H. Ballis, 'Seventh-day Adventists and New Zealand Politics, 1886–1918', in *In and Out of the World: Seventh-day Adventists in New Zealand*, edited by Peter H. Ballis (Palmerston North: Dunmore Press, 1985), 65–71.

13 *Sun*, 6 February 1917.

14 For example, AS, 14 August 1911.

15 *Press*, 9 June 1916.

16 *New Zealand Herald* (NZH), 22 June 1916.

17 *Press*, 3 July 1916.

18 *Otago Daily Times* (ODT), 26 August 1916.

19 *Timaru Herald*, 30 December 1916.

20 *Mataura Ensign*, 16 May 1917; *Sun*, 26 July 1917.

21 *Star*, 25 July 1917; *Waikato Times*, 27 November 1917.

22 For example, *Dominion*, 19 June 1918.

23 Deborah Payne and Suzanne Beer, eds., *In Defence of Our Conscience: A History of Conscientious Objection among the New Zealand Ecclesias* (Torrens Park: Christadelphian Study Service, 1988), 37.

24 'Draft Regulations Regarding Religious Objections, Christadelphian', R3090779 (ADRE 17315 NEB1/5, 112), ANZ.

25 *Star*, 14 July 1917; also *Sun*, 14 June 1917; 12 June 1918.

26 *Press*, 6 February 1917.

27 Mary Petersen, *To the Glory of the Lord Who Called Them to Serve: A History of the Richmond Mission, Christchurch, 1911–1984* (Christchurch: North Avon Baptist Church, 1995), 29–30.

28 *New Zealand Truth*, 12 March 1910.

29 *Star* (Christchurch), 12 March 1917.

30 NZH, 28 February 1941.

31 Baker, 243.

32 *Evening Post* (EP), 2 September 1941.

33 NZH, 5 June 1941, p. 8; EP, 16 June 1941.

34 EP, 7 May 1942; AS, 26 July 1945.

35 Grant, *Out in the Cold*, 159, citing George Laird.
36 EP, 23 July 1941.
37 AS, 11 July 1914; *Ashburton Guardian*, 15 January 1919.
38 AS, 5 November 1941; NZH, 5 December 1941.
39 NZH, 21 February 1941.
40 EP, 11 June 1941.
41 Taylor, 234–43.
42 AS, 19 July 1945; NZH, 20 January 1945.
43 Grant, *Out in the Cold*, 157–58.
44 See Peter J. Lineham, *There We Found Brethren: A History of Assemblies of Brethren in New Zealand* (Palmerston North: G.P.H. Society, 1977).
45 J. G. Harvey, 'The War in Europe', *Treasury* 16 (1914): 136. On the Brethren see Elisabeth Wilson, '"The Eyes of the Authorities Are Upon Us": The Brethren and World War I', *Brethren Archivists and Historians Network Review* 3, no. 1 (2004): 2–17.
46 *Press*, 12 June 1916; ODT, 24 September 19152; AJHR, H1-19C, 1917.
47 *Sun*, 27 November 1916; *Press*, 28 November 1916; 29 November 1916; *Feilding Star*, 29 November 1916.
48 *Dominion*, 2 December 1916; *Feilding Star*, 5 December 1916.
49 *Press*, 9 January 1917; *Sun*, 9 January 1917; ODT, 10 January 1917; *Press*, 10 January 1917.
50 Baker, 243.
51 W. Johnson, T. W. Hunter, G. Russell et al., Circular Letter to Assemblies, 19 January 1917, with enclosure to the Governor (copy sent to the Assembly in Christchurch in author's possession).
52 *Evening Star*, 27 July 1917.
53 'Military Exemption', *Treasury* 19 (1917): 20–21.
54 *Oamaru Mail*, 2 April 1917.
55 J. W. Clapham, *John Olley, Pioneer Missionary to the Chad* (London: Pickering and Inglis, 1966).
56 Sawyer, McIlwaine, Salter and Reese per Savill to Government, response, 27 September 1939. AD ser. 1 227/9/1 vol. 1, ANZ.
57 EP, 3 February 1941; 4 February 1941.
58 Elisabeth Kay Wilson, 'Brethren Attitudes to Authority and Government with Particular Reference to Pacifism' (MA thesis, University of Tasmania, 1994), 60, citing *List of War Conscientious Objectors in Detention Camps*, private photocopied list supplied by Owen McKirdy, Hamilton, New Zealand, with Brethren names marked. See Peter Lineham, 'The Religious Face of Patriotism', in *Kia Kaha: New Zealand in the Second World War*, edited by John Crawford (Auckland: Oxford University Press, 2000), 26. I have been unable to trace the Brethren statement in Archives New Zealand.
59 See letter by Vigilant, AS, 27 February 1941.

60 EP, 7 February 1941; undated statement, 'The Question of the Christian's Duty' (in author's possession, supplied by J. Dixon).
61 EP, 5 June 1941; 21 June 1941; A. Read to E. Wilson, in Wilson, 'Brethren Attitudes', 68.
62 *Ellesmere Guardian*, 17 June 1941; EP, 9 April 1942.
63 NZH, 21 January 1926.
64 Doug and Helen Parker, *The Secret Sect* (Pendle Hill: D. Parker, 1982), 1–11, 59–81. For the tone of the movement in New Zealand see Lyn Cooper, *The Church with No Name: Known as the Cooneyites, Two by Twos* (Wellington: L. Cooper, 1996); for theological criticism see Lloyd Fortt, *A Search for "the Truth": The Workers' Words Exposed* (Bend: Research & Information Services, 1994).
65 See www.tellingthetruth.info/history_pioneering/australia-nz.php#first.
66 *Dominion*, 1 February 1917; EP, 1 February 1917; AS, 22 May 1917; *Lake Wakatip Mail*, 22 May 1917; *Dominion*, 26 July 1917; also NZH, 21 January 1926.
67 AS, 18 August 1921.
68 EP, 21 May 1942.
69 Parker, 53, 120
70 For example, *Manawatu Standard*, 2 July 1917.
71 Stan Thorburn, who was raised in the movement, provided me with information on this and other points.
72 *Waikato Times*, 26 May 1917.
73 AS, 18 August 1921.
74 NZH, 19 January 1926.
75 *Hawera and Normanby Star* (HNS), 31 January 1917.
76 *Hastings Standard*, 5 June 1917.
77 *Press*, 4 January 1917; 8 February 1917; *Sun*, 8 February 1917.
78 ODT, 29 September 1917.
79 See AD ser. 1 227/9/1, ANZ, which includes clippings from 22 February 1919, note by Colonel Potter (25 March 1919), reports from 30 October 1916 and Captain H. L. Garlick to HQ, 4 May 1920 (concerning military training).
80 EP, 26 July 1917; also *Star* (Christchurch), 4 January 1917.
81 NZH, 16 May 1918.
82 For example, HNS, 22 February 1917.
83 NZH, 15 March 1917; *Waikato Times*, 15 March 1917.
84 HNS, 17 July 1917.
85 AS, 18 July 1923.
86 AS, 19 March 1924.
87 For example, NZH, 21 July 1917.
88 For example, HNS, 20 March 1917; NZH, 10 July 1917.
89 *Waikato Times*, 26 May 1917.
90 EP, 25 July 1917.

91 *Dominion*, 26 July 1917.
92 EP, 26 July 1917.
93 EP, 3 August 1917.
94 *Feilding Star*, 4 August 1917; NZH, 21 August 1917.
95 EP, 26 October 1917; *Free Lance*, 2 November 1917; *Press*, 27 October 1917.
96 EP, 3 May 1918.
97 *Dominion*, 26 February 1918.
98 David Grant, *Field Punishment No 1: Archibald Baxter, Mark Briggs and New Zealand's Anti-militarist Tradition* (Wellington: Steele Roberts, 2008), 45, 47.
99 NZH, 18 September 1917; Baker, 173.
100 AS, 9 January 1919; NZH, 3 September 1919.
101 AS, 15 July 1921.
102 AS, 18 August 1921.
103 McClung to Massey 15 June 1920; Massey to McClung, 18 June 1920; Coates to McClung, 12 July 1920; McClung to Coates, 29 July 1920. AD ser. 1 227/9/1, ANZ.
104 NZH, 19 February 1941.
105 W. J. Hughes, cyclostyled list 1946, from the collection of Stan Thorburn.
106 NZH, 30 June 1945.
107 AS, 3 August 1945.
108 NZH, 1 March 1941.
109 NZH, 29 January 1942.
110 NZH, 3 February 1942. For their location, see AS, 11 July 1945; W. J. Hughes, cyclostyled list 1946.
111 EP, 12 December 1940; EP, 17 December 1940. The newspaper reports did not name the evangelist.
112 For example, AS, 11 July 1945.
113 AS, 10 July 1945.
114 Grant, *Out in the Cold*, 165–66.
115 AS, 27 June 1945.
116 EP, 5 July 1945.
117 NZH, 11 July 1945; AS, 10 July 1945.
118 Hughes to Prime Minister Peter Fraser, 2 July 1946, cyclostyled statement supplied by Stan Thorburn.
119 EP, 4 July 1945.
120 AS, 9 July 1945.
121 AS, 9 July 1945; NZH, 10 July 1945.
122 NZH, 18 July 1945.
123 AS, 23 July 1945.
124 NZH, 8 August 1945.
125 AS, 3 August 1945.
126 Hughes, cyclostyled material supplied by Stan Thorburn.

127 AS, 17 July 1945.
128 AS, 7 September 1917.
129 For example, *Evening Star*, 29 September 1917.
130 See W. J. Foote, *The Decision: Behind the Wire in New Zealand* (Nelson: Glen Press, 1983), 64–65.
131 Foote, 75.
132 Handyside, 25.
133 See AJHR, 1917, H-19B, which reports the religious denominations of those on active service in the New Zealand Expeditionary Force; see also H-19C, on the Expeditionary Force Reserve.

10. Adventist Conscientious Co-operators and Jehovah's Witness Neutrals in New Zealand during the Second World War – Peter H. Ballis

1 L. Fraser Jackson, 'Seventh-day Adventists in New Zealand: Towards a Demographic History', in *In and Out of the World: Seventh-day Adventists in New Zealand*, edited by Peter H. Ballis (Palmerston North: Dunmore Press, 1985), 133.
2 'Statistical Report of Seventh-day Adventist Conferences, Missions and Institutions', General Conference of Seventh-day Adventists, 31 December 1940; *1940 Yearbook of Jehovah's Witnesses Containing Report for the Fiscal Year of 1939* (Brooklyn: Watch Tower Bible and Tract Society, 1940).
3 See Ken Jubber, 'The Persecution of Jehovah's Witnesses in Southern Africa', *Social Compass* 24, no. 1 (1977): 121–35.
4 *New Zealand Observer* (*Observer*), 14 August 1940.
5 *Church Chronicle*, 1 December 1940, 9.
6 *Time*, 24 June 1940, 54.
7 *Smith's Weekly*, 20 July 1940; 27 July 1940; *New Zealand Truth* (NZT), 4 September 1940.
8 *The Protestant World*, 15 August 1940; *Observer*, 7 August 1940.
9 *Dominion*, 25 March 1940; *Observer*, 7 August 1940.
10 See *1981 Yearbook of Jehovah's Witnesses* (Brooklyn: Watch Tower Bible and Tract Society, 1980), 234ff; Nancy M. Taylor, *The Home Front: The New Zealand People at War*, vol. 1 (Wellington: Government Printer, 1986), 234–43.
11 I. S. Keltie, 'Report on the Lecture, Government & Peace, at Oamaru, 22 October 1940', unpublished manuscript, Jehovah's Witness Headquarters, Manurewa (JW Headquarters).
12 F. McAuley to H. Gill, undated letter from Hospital (copy in author's possession). See also *Evening Post* (EP), 14 October 1940; *Daily Telegraph* (DT), 14 October 1940; *Hawke's Bay Herald-Tribune* (HBHT), 14 October 1940; Keltie, 'Report on the Lecture'; H. Ridling to P. H. Ballis, 16 July 1986.

13 H. Gill to Prime Minister Peter Fraser, 14 October 1940, cited by H. Gill to A. MacGillivray, 14 October 1940; H. Gill to A. C. Piper, Secretary, Oamaru RSA, 26 October 1940, JW Headquarters.
14 The RSA changed its name to the Returned Services' Association in 1941.
15 H. Gill to A. MacGillivray, 2 November. 1940; D. Keoghan to P. H. Ballis, 21 June 1986.
16 EP, 25 October 1940.
17 *New Zealand Gazette*, 24 October 1940; DT, 25 October 1940.
18 R. Lazenby to A. MacGillivray, 8 November 1940.
19 *Otago Daily Times* (ODT), 5, 6, and 7 February 1941.
20 H. Gill to A. MacGillivray, 2 November 1940.
21 R. W. Johnston to P. H. Ballis, 21 June 1986.
22 NZT, 20 November 1940.
23 D. Keoghan to P. H. Ballis, 21 June 1986; H. Ridling to P. H. Ballis, July 1986.
24 R. W. Johnston to P. H. Ballis, 8 June 1986.
25 *1981 Yearbook*, 236; R. W. Johnston to P. H. Ballis, 8 June 1986.
26 R. W. Johnston to Watch Tower, Strathfield, November 1940; R. Lazenby, General Letter to New Zealand Witnesses, 22 October 1940, JW Headquarters.
27 *1981 Yearbook*, 237.
28 D. Keoghan to P. H. Ballis, 21 June 1986.
29 H. Gill to A. MacGillivray, 2 November 1940; A. MacGillivray to H. Gill, 15 November 1940.
30 H. Gill to A. MacGillivray, 2 November 1940; *1981 Yearbook*, 238.
31 DT, 2 December 1940; H. Gill to A. MacGillivray, 4 December 1940; R. W. Johnston to P. H. Ballis, 24 June 1986.
32 NZT, 11 December 1940.
33 R. T. Reid to Attorney-General, 31 October 1940; DT, 29 October and 8 November 1940, JW Headquarters.
34 A. MacGillivray to Lord Galway, undated, JW Headquarters.
35 R. T. Reid to Attorney-General, 5, 7, and 9 November 1940; H. G. Mason to R. T. Reid, 4 November 1940. Telegrams: Mason to Reid, 5 and 8 November 1940; H. Gill to Attorney-General, 15 November 1940.
36 R. Lazenby to A. MacGillivray, 21 November 1940; cf. 8 November 1940; 'Details of New Zealand Court Cases, 9 November–5 March 1941', unpublished manuscript, JW Headquarters.
37 DT, 11, 12, and 19 November 1940; HBHT, 18 and 19 November 1940; 11 and 19 November 1940; *Dominion*, 12 and 19 November 1940; EP, 19 November 1940; NZT, 27 November 1940. Also W. A. Roberts to P. H. Ballis, 16 July 1986; E. Ridling to P. H. Ballis, 25 July 1986; R. W. Johnston to P. H. Ballis, 8 June 1986.
38 DT, 21 November 1940.

39 H. Gill to A. MacGillivray, 2 November 1940.
40 R. Lazenby to A. MacGillivray, 8 November 1940; A. MacGillivray to R. Lazenby and H. Gill, 15 November 1940.
41 *Dominion*, 19 November 1940; EP, 19 November 1940; DT, 19 November 1940; HBHT, 19 November 1940, JW Headquarters; *Auckland Star* (AS), 20 November 1940; Telegram: H. Gill to His Majesty, King George, 19 November 1940.
42 EP, 20 November 1940; AS, 20 November 1940; DT, 20 November 1940.
43 DT, 20 November 1940.
44 *New Zealand Parliamentary Debates* (NZPD), 1940, 258, 500.
45 *New Zealand Herald* (NZH), 7 May 1941.
46 NZPD, 1940, 258, 503.
47 *New Zealand Gazette*, 8 May 1941, 1298; EP, 9 May 1941; DT, 9 May 1941. H. G. R. Mason to A. MacGillivray, 8 May 1941; H. G. R. Mason to R. T. Reid, 10 May 1941.
48 *Taranaki Daily News* (TDN), 9 July 1942; *Taranaki Herald*, 8 August 1942; NZH, 11 August 1942.
49 ODT, 16, 21 November 1942; *Dunedin Evening Star* (DES), 17 and 20 November 1942; C. J. L. White to R. T. Reid, 14 and 29 October 1942; R. W. Johnston to P. H. Ballis, 8 June 1986.
50 NZH, 13 June 1941; DT, 16 June 1941.
51 *New Plymouth Herald*, 2 June 1942 (Leslie Ward); DES, 1 April 1942 (Silas Martyn); R. W. Johnston to P. H. Ballis, 8 June 1986.
52 'The President's Symposium', *Australasian Record* (AR), 6 October 1941, 3.
53 R. P. Brown to P. H. Ballis, 7 August 1986; S. R. Goldstone, *Nothing to Fear: Stories of the Seventh-day Adventist Church in North New Zealand* (Napier: Max Printing, 1983), 103–6.
54 Minutes, North New Zealand Conference Session (NNZCS), 1 January 1940, 200; 19 January 1941, 219; R. P. Brown to P. H. Ballis, 30 July 1986.
55 A. W. Anderson, 'Religious Liberty Department', AR, 21 October 1918, 12.
56 Newspaper reports concerning Witnesses in Adventist Religious Liberty Files and references to Adventist negotiations with government authorities in Jehovah's Witness correspondence suggest that the two movements were acutely aware of each other's position.
57 AR, 13 February 1939, 1–2.
58 E. N. Dick, 'The Adventist Medical Cadet Corps as Seen by Its Founder', *Adventist Heritage* 1 (July 1974): 18–27.
59 A. J. Dyson, 'The Head and Not the Tail', AR, 31 July 1939, 3; E. E. Roenfelt, 'Autumn Council Notes', AR, 1 May 1939, 8; R. Hare, 'Disarm Prejudice', AR, 24 July 1939, 2.

60 C. H. Watson, 'The Significance of World Events', AR, 9 October 1939, 1–2.

61 Minutes, Wellington Church Quarterly Meeting, Book D, 1939, 4–5, Seventh-day Adventist Church, Wellington.

62 Minutes, National Emergency Council, South New Zealand Division, 23 May 1939, Seventh-day Adventist South New Zealand Conference.

63 Minutes, South New Zealand Conference Session (SNZCS), 10 January 1940; L. C. Naden, 'A Year of Progress', AR, 11 March 1940, 5.

64 Minutes, Wellington Church Quarterly Meeting, Book D, 1939, 5, 11; Minutes, Wanganui Church Board, 22 July 1940, 146, and 26 August 1940, 149; Minutes, SNZCS, 9 January 1941.

65 H. G. Moulds et al. to F. Jones, 17 August 1939; Minutes, National Emergency Council, 20 August 1939; Minutes, Australasian Union Conference (AUC), 11 August and 8 September 1939, 620.

66 'Notes of a Deputation from the North New Zealand Conference of Seventh-day Adventists which Waited on the Hon. F. Jones, Minister of Defence, on 17 August 1939', WArc. AD Series 227, 9/1 1942, Archives New Zealand (ANZ), Wellington; Peter Fraser to Australasian Union Conference, 5 September 1939; Minutes, AUC, 14 September 1939, 686.

67 A. W. Anderson, 'Religious Liberty Department', *Australasian Union Conference Bulletin*, no. 3, 1941, 12. At the 1941 North New Zealand Conference Session, H. G. Moulds reported that during the previous twelve months 'some exceptional contacts [had] been made . . . with Government authorities which had made very favourable impressions'; Minutes, NNZCS, 17 January. 1941, 214.

68 *Dominion*, 8 January 1940; *Star* (Christchurch), 19 January 1940; Minutes, AUC, 21 November 1939, 684.

69 Minutes, North New Zealand Conference Executive Committee (NNZCE), 29 May 1940, 557.

70 H. G. Moulds and L. C. Naden to F. Jones, 5 June 1940; H. Turner to H. G. Moulds, 25 June 1940, WArc, AD Series 27, 9/1, ANZ.

71 Minutes, NNZCE, 22 July 1940.

72 Minutes, AUC, 7 June 1940, 753; H. G. Moulds to R. Semple, 19 June 1940; Minutes NNZCE, 23 June 1940, 563.

73 R. Semple to H. G. Moulds, 8 July 1940; Minutes, NNZCE, 22 July 1940, 566.

74 Minutes, AUC, 24 December 1940, 854; *Dominion*, 7 September 1940; H. E. Piper, 'Ambulance Presented to Government', AR, 6 January 1941, 5.

75 'Facing A Grave Situation', AR, 1 July 1940, 8; Minutes, AUC, 7, 8, and 25 June 1940, 753, 747, and 759; Minutes, NNZCE, 23 June 1940, 563.

76 Minutes, NNZCE, 23 June 1940, 564; Minutes, AUC, 7 June 1940, 753; H. G. Moulds to R. Semple, 19 June 1940; R. Semple to H. G. Moulds, 8 July 1940.
77 F. Jones to H. G. Moulds, 18 July 1940.
78 L. C. Naden, 'South New Zealand Conference', *Australasian Union Conference Bulletin*, no. 3, 1941, 24; AR, 1 June 1942, 8; Minutes, NNZCE, 22 July 1940, 566.
79 Minutes, Wanganui Church Board, 22 August 1940, 147, and 25 February 1941, 165; Minutes, Gisborne Church Board, 1 February 1941, 2.
80 L. C. Naden, 'South New Zealand Conference', *Australasian Union Conference Bulletin*, no. 3, 1941, 24.
81 Memorandum for Record Clerk, Army Department, 19 July 1940; F. Jones to M. R. Wilson, 30 July 1940, WArc. AD Series 227, 9/1, ANZ.
82 L. C. Naden, 'The Military Position in New Zealand as it Relates to Seventh-day Adventists, 25 September 1941', unpublished paper; H. G. Moulds, 'Circular for Young Men of Military Age', undated newsletter (copies in author's possession).
83 O. H. Mead to the Director of National Service, 6 August 1940, WArc. AD Series 227, 9/1, ANZ.
84 F. Jones to H. G. Moulds, 15 July 1940; *Dominion*, 14 February 1941.
85 *Dominion*, 5 and 14 February 1941; Memorandum for the Adjutant-General, re Exemptions from Military Service—Seventh-day Adventists, 13 February 1941, WArc. AD Series 227, 9/1, ANZ.
86 Minutes, NNZCE, 14 February 1941, 657; P. H Ballis interview with D. Stock, Auckland, 11 January 1985.
87 H. G. Moulds to the Minister of National Service, 18 February 1941; H. G. Moulds, 'Circular to Young Men of Military Age'; *Press*, 16 May 1941; V. G. Jervis, Adjutant-General, Memorandum for the Director of National Service, 3 April 1941; J. H. Hunter, Memorandum for the Army Secretary, 17 March 1941, WArc. AD Series 227, 9/1, ANZ.
88 P. H. Ballis interview with J. B. Keith, Napier, 1 March 1984. Keith encouraged Adventist young men to appeal against conscription on the grounds of Sabbath observance rather than on the grounds of not carrying arms.
89 ODT, 13 February 1941.
90 C. H. Watson, T. W. Hammond, R. H. Adair and H. G. Moulds. See L. C. Naden and R. E. Hare to Prime Minister M. J. Savage, 16 May 1939, ANZ.
91 H. G. Moulds to Minister of Defence, 19 June 1940, WArc. AD Series 227, 9/1, ANZ; Minutes, AUC, 30 May and 7 June 1940, 753.

92 H. G. Moulds, 'Circular to Young Men of Military Age' (in author's possession).
93 Minutes, AUC, 6 February 1941, 870.
94 D. M. Robinson, Adjutant-General, Memorandum for Army Headquarters, 14 February 1941, WArc. AD Series 227, 9/1, ANZ; Minutes, NNZCE, 20 May 1941, 629, and 24 February 1942. The only exceptions were Watts and Robertson of the 9th Field Ambulance Unit, Kaikohe, who refused to parade on the Sabbath and were charged with disobeying orders. This situation was corrected following communication with H. G. Moulds (T. H. Petit to H.G. Moulds, 15 and 21 April 1942; H. G. Moulds to T. H. Petit, 17 April 1942). A. W. Archer's difficulties were different again. He did not appeal against military service, but had hoped the Army would respect and accommodate his religious convictions as a Sabbath observer. Only after some considerable difficulty was his conscientious position recognised: A. W. Archer, 'Active Service Notebook, 1943–44' (in author's possession); A. W. Archer to P. H. Ballis, 20 September 1985; P. H Ballis interview with A. W. Archer, Hastings, 20 September 1985.
95 F. Jones to H. G. Moulds, 17 January 1942; P. H. Ballis interview with D. Stock, Auckland, 11 January 1985.
96 L. R. Franks, 'A Letter from the Middle East', AR, 4 January 1943, 6; M. McLoughlin, 'A New Zealander in the Desert', AR, 8 March 1943, 6; 'All Things Work Together for Good', AR, 17 May 1943, 6; F. McCusker to N. G. Knowles, 29 June 1943.
97 Taylor, 275.
98 Paul Oestreicher, 'They Would Not Fight: Being a Survey of the Position of Conscientious Objectors and Military Defaulters in New Zealand during World War II' (MA thesis, Victoria University College, 1955), 6.
99 AS, 29 May 1941; *Nelson Evening Mail*, 28 June 1945.
100 Taylor, 275, describes Jehovah's Witnesses in camps as 'docile and cooperative' and 'often fanatical in their religion'. Although this comment reflects a degree of prejudice on her part, it does, nevertheless, reflect accurately the tenacity of Witnesses to their ideology.
101 DT, 15 February 1941, 15 September 1941 and 24 November 1941; DES, 20 November 1942; NZH, 7 March 1942; AS, 24 November 1941; *Waikato Times*, 25 June 1941.
102 AS, 20 June and 6 November 1941; NZH, 21 April 1942.
103 *Dominion*, 2 February 1941.
104 DT, 27 November 1941.
105 DT, 10 October 1941.
106 TDN, 3 September 1942.
107 F.L.W. Wood, *The New Zealand People at War: Political and External Affairs* (Wellington: A. H. & A. W. Reed, 1971), 147.

108 AS, 13 September 1945; NZH, 18 November 1941; *Dominion*, 29 June 1945.
109 AS, 8 November 1945.
110 'Neutrality', *Watchtower*, 1 November 1939, 323–33; *God and the State* (Brooklyn: Watchtower Bible and Tract Society, 1941); L. R. Franks, 'Pursuing My Purpose in Life', *Watchtower*, 15 November 1958, 700ff.
111 Ian Hamilton, *Till Human Voices Wake Us* (Auckland: Auckland University Press, 1984 (first published 1953)), 217.
112 P. H. Ballis interview with Tom Harrison, 22 July 1986; 'United Announcers Theocratic Assembly, Whitanui Detention Camp, August 9–14, 1944' (in author's possession).
113 Hamilton, 218.
114 R. Lazenby to R. Pope, 13 June 1945; Tom Harrison, Interview 22 July 1986.
115 H. Thompson to P. H. Ballis, 7 September 1986; F. Slade to P. H. Ballis, 14 September 1986; Taylor, 275.
116 W. Archer to P. H. Ballis, 20 September 1986. According to the *Pitcairn Miscellany* 3, no. 4 (30 April 1960), at least fifteen Pitcairn Islanders in New Zealand enlisted during the Second World War.
117 Minutes, AUC, 9 April 1940, 728; 30 May 1940, 750; and 12 September 1940, 821; Minutes, Wellington Church Quarterly Meeting, Book D, 1940, 20; Minutes, Gisborne Church Board, 28 February 1942, 85; F. M. de Vaynes Jones, 'Auckland Combined Meeting', AR, 17 June 1940, 4.
118 C. B. Haynes, 'Conscientious Objectors Who Do Not Object', *Youth's Instructor*, 18 November 1941.
119 R. J. Burns to Secretary, Conscientious Objectors Committee, Wellington, 16 May 1950, in SNZCS. Although this statement postdates the Second World War, the comments are possibly based upon, and reflect, the sentiments of J. P. Neff, *Our Youth in Time of War*, revised and approved by the General Conference of Seventh-day Adventists (Takoma Park: Review and Herald, 1942 (first published 1934)).
120 A. W. Anderson, 'Denominational Definition of Noncombatancy', AR, 28 April 1941, 3–4; A. W. Anderson, 'Denominational Definition of Noncombatancy Challenged', AR, 9 June 1941, 4–6; A. W. Anderson, 'Loyal Seventhday Adventists Please Take Notice', AR, 16 June 1942, 5–6; A. W. Anderson, 'Our Noncombatant Attitude to War', AR, 11 May 1942, 3–5; R. Smith to A. Smith, 23 November 1941 (in author's possession).
121 F. Slade to P. H. Ballis, 14 September 1986.
122 *Press*, 24 July 1942; *Star* (Christchurch), 25 July 1942.
123 E. J. Johanson to Secretary, No. 1 Armed Forces Appeal Board, 24 July and 8 October 1942, SthNZSDA.

124 *Smith's Weekly*, 18 January 1941. For detail on the SDA Reform Movement, see L. Tarling, *The Edges of Seventhday Adventism* (Bermagui South, NSW: Galilee Publications, 1981), 100–22; R. Schwarz, *Light Bearers to the Remnant* (Mountain View: Pacific Press Publishing Association, 1979), 452–54; H. E. Piper, 'LastDay Deceptions', AR, 1 April 1940, 1–2; R. Bullas, 'Fifth Columnists in Israel', AR, 2 December 1940, 1; C. H. Watson, 'A Serious Charge Refuted', AR, 14 April 1941, 1–2; 21 April 1941, 1–2; 28 April 1941, 1–3; C. H. Watson, *A Serious Charge Refuted* (Warburton: Signs, 1941).

125 L. Benton, 'Importance of Organisation', AR, 9 January 1939, 1; F. Lee, 'The Unity of the Church', AR, 8 April 1940, 1; A. W. Anderson, 'A Plea for Tolerance', AR, 28 November 1938, 1.

126 H. G. Moulds, 'Circular to all Seventhday Adventist Believers in North New Zealand Conference', 1940, cyclostyled (copy in author's possession); R. P. Brown to P. H. Ballis, 13 August 1986; F. Slade to P. H. Ballis, 14 September 1986; Minutes, NNZCE, 14 June 1940, 561; 2 December 1941, 674; 18 May 1943, 789–90; 4 December 1944, 889; L. C. Naden, 'South New Zealand Conference', *Australasian Union Conference Bulletin*, no. 3, 1941, 23.

127 *Constitution of the North New Zealand Conference of Seventhday Adventists (adopted October 19th, 1942), and Statement of Fundamental Beliefs* (Auckland: The Brookdale Press, 1942).

128 Minutes, NNZCS, 11 February 1923, 298; 9 October 1942, 230ff; Minutes, SNZCS, 22 October 1942, 11ff.

129 Circular letter, 26 April 1945.

130 A. W. Anderson, 'Religious Liberty Department', *Australasian Union Conference Bulletin*, no. 3, 1941, 12.

131 'South New Zealand Conference', AR, 18 August 1941, 4.

132 Minutes, NNZCS, 21 October 1943, 261; H. G. Moulds, 'North New Zealand Conference', *Australasian Union Conference Bulletin*, no. 3, 1941, 16.

133 *Dominion*, 3 July 1941; 'Garments for British Air Raid Victims', *Dominion*, 11 August 1941, 5.

134 D. Keoghan to P. H. Ballis, 21 June 1986.

11. The Reverend Ormond Burton and his Antagonists during the Second World War – David Grant

1 The following information on Burton's life and career is drawn from my biographical sketch: David Grant, 'Burton, Ormond Edward', *Dictionary of New Zealand Biography. Te Ara –The Encyclopedia of New Zealand*, www.teara.govt.nz/en/biographies/5b53/burton-ormond-edward; also Ormond Burton, 'A Rich Old Man' (typescript

autobiography), MS-Papers-0438-059, Alexander Turnbull Library, Wellington (ATL); Ernest Crane, *I Can Do No Other: A Biography of Ormond Burton* (Auckland: Hodder and Stoughton, 1986). See further my works: 'To Turn the Other Cheek: A History of Anti-Militarism in New Zealand Before and During World War Two' (MA thesis, University of Auckland, 1983), 62–64; *Out in the Cold: Pacifists and Conscientious Objectors in New Zealand during World War II* (Auckland: Reed Methuen, 1986), 34–39; *A Question of Faith: A History of the New Zealand Christian Pacifist Society* (Wellington: Philip Garside Publishing, 2004), 18–20.

2 Burton 'Rich Old Man', 23.

3 *Our Little Bit: A Brief History of the New Zealand Division* (Norwich: NZYMCA, 1918), later published as *The New Zealand Division* (Auckland: Clark and Matheson, 1920); *The Auckland Regiment* (Auckland: Whitcombe and Tombs, 1922).

4 *The Silent Division: New Zealanders at the Front, 1914–1919, and, Concerning One Man's War*, edited by John H. Gray (Christchurch: John Douglas Publishing, 2014).

5 A. C. Barrington, 'Ormond Burton Obituary', *NZCPS Bulletin*, January/March 1974, 1. There were slight changes in the name of NZCPS's periodical during and after the war; the wartime and post-war issues are referred to hereafter as the *Christian Pacifist Bulletin* and *NZCPS Bulletin* respectively.

6 Crane, 89–90.

7 Burton to Superintendent of Central Methodist Circuit, 25 January 1937, Ormond Edward Burton Papers, MS-Papers-0438-041, ATL.

8 Author interview with A. C. Barrington, 31 March 1982.

9 Grant, *Out in the Cold*, 36.

10 *Dominion*, 5 September 1939. Barrington was also present on the parliamentary grounds; he did not speak, but recorded the events for the movement. Thus began the NZCPS's *Bulletin*. See A. C. Barrington, *Trials of a Pacifist: Being Two Broadcast Talks Over New Zealand YC Stations* (Christchurch: New Zealand Christian Pacifist Society, 1970), 9.

11 Crane, 69–70, 80; Grant, *Out in the Cold*, 34.

12 Burton, 'Rich Old Man', 384.

13 *Dominion*, 12 September 1939.

14 *Evening Post*, 17 December 1939.

15 *Auckland Star*, 31 January 1940; 1 February 1940; Burton, 'Rich Old Man', 392.

16 *Christian Pacifist Bulletin*, W-10, 10 February 1940; Burton, 'Rich Old Man', 395; Barrington, *Trials*, 9; *Tomorrow*, 21 February 1940.

17 Burton, 'Rich Old Man', 376.

18 *Tomorrow*, 24 February 1940; *People's Voice*, 26 February 1940.

19 Paul Baker, *King and Country Call: New Zealanders, Conscription and the Great War* (Auckland: Auckland University Press, 1988), 166–67.
20 *Dominion*, 2 April 1940.
21 Cited in 'Christian Pacifist Society, Conference Circular', October 1940, Archibald Charles Barrington Papers, Publications—Miscellaneous CPS, MS-Papers-0439-235, ATL.
22 'Christian Pacifist Society, Conference Circular'.
23 'Christian Pacifist Society, Conference Circular'.
24 The Christian pacifists present included Barrington, E. S. Hoddinott, the Reverend Arthur Penn, Arthur Carman and Basil Dowling. The government officials were: the Minister of National Service, Rex Mason; the Commissioner of Police, D. J. Cummings; the Director of the National Service Department, J. S. Hunter; and the Chief Censor, J. T. Paul. See 'Notes on Deputation of New Zealand Christian Pacifist Society to Prime Minister, Colleagues and Government Officials, 18 November 1940', Justice Department File 1940/135/140, Archives New Zealand.
25 'Notes on Deputation of New Zealand Christian Pacifist Society'.
26 'Notes on Deputation of New Zealand Christian Pacifist Society'.
27 Author interview with John Boal.
28 Grant, *Out in the Cold*, 90–95.
29 Burton, 'Rich Old Man', 449.
30 *A Testament of Peace* (Wellington: New Zealand Christian Pacifist Society, 1940).
31 Burton, 'Rich Old Man', 403–5.
32 Information on Burton's expulsion comes from: Barrington, 'Ormond Burton', 1–2; Burton, 'Rich Old Man', 444–50; also Grant, 'To Turn the Other Cheek', 127–28; Grant, *Out in the Cold*, 77–79.
33 Barrington, 'Ormond Burton', 2.
34 E. W. Hames, *Coming of Age: The United Church, 1913–1972* (Auckland: Institute Press, 1974), 89.
35 Cited in *Christian Pacifist Bulletin*, W-47, November 1942.
36 Burton, 'Rich Old Man', 456.
37 Information on the Burton trial comes from: *Christian Pacifist Bulletin*, W-47, November 1942; author interview with A. C. Barrington, 31 March 1982; Jeremy Pope, 'Mockery of Mercy', *New Zealand Law Journal* (4 May 1976): 188–91; Burton, 'Rich Old Man', 456–58.
38 Pope, 189.
39 Crimes Amendment Act 1910, 3.b.
40 B. L. Dallard to Barrington, 20 November 1942, Barrington Papers, MS-Papers-0439-017, ATL.
41 John Pratt, *The Prison Diary of A. C. Barrington: Dissent and Conformity in Wartime New Zealand* (Dunedin: Otago University Press, 2016), 167.

42 On Niebuhr, Barth and Burton, see Crane, 95.
43 Burton 'Rich Old Man', 437.
44 *Bart, The Story of a Dog* (London: James Clarke, 1944); *In Prison* (Wellington: Reed, 1945). Along with a number of pacifists and released conscientious objectors he would become active in the Howard League for Prison Reform after the war.
45 *New Zealand Observer*, 7 February 1940.
46 On treatment of the fourteen New Zealand conscientious objectors sent to the Front in 1917, see Archibald Baxter, *We Will Not Cease* (Auckland: Cape Catley, 2003); H. E. Holland, *Armageddon or Calvary: The Conscientious Objectors of New Zealand and 'The Process of their Conversion'* (Wellington: Maoriland Worker, 1919); David Grant with paintings by Bob Kerr, *Field Punishment No. 1: Archibald Baxter, Mark Briggs and New Zealand's Anti-militarist Tradition* (Wellington: Steele Roberts, 2008), 41–97.
47 *New Zealand Parliamentary Debates*, vol. 256, 1939, 90–113.
48 Grant, 'To Turn the Other Cheek', 77–79.
49 Grant, *Out in the Cold*, 46.
50 Cited in 'Some British opinions on pacifists and conscientious objectors', a circular printed by the Christchurch Branch of the Fellowship of Conscientious Objectors, n.d., Lincoln Efford Papers, MS-Papers-0445, Box 2, Folder 34, ATL.
51 Miller to Barrington, 10 March 1941, cited in *Christian Pacifist Bulletin*, W27, March 1941.
52 Cited in Martin Ceadel, *Pacifism in Britain 1914–1945: The Defining of a Faith* (Oxford: Oxford University Press, 1980), 206.
53 *Peace News*, 5 April 1940, cited in Ceadel, 304.
54 *Commonwealth Debates*, vol. 161, 1939, 164–65, cited in Paul Hasluck, *The Government and the People 1939–1941* (Canberra: Australian War Memorial, 1952), 174.
55 Hasluck, 178.
56 Armstrong to Burton, 9 October 1939, Burton Papers, MS-Papers-0438-046, ATL.
57 Ormond Burton, *Into the Way of Peace: An Address Given at the University Congress, January 1950* (Auckland: Forward Books, 1950), 3.
58 See Grant, 'To Turn the Other Cheek', 75–145.
59 Burton, *Way of Peace*, 5.
60 Ceadel, 206, 210, 295, 310; A. H. Nordmeyer to A.H. Carman, n.d., cited in A. C. Barrington to Leslie Artingall, 17 April 1944, Barrington Papers, MS-Papers-0439-028, ATL. Similarly, G. H. C. MacGregor's influential book, *The New Testament Basis of Pacifism* (London: Fellowship of Reconciliation, 1936) was still freely available in Britain during the war, but banned in New Zealand from early 1941.

61 Grant, 'Ormond Burton'; Grant, *Out in the Cold*, 250–52.
62 Ormund Burton, *To Whom Shall We Go?* (Auckland: Forward Books, 1973).
63 Ormund Burton, *Hadfield of the Kapiti Coast* (Otaki: O. E. Burton, 1972).
64 *The King v Barrington* [1942] NZLR 502, 518.

Index

Page references in bold refer to photographs and illustrations